A BACKGROUND TO
CHINESE PAINTING

I. CHILDREN AT PLAY ON A WINTER DAY

By an unknown artist of the Sung dynasty (960–1279)
The National Collection, Peiping. (7' 2½" × 3' 10¼")

A BACKGROUND

TO

CHINESE PAINTING

BY

SOAME JENYNS

ASSISTANT KEEPER, DEPARTMENT OF ORIENTAL ANTIQUITIES,
BRITISH MUSEUM

WITH A PREFACE FOR COLLECTORS BY

W. W. WINKWORTH

LONDON

SIDGWICK & JACKSON, LTD.

1935

PRINTED IN GREAT BRITAIN BY
WILLIAM CLOWES AND SONS, LIMITED, LONDON AND BECCLES.

To

M. J.

WITHOUT WHOSE ENCOURAGEMENT AND
CRITICISM THIS BOOK WOULD
NOT HAVE BEEN WRITTEN

AUTHOR'S NOTE

It has not been an easy task to select suitable illustrations for this book. Many old paintings with important attributions are either so dimmed or damaged by time as not to permit satisfactory reproduction; others depend on their colours. I have been inclined to pass over both of these in favour of less well-known or even anonymous painters whose works lent themselves more happily to the photographer. I have included measurements whenever they were available.

I have to thank Dr. Lionel Giles and Mr. William King of the British Museum, and Mr. Ian Anderson for the laborious task of reading my proofs. Dr. Giles has given me frequent assistance in Chinese translations; but I would hasten to point out any inaccuracies are entirely my own. Mr. A. G. Cook has most kindly undertaken all the typing. Lastly I am deeply indebted to Mr. W. W. Winkworth for criticism and for a preface which no pen but his could supply.

TO COLLECTORS

By W. W. WINKWORTH

I AM writing to introduce Mr. Jenyns; but it is really I myself who need introduction, and it is of myself I intend to speak. It seems a good opportunity. Taking a deep breath, I shall therefore put on my most mysterious, my deepest look, and prepare to explain what Chinese Art has meant to me. But on second thoughts it occurs to me that the literature of artistic piety is, perhaps, already rather milky. The fact is, people get into certain habits, and I happened to get into the habit of looking at pieces of china and reproductions of Chinese paintings. I have never been to China; it is an accident that I happened to prefer poring over porcelain rather than postage stamps. It was partly because I found some of my fellow-loiterers congenial that the habit became a confirmed one.

It so happened also that London's museums, shops and auction-rooms happened to be very rich in good Chinese things, just before and just after the war. While the war was in progress I used to see as much as I could when on leave; and Mr. Eumorfopoulos sent me some photographs, too, I remember, of some of his latest finds, including the *famous bronze owl*, now one of the principal objects of reverence and interest in that great fetich-house in Bloomsbury, the British Museum.[1] This place is a specially useful centre for

[1] This is a mistake. Curiously enough, the owl, which being Athenian as well as Chinese, is obviously of the company of Sir Frederick Kenyon and Sir George Hill, is actually at the Victoria and Albert Museum. Is this an omen? Livy would have thought so.

the acquisition of virtue at the present moment; the faithful have seldom had a guarantee of Paradise offered them so cheap. For half a crown, in fact if you like to descend to such unworthy details, for twopence (I scorn to mention pennies except in pairs) any member of the British public —in fact any member of the human race—can obtain the privilege of placating that owl. You have only to look at him before and after you have decided to put your pennies in the slot, to see the difference they make.

In previous years, the pleasure of patronizing the British Museum was much more troublesome. You had to write to the Director and ask for an interview; you had to wrap the skull of your great-grandfather in a parcel and take it round, and submit it to the eye of an expert; and when you had convinced him that it really was your ancestor, and not a prehistoric horse, and that you wished it to become the nation's property, he would explain that being perfectly normal, it was of no interest at all. Then you had to begin all over again. But now you can go and buy them a bit of the Eumorfopoulos Collection, which they have rashly decided to have before they were sure that they could afford it. Your position is therefore splendid: you can deliver one of those lectures on extravagance which make one feel so virtuous, and then, graciously unbending, extend your patronage as far as you like, and no further.

I have now patronized Chinese art in one way or another for quite a long time, and I can recommend this method as one of the best. There are other ways, of course. One can, for instance, become a collector, a miniature Eumorfopoulos oneself. It is usually believed that for this it is necessary to be also a miniature millionaire. That is not quite true. At Sotheby's auction-rooms, or Christie's, it is notorious that by merely nodding your head you can become the possessor of almost anything any day of the week. It is certainly true that there is a most interesting stream of objects flowing through the London sale-rooms every week in the season; and though you have to pay, as well as nod, for the price of a couple of stalls at the theatre it is quite possible to get something knocked down to you which is just as interesting to look at when the fun of the sale is over as your theatre programme is after even a very good performance; and even sale catalogues are interesting things, and those are free. Yes, it is a fallacy to suppose that collecting is a hobby for the very rich only.

I do not hesitate to confide to the public that Mr. Jenyns is himself a collector. Indeed the whole subject of Chinese art is in that interesting and human, all too human, stage when the collector dominates the field. It is, of course, quite otherwise with the arts nearer home. Here the expert, the historian, the Walter Paters, Roger Frys and Clive Bells have it all their own way; and besides that, the arts of less remote times and places actually affect the behaviour of living artists. Many people suppose that modern artists never go to the National Gallery. This is a great mistake. Not only do they go there, but their opinions and practice actually influence policy. I often wonder if it would not be better if the influence were more direct; but when you consider that the last two Directors are rather exceptions to the rule in not being in some degree practising artists, the fact that the influence exists is clear. Even the last two, Sir Augustus Daniel and Mr. Kenneth Clark, are both collectors of modern pictures and are intimate with many living artists. But in the Chinese art world the state of things is bound at present to be different. Personally I regret this. I hold the view—and I am at present one of the very few who do—that modern Chinese art is if anything more interesting than ancient; certainly not less so. I don't deny that if the walls on which Wu painted his frescoes were still standing, they would be as well worth a pilgrimage as Rome or Florence. But all that phase of Chinese painting, even the art of the Sung dynasty, has, in my opinion, survived in too slight a form to be worth attention except from a few specialists, and is far more remote even than the painting of classical antiquity, because the tradition has not survived to the same extent. The present tradition (the only tradition, I mean, which is alive), in its way an excellent one, dates, in my view, from the Yüan and Ming periods at earliest. One has only to remember the modern Chinese art exhibitions which this year and last were to be seen in many European towns, where they had been taken by Professor Liu Hai-su of Shanghai. It was evident from the Professor's reasonable and well-considered statements in print and otherwise, that the living tradition in China to-day is that embodied in the school known as the "Literary man's school." This type of painting is particularly hard for Europeans to understand, and not unnaturally only a few people were at all impressed by it, those, in other words, whose experience of art in all its forms was very wide: lecturers and professors of art at various Universities, scholars in Oriental languages and other people not necessarily Orientalists, who were deeply versed in the technique of painting and handwriting.

By such people the interest of this kind of art is bound to be felt once good examples are seen. Up till now, almost none have been available. Our collections of Chinese paintings have been formed on quite other lines, inevitably. The British Museum, therefore, contains hardly any examples. For instance, it possesses only two very slight sketches by Chu Ta, that remarkable genius who flourished in the seventeenth century. The reasons for this are clear when one knows the circumstances. Chu Ta's paintings are

xii

highly valued in China and eagerly collected at the present day. Now it might be supposed that securing examples of his art was only a matter of paying the price asked. The prices of his best works were certainly not beyond the reach of the British Museum. If there were an organized art market in China as there is in Europe, it would only be necessary to write to some reliable firm corresponding to those respectable institutions we have in London such as Agnew's or Colnaghi's ; they would then either supply a selection of examples from their stock, sending photographs first, or would look out for them at the sales. But in China there are no firms like Agnew's and Colnaghi's, no sale-rooms like Christie's and Sotheby's. There are no art magazines in which the prominent dealers advertise their latest acquisitions, no newspapers in which forthcoming auction sales are announced. In practice we have simply got to wait until by the devious channels of trade examples of Chinese painting reach us. One of the most usual ways is through European dealers. These dealers are often men of high integrity and considerable knowledge; but before they can offer us things they have to buy them from the Chinese.

Now the Chinese have a great many works of art to sell. They naturally offer to European clients the sort of thing they think will appeal to them. Knowing as they do that the interest in Chinese painting is governed by the taste of collectors, they offer to Europeans the sort of thing they think will suit. Naturally they do not offer us first those things for which there is an immediate demand in their own country. Another fact is that China is still an old-fashioned country as regards the art trade. In Europe, if there are two or three wealthy men and perhaps one museum official who have discovered (the museum official usually, but not always, does the discovering) that the

b

drawings, let us say, of G. B. Tiepolo (an artist who was in Ruskin's time regarded as inferior) are desirable and rare, it does not take more than a few months for that fact to register itself in the sale-room value of Tiepolo drawings; I am quoting an actual instance from recent history. One or two high prices at auction for Tiepolo drawings attract the attention of all sorts of people who have, perhaps, hardly heard of the Venetian ceiling-painter as a draughtsman; the merit of the drawing is at once recognized, and in future a good Tiepolo is as good as a banknote.

A reasonable relation exists on the whole between the market prices of nearly all European objects; the scale of values so established facilitates exchange and makes it possible for the demands of collectors to be satisfied in a reasonable way. But in China it is evidently quite otherwise. There is no publicity, no reliable market, no sale-rooms, and comparatively few great capitalist firms. There are, moreover, no museums and no art experts of recognized status, no art magazines, no art libraries. Obscurity reigns; confidence is slow to establish itself. If one of the European dealers who visit China were sure of being able to go to a national institution like our British Museum and get a disinterested opinion from a student of the subject, the situation would be very different.

The Chinese art trade has in the past thirty years enormously developed, and our knowledge of Chinese art has correspondingly increased. But with regard to painting, there are certain facts which have hitherto prevented what I should describe as a sane situation. To understand Chinese painting it is really necessary to know a good deal about the Chinese language, and not only that, but about artistic calligraphy. A very large number of paintings have inscriptions by the artist which form part of the artistic effect of the picture—they do not correspond merely to the notes

xiv

which a European draughtsman puts on a drawing sometimes. It must be explained here, too, that all Chinese
paintings, frescoes excepted, correspond to our drawings;
some it is true are coloured, but the colours are simply more
or less water-colour pigments. They would in England be
classified as drawings, and in the British Museum all the
Chinese and Japanese paintings are in the Department of
Prints and Drawings, or have been till recently—a new
Department of Oriental Antiquities will perhaps now
claim them.

In addition to this, many Chinese paintings have a sort
of autograph value; they include, mounted on the same
roll of silk or paper, inscriptions by artists or literary men
—in China the two terms are nowadays largely interchangeable. To understand not only the meaning of these inscriptions, but their value or authenticity as autographs, is a
task which for many years to come is bound to be beyond
all but a very few Europeans. Indeed, the judgment of
handwriting is a matter which in the absence of an easily
available literature and a scientifically arranged and classified
body of original material is bound, even in China, to depend
largely on the authority of a few people who have chanced
to have opportunities for forming opinions. In practice
there are few Europeans who can undertake to form such
opinions; outside China and Japan, it is unlikely that there
will be any for some time.

This brings me to another consideration. To the Japanese
Chinese literature, calligraphy and painting have the same
enormous interest that classical scholarship and the study
of Greek and Roman subjects have among ourselves.
Naturally Japan has in recent years absorbed a large number
of Chinese paintings and autograph writings as these have
become available owing to political uncertainty in China.
The position of Japan in this problem is of great importance.

Twenty or thirty years ago, almost the only knowledge we had of the paintings of China (apart from merely commercial products such as wallpapers, " rice-paper pictures " and other pretty trifles) was through a Japanese art magazine called *The Kokka*. At that time the Japanese were our allies politically, and there was a strong pro-English sentiment. Many numbers of *The Kokka* were printed in excellent English as well as in Japanese (now the English section is reduced, but it still exists). But unfortunately at that time the realization of China as a civilization whose painting was one of its paramount arts was not yet general in Europe. Indeed many people actually supposed, at the end of the nineteenth century, that Japanese painting was much superior to Chinese. I am a great lover of Japanese painting, but I know that this is not true ; in Japan no one would uphold such a view. But no one in Europe would have at any time maintained that in the minor arts Japan was superior, though actually I think that that is much nearer the truth. But by an accident of history Japan has been Europeanized now in many ways for fifty years or so, which is not true of China, and this has had at least one result, namely, that a Japanese firm of art dealers has long been established in London, in fact, if we remember the late Mr. Kato and his successor, two. It is true that there have been from time to time Chinese dealers in London; but for whatever reason, the best-known one has now returned to China. He did not, however, deal at all extensively in Chinese paintings. But the Japanese firm has done so. These facts of commerce, perfectly well known to all who are interested in the subject, have actually and inevitably influenced the whole situation ; they are a powerful and wealthy firm, and many fine paintings have reached our collections through them. But one cannot help noticing that the source of supply is indirect. They have, it

xvi

is true, made valiant efforts to interest the British public in Chinese art. But it has not been easy. Chinese paintings are not easily placed in our homes; and though every effort has been made to show us the sort of pictures most likely to appeal to us, there has been little response. It is hardly to be expected, therefore, that the type of picture most admired in Japan should often be seen here; and when one remembers that it is only recently that the Japanese have been able to secure paintings from China at all (I do not refer to the more remote past, of course) it is easily seen that many types of Chinese paintings are never likely to reach us. There is at present a great deal of enthusiasm in Japan for the more recent schools of Chinese art, dating from the sixteenth century onwards. This is natural because during the eighteenth and nineteenth centuries these schools had a great influence on Japanese art. Many learned Japanese, scholars in the classical language of China, found the style of the literary school congenial; and among these men one may count some of the greatest artists Japan has produced. Their work—the work of men like Taiga, Buson, Chikuden and Tomioka Tessai, to name but a few—is now highly esteemed. Moreover, the artists of present-day China, some of whose work was introduced to Europe during the summer of this year, are many of them also much admired; and their pictures are eagerly collected.

It will thus be even more obvious that as far as Chinese painting is concerned, viewed as a living tradition, Europe is at the other end of the world, and very little filters through, or is likely to filter through at present.

Our collectors and museums have therefore had to rely on all sorts of chance sources of supply for the accumulation of specimens. For the acquisition of knowledge, on the other hand, Chinese literature has been available, and this has had the very natural result of concentrating our attention on the glorious past of Chinese art, the T'ang and Sung dynasties, rather than on more recent times. We know much from literature about the great masters of these times. Professor Giles and Mr. A. D. Waley have translated much valuable material for their study. It becomes, it is true, increasingly clear that very few reliable examples of the painting of those times have survived. But the intelligentsia of our country, and the learned world in general, are prone to attach more value to what they read about than to what they see. Indeed, it is only in very recent times that with regard to our own old masters the importance of having numerous and tangible documents, actual pictures of undoubted worth, has become generally appreciated; or even considering the absence, until recent times, of museums and galleries, at all possible. Connoisseurship as a scientific study is almost entirely a modern growth. Even now old-fashioned people are hardly aware of its existence. The small dealers who still, I am glad to say, flourish in London, still think that a copy of Bryan's dictionary and a little sale-room experience is quite enough to equip them to decide whether a picture is "by the master" or not. It is not unnatural, therefore, that many people should suppose that if they like a picture and it is signed by a well-known Chinese artist, all they have to do is to consult Mr. Waley's *Index* (published by the British Museum) and that they can then consider themselves in possession of an old master. But these are, perhaps, too unsophisticated a public to concern readers of this book. There is another class of error which will to them be more dangerous, I fear. This is to suppose that there is at present any standard of connoisseurship in China, Japan or elsewhere that will enable them to decide on the authenticity of reputed works by Chinese artists of the T'ang and Sung dynasties. It is true that in China and Japan a great deal of

xviii

work is being done which will eventually make the situation clearer. But it is doubtful whether there will ever be the same certainty as exists about European works of art; the Sung dynasty ended in A.D. 1279 and much has happened in the East since then.

The reason, therefore, why I am interested in comparatively modern Chinese art rather than in that of these great but remote epochs will be clear. My instincts are those of a connoisseur. I like to see and compare, and to form my own tastes and judgments. I have said that Mr. Jenyns also shares my tastes. I think that they will stand him in good stead. I believe that the future of the study of Oriental art lies for us far more in the hands of the practical expert, the connoisseur, than in those of the art historian proper. Unless we are prepared to establish in London a body of learned Chinese and Japanese, working along the most modern lines, and equipped with the best possible libraries, not to mention unobtainable museums of specimens, I think that we shall never be able to make Far Eastern art scholarship a respectable, scientific and spiritually valuable body of knowledge and opinion.

We shall at most be able to study it at second-hand and at a wide remove of sympathy, with an intelligence necessarily less ready than is possible for men to whom the brush is still the natural implement of expression. Oriental art is not a department of ethnography (except in so far as all art is). It cannot be rightly regarded except by those to whom its practice is a sacred trust, a living enthusiasm.

Our policy ought, I think, to be to approach it with a spirit of humility far different from that in which we have attempted to proselytize the East with religious missions. This is a hard task for us; humility is a virtue which as a nation we may, perhaps, in recent years have learnt more about than ever before; but it is still in Europe confined to a few chosen wise men. It is difficult to suppose that it will in the near future become the governing principle even in matters so trifling as our policy towards the culture of China and Japan.

But I must here point out that the problem is even more complicated. In all matters of what one might, on the analogy of the phrase "dead languages" call the "dead arts," we are certainly better equipped than those in whose native land the material for the study of these dead arts is found. Archæology is a European science, in so far as it is scientific at all. Our knowledge of all those matters to which the scientific intelligence, the art of correct classification, of scientific analysis of specimens, of scientific recording of sites, can be applied, is equal or superior to that of the Chinese. In the domain of all the minor arts, too—porcelain, pottery, bronze, jade, etc.—our museums are now very well equipped. An occasional inscription puzzles us by a reference, perhaps, to some historic fact at present inaccessible; problems of style have as yet not had time to sort themselves out completely; but on the whole we are well on the way to order and comprehension. Here again the trend of the art trade has helped us.

It is when we come to the arts where personality is paramount, where genius and intellect of the highest order are in question, where biography matters, that our task is, I think, of a wholly different kind. We are at grips with a civilization, a civilization still alive, changing and growing; a world of thought, not wholly familiar, and yet wholly human, fallible, sublime, abysmal, the world of the humanities, in a land where that word has a significance quite as real as it has among us, but where correspondences must be sought not with the tally and gauge, not with the apparatus of conscious science and conscious reasoning only, but with the whole of the spirit, with all the emotions that go to make up man.

We are seeking to storm the inmost citadels of the soul of another people; we are in a contact, not on the level either of war or of commerce, relationships which are neither perhaps quite valueless, but on a level far less simple, where even the commerce of the intellect, the interchange that goes on between scholars in pursuit of common aims, the impersonal relationships of fellow-researchers, will not do more than mitigate slightly the solemnity, the portentousness of our undertaking.

It is a thing which it is hard to avoid becoming too serious about. Hardly any one can escape sentimentality in such circumstances, certainly not myself. I very easily get into a state in which the very thought, for instance, of Professor Liu Hai-su brings tears to my eyes. He himself, I think, is luckily comparatively sane.

CONTENTS

LIST OF ILLUSTRATIONS

LIST OF ILLUSTRATIONS

I

A General Survey

"ABOVE is Heaven, below are Hangchow and Soochow" runs a Chinese proverb. China is still distant enough from our lands to be invested with the glamour of an undiscovered country. The customs of the Chinese, their manners, their methods of life, their wars and their politics, their art, have an engaging quality; yet they are so far remote from our own habits of thought and life as to make it difficult for us to appreciate the problems of their society. To the larger part of the British public China is still a fantastic and decorative country of make-believe: a land of pigtails and pagodas and the willow-pattern plate. It is a sad illusion—the pigtails have gone, the pagodas are in ruins, the willow-pattern plate was a foreign invention.[1] It is a picture of China as conceived by England of the eighteenth century that lingers. Most of us think and speak of China in terms of the *chinoiserie* which our ancestors collected. The Chippendale furniture in the Chinese manner, the immense armorial dinner services ordered through the good offices of the East India Company, the pretty but trivial wallpapers that still cling to the walls of our country houses, are the popular idea of Chinese art. We are prepared to judge its merits on the materials that appealed to the taste of the eighteenth century, and whatever charming bric-à-brac

[1] First used at Caughley on Salopian porcelain towards the end of the eighteenth century. See Honey. *English Pottery and Porcelain*, p. 190.

B   I

the Chinese were willing to export to Europe at that time. We are apt to forget how very recent is our knowledge of China previous to the eighteenth century. It is not an exaggeration to say that it is only the last thirty years that have revealed to us the existence and extent of the art of earlier periods; they should have fundamentally changed our outlook. The recent purchase of the Eumorfopoulos Collection by the British nation implies at last a generous acceptance of the importance of Chinese civilization. It is a final, if somewhat belated, recognition that the great culture of China is fit to take its place beside that of Greece and Egypt.

But since the great bulk of Chinese painting in this country dates from the eighteenth century, an affection for European art of that period is the best passport to the work of Chinese painters the public is likely to encounter. Eighteenth-century Europe and eighteenth-century China shared the same tastes, for Europe at that time, under the domination of French taste, was particularly open to Chinese influence. "European taste indeed had at last been so closely disciplined in the classic style that a reaction in favour of the outlandish was experienced. Some alternative was needed to academic classicism. Something that should be different in style, in scale, and in association but should none the less appeal to tastes trained in the canons of Le Brun's Academy and the Court of Versailles. The East offered exactly what was needed: an art associated with a mighty empire, and therefore not ignoble; an art of pure and glowing colour and of rare and precious material; an art of exquisite finish and infinite sophistication, yet one neither solemn nor pompous nor (to European eyes) consistent; an art, moreover, which had never been measured by the five orders and had never felt the heavy impress of Rome. All this China offered, 'enwrapped in an exquisite sense of the strange.' It is exactly this quality which is seized upon by De la Loubère in his contemporary analysis of Chinese art. 'Ils veulent donc de l'extraordinaire dans la peinture, comme nous voulons du merveilleux dans la poésie. Ils imaginent des arbres, des fleurs, des oiseaux et d'autres animaux qui ne furent jamais. Ils donnent quelquefois aux hommes des attitudes impossibles et le secret est de répandre sur toutes ces choses une facilité qui les fasse paraître naturelles.' " [1] At no other date were the two civilizations nearer each other. The reigns of Louis XV and XVI found their natural parallel in those of the Chinese emperors K'ang Hsi and Ch'ien Lung. The temper of both countries in the eighteenth century was tolerant, rational, a little sceptical, supremely confident and intellectually discriminating. The taste of the eighteenth century was gracious and gay, extravagant, curious and more than a little worldly ; for it was dominated by the brilliance of cosmopolitan courts and the fancy of the *poule de luxe*. That century had no wish to understand the Chinese art of earlier periods; it sought to stir the imagination with extravagant pictures of a distant and exotic civilization. It did not even obtain good examples of contemporary Chinese painting, but was content with the Chinese "rice paper" paintings, the carved ivory balls and the other charming rubbish that the Chinese were prepared to send overseas. An enormous export trade sprang up in articles which were especially manufactured for foreign amusement and which the Chinese would have scorned to use themselves. By the middle of the eighteenth century, in her indiscriminate admiration for everything Oriental, Europe was ready to consume anything that the East might offer.

The taste for *chinoiserie* was first established in France ; in 1667 Louis XIV appeared at a court ball in a costume half

[1] Joan Evans. *Pattern*, vol. ii, ch. vii, pp. 64–65.

Persian and half Chinese ; by the end of the seventeenth century it was in full bloom and by 1725 it was international. The enormous porcelain rooms in the rococo palaces of Vienna, Munich and Berlin still exist to remind us of its close. An engraving by Jollein supplied Louis XIV with the model for a *trianon de porcelaine* in imitation of the porcelain tower of Nanking.[1] In 1756 Louis XV, at the suggestion of the Pompadour, and in imitation of the Chinese emperor, guided the plough at the opening of the spring tilling: [2] as early as 1707 the Duchess of Namur had herself conveyed in her chair to her country estate at Neufchâtel by relays of French coolies that followed her in carts.[3] England was not long in adopting these exotic tastes. In 1682 Evelyn wrote, "Went to visit our good neighbour Mr. Bohun whose house is a cabinet of all elegancies, especially Indian, in the hall are contrivances of Japan Screens instead of wainscoat . . . the landscapes of the screens expressed the manners of living and country of the Chinese." Pagodas rose at Kew Gardens, at Het Loo in Holland, and on the property of the Duc de Choiseul beside the Loire. Ludwig of Bavaria contemplated the erection of a reproduction of the Summer Palace, while the Landgrave of Kassel in 1781 established at Weissenstein on the shore of Lake Wilhemshöhe a model Chinese village in which black women masqueraded as Chinese milkmaids.[4]

Meanwhile Jesuit scholars had made themselves indispensable at the Chinese court, but it was their secular accomplishments that enabled them to keep their positions, and their religion was only tolerated as long as they did not interfere with the government of the country. Yung Chêng,

[1] Reichwein. *China and Europe,* p. 60.
[2] *Ibid.,* p. 106.
[3] *Ibid.,* p. 35.
[4] *Ibid.,* p. 121.

in the second edition (1724) of his father's edict against
heterodox beliefs, speaks of "the doctrine of the Occident
which honours T'ien Chu. Neither is this orthodox. But
because the men who prefer it are well versed in astronomy,
they are employed by the throne, all must know it." [1] It
was these learned and adventurous priests who tended the
clocks, astronomical instruments and mechanical toys, and
introduced medicine and mathematics, for the benefit of
the late Ming and the early Ch'ing emperors; and it was
they who fed the curiosity of the West with descriptions
of Chinese life. The first of them, Matteo Ricci, arrived in
China in 1583. His enterprise, tact and ability earned him a
place in the Imperial annals.[2] On Jan. 28, 1601, a petition by
Ricci enumerates among other presents sent to the emperor
"an image of the Lord, two images of the Holy Virgin, a
prayer book in one volume, a crucifix inlaid with pearls,
two striking clocks, a map of the world and a Western
lute." [3] But the Board of Rites began to look askance at

---

[1] Wieger. *Moral Tenets and Customs in China*, p. 131.

[2] Chang Keng, the author of the *Hua-shi-hui-chuan*, writes: "In the
time of the Ming dynasty, there came to this land a European artist by
the name of Li Ma-Tao (Ricci). He had a good working knowledge of
our tongue, and resided in the Western Camp near the Cheng-yan-men
Gate in the Southern Capital. Among his paintings there is one representing a woman holding a babe in her arms. It is a masterly work full
of life and spirit, and especially attractive in brilliance of colours. He
once remarked that 'Chinese paintings for the most part are shadeless,
and hence are always flat: on the contrary Western art deals with both
light and shade, so it is full and perfect. Objects when seen from the
front are shadeless, but viewed sideways they necessarily look dark and
in art should be treated accordingly. The front view being exposed to
full light looks conspicuous, so it is drawn raised. Our own Ping-Cheng
mastered this principle and applied it to his art, though in so doing he
went against the taste of his own countrymen to whom the orthodox
native methods were sacred and inviolable.' " (*The Kokka*, No. 222,
vol. xix, 1908-9, p. 133: "Influence of Western Art upon Chinese
Painting," by Kyûshirô Nakamura.)

[3] Laufer, B. *Christian Art in China*, p. 7.

his strange doctrines; we find them remonstrating at his gifts, "for instance the pictures of the Lord of Heaven and his Mother, also bones of the transfigured, as if those ascending to heaven needed bones. Han Yü of the T'ang said such unclean things can only bring ill-luck and should therefore be kept out of the palace . . . let him (Ricci) be given a cap and belt and sent away to Kiangsi."

In 1696 an edict of toleration promoted the spread of Christianity. Soon after it was said that the provinces of Kiangsi, Kiangsu and Anhwei alone could boast of a hundred churches and a hundred thousand converts. The Jesuits Belleville and Gherardini arrived in 1699, and Castiglione and Attiret under Ch'ien Lung.[1] But in 1742 Benedict XIV in a Papal Bull condemned ancestor-worship, which the Jesuits had tolerated; and this entirely undermined the position that the Jesuits had established. This action was attributed to the ignorance and jealousy of the Dominicans. But even before this date anxiety had been growing among Chinese officials at the extent of Christian influence, which had led in 1733 to an edict forbidding the propaganda of Christianity and in 1736 to a prohibition of the teaching itself. Ch'ien Lung resented the Papal Bull, which he regarded as an intrusion, and withdrew all protection from the Christian community; but the Jesuits were permitted to remain in the palace, and continued to paint portraits of his hawks and hounds, to manufacture and manipulate his mechanical toys, to wind the clocks and to draw up the plans of the Yüan Ming Yüan (a Chinese copy of Versailles) and to arrange for the striking of a series of copper engravings in Paris to celebrate his campaigns. And so, by a strange reversal of circumstances, while Ludwig of Bavaria contemplated a model of the Summer Palace,[2]

[1] 1736-96.
[2] Reichwein. *China and Europe,* p. 59.

II. BROCADE STRIPED HOUND
by Lang Shih-Ning (*b.* 1688, *d.* 1766).
(Guiseppe Castiglione.)
The National Collection, Peiping.   (9′ 11″ × 6′)

Ch'ien Lung with the help of the Jesuits built a Chinese edition of Versailles, and while the Landgrave of Kassel played at Chinese life in a model hamlet, the emperor Ch'ien Lung dressed up his own coolies to masquerade as the inhabitants of a European village. At the same time that Chinese artisans laboured to supply the silks the wallpapers and the porcelains that the West demanded, Castiglione and Attiret painted pictures for the Chinese imperial pleasure; and "in the imperial palaces of Peking, Yüan Ming Yüan and Jehol the passage of hours was marked by the fluttering of enamelled wings, a gushing of glass fountains and a spinning of paste stars, while from a thousand concealed and whirring orchestras the gavottes and minuets of London rose strangely in the Chinese air." [1]

But by 1780 the taste for *chinoiserie* was on the wane. Elizabeth Montagu wrote in 1749 slightingly of the "barbarous gaudy gout" of the Chinese.[2] Fanny Burney, on Dec. 19, 1785, confides to her diary that she was taken to see the Chinese curiosities of a certain Dr. Lind, among them a book of paintings of Chinese plants "very finely executed and brightly coloured (which) showed how little their artists want patience, though everything shows how little is the pleasure to be given by any pains without taste." Chinese taste stood condemned as flippant and extravagant. In 1816 Ellis of the Amherst Mission speaks of Chinese painting as "grotesque and uselessly laborious," and Macaulay, writing in the middle of the last century of the foibles of William and Mary, says " Mary had acquired at the Hague a taste for the porcelain of China, and amused herself by forming at Hampton a vast collection of hideous

[1] S. Harcourt Smith. *Catalogue of Various Clocks, Watches, Automata and Other Miscellaneous Objects of European Workmanship dating from the XVIII and early XIX Century in the Palace Museum and the Wu Ying Tien.*

[2] P. McQuoid and R. Edwards. *Dictionary of English Furniture*, vol. ii, p. 92.

7

images and of vases on which houses, trees, bridges, and mandarins were depicted in outrageous defiance of all the laws of perspective. The fashion, a frivolous and inelegant fashion, it must be owned, which was thus set by this amiable queen spread fast and wide. In a few years almost every great house contained a museum of these grotesque baubles. Even statesmen and generals were not ashamed to be renowned as judges of teapots and dragons, and satirists long continued to repeat that a fine lady valued her mottled green pottery quite as much as she valued her monkey, and much more than she valued her husband."

By 1863 Japan had been opened,[1] and the latter half of the nineteenth century saw a rage for Satsuma porcelain, *tsuba, netsuké* and Japanese prints which entirely eclipsed the Chinese taste to which it was considered immensely superior. It is only during the last thirty years that taste for Chinese art has returned. The bronzes of the Chou dynasty and the Han, the tomb figures of the T'ang and porcelain of the Sung, even the rough blue and white underglaze wares of the Ming are what is sought for now. The *chinoiserie* of the eighteenth century has had its day.

But the reason why Chinese painting is so often dismissed as a beautiful trifle cannot be explained entirely by the false emphasis that the taste of eighteenth-century Europe has placed upon it. Of the great figure-paintings of the Han period nothing but a few engravings on stone has survived. The Sui dynasty and the Five Dynasties that preceded the T'ang, by which Chinese painting is supposed to have been fully developed, have left a few tentative remains, while the T'ang dynasty has reached us mainly in the provincial [2] and archaic material that the Tun Huang caves have supplied. It is not until we arrive at the Sung dynasty that there are

---

[1] To foreign trade.

[2] The famous French sinologue Pelliot does not agree with this.

8

sufficient numbers of paintings to give us a clear picture of the Chinese tradition, but by that time, it is widely believed, it was almost a spent force. It seems likely that the Chinese themselves must be content with an incomplete knowledge from scattered fragments of their own greatest periods. It is so rare for these fragments to reach Europe that most Europeans have not only been misinformed, but have had no opportunity of correcting their ignorance. Since they are unable to distinguish the genuine from the counterfeit European collectors are not prepared to pay sufficiently high figures to attract even the best of the later paintings to our shores. The situation is not likely to change until a much higher standard of connoisseurship has arisen. There are but a few Americans and a mere handful of Europeans who have the least idea how to begin to distinguish good Chinese paintings from bad, genuine calligraphy from the counterfeit, live from dead ink. There are comparatively few facilities provided by our museums for the student. The British Museum is the only museum in this country that possesses more than a handful of Chinese paintings, and the great bulk of that collection is not good enough to put on exhibition. Chinese painting on the continent is even less well represented. The poverty of private collections (they are almost non-existent) and the difficulty of obtaining reproductions from China [1] have all contributed to the obscurity which shrouds this subject. In China itself the absence of any public collection of importance, except the ex-Imperial Palace treasures (which have never yet been properly exhibited and which down to the fall of the Ch'ing dynasty were only accessible to a narrow circle round the throne), has meant that enthusiasts have had to rely on the pictures in private collections, which are scat-

[1] This has recently been corrected by the publication of the Ku Kung Shu Hua Chi (Calligraphy and Paintings from the Palace Collections).

tered at vast distances over the country, and whose owners are never anxious to exhibit their possessions to a stranger. For a foreigner to obtain the entrée to such collections, it requires social position, considerable tact, and a knowledge of the Chinese language and Chinese etiquette, besides an endless series of appointments and unlimited patience. Nor does the European understand the trouble that he is causing. Chinese pictures are not unrolled and rolled up in a minute or suspended without effort. Chinese etiquette demands polite overtures, an exchange of tea and compliments over each picture. Moreover, it is an excellent Chinese habit to withhold the best until the host feels sure his visitor is able to appreciate it. Mi Fei, whose collection was famous, kept a number of poor paintings especially for the benefit of the ignorant and troublesome.

The native literature on painting is considerable, informative, but entirely unscientific, and it never gives us a sufficiently clear account to enable us to distinguish the work of great masters. Chinese books are full of charming anecdotes of the lives of painters and of instances of their skill. They tell us of horses that were painted so vividly that they left their frames to range the fields at night, and of painted dragons that flew away. We are told that Chang Sēng-Yu, when the monks of a monastery complained to him that the pigeons under the temple eaves would foul the gilt faces of the Buddhist images beneath, covered the east wall with a painting of hawks and the western one with kites. The pigeons promptly left, and peace and cleanliness was restored. While Li K'ung-Hsiu could paint cats which would keep any home free of mice.

It is difficult to resist the conclusion that it is not at all easy for the educated classes in China to obtain a real knowledge of their own painting. But at least they have not to strive with the difficulties of the Chinese language and the

10

intricacies of Buddhist and Taoist iconography (which
deters a great number of Europeans). Most of the Chinese
sources must be tackled in the original, and the sinologue is
not always, alas, a competent art critic.

Moreover, the enormous number of imitations have
made it impossible to identify the originals with any certainty, if they still exist. We are able to recognize, for
instance, the style in which Hsia Kuei painted, but there is
probably no one who is in the position to make a definite
attribution. A very intimate knowledge of the paintings
attributed to him in the Palace Collections would supply the
best criterion, but even so in the case of many artists it is
impossible to be certain that the imperial attributions were
correct. Ch'ien Lung inscribed many pieces of porcelain
with attributions which would not be accepted to-day.
Most of the imperial collections of the past have come to
unfortunate ends. This is the sad consequence of assembling
many pictures in one place. Chou Hsin burnt himself and
his treasures on the Deer Terrace before his dynasty was
replaced by the Chou's. Hui Tsung's wonderful collections
were looted and dispersed (where they were not destroyed)
at the fall of the Northern Sung, and Ch'ien Lung's collection must have suffered during the Boxer troubles and
the turmoil that surrounded the collapse of the Ch'ing
dynasty; but a very extensive national collection still survives and it is upon this that future standards will have to
be based. Each generation has gone out of its way to lament
the decadent art of the present and the glorious paintings of
the past dynasties. "The mountains of our time are not as
lofty as the mountains of the days of old." Chang Yen
Yüan of the T'ang dynasty said in his day, "even things as
poor as a dead rat were gems." [1]

It is not surprising in view of the rarity of early paintings

[1] Osvald Sirén. *A History of Early Chinese Painting*, vol. i, p. 28.

that the desire for Sung paintings in Europe has entirely outweighed the supply. There is a Chinese saying "out of every ten Sung paintings, eleven are spurious," and the majority of Chinese paintings date from the Ming and later.[1] Critics have asserted with some truth that the seventeenth- and eighteenth-century paintings are imitative, with the result that a large number of dingy paintings bearing appropriate signatures of the Sung period have been cooked for the foreign market. It is a great mistake to dismiss all the late paintings as decadent. The word may blind the eye to changes that were not possible under earlier conditions. It would be comparatively easy to assemble a collection of genuine paintings of the best artists from the Ming and Ch'ing, and they are not nearly so expensive. By a swing of the pendulum the habit of decrying Chinese art of the eighteenth century has succeeded the taste for *chinoiserie*. An archæological flavour has crept into collecting. But the snobbery of the "older the better" school is just as insidious as the shallowness of those who cannot appreciate any porcelain other than that decorated in the gay enamels of *famille verte* or *famille rose*.

As Waley has pointed out, the vicissitudes that many paintings had to endure did not make for their survival. To the dry climate of the north we owe the preservation of the Tun Huang paintings, but the damp heat and white ants of the south must have destroyed many others, and the ravages of civil war and fire, and the vicissitudes of travel accounted for more. A Chinese official was likely to take his paintings on tour with him. (We are told that an album of flower and bird paintings belonging to the eighteenth-century collector Yuan Yuan fell into the Yangtze, when he was on his way to a new post; later it disappeared in

[1] Waley, A. *Burlington Magazine,* vol. xxx, No. clxxi, June 1917, pp. 209–214.

the Boxer troubles.[1]) The Chinese are careless of preservation. Worm-holes and mould are constantly pointed out
by Chinese dealers with pleasure as evidence of age. China
leaves her ruins to fall to dust carrying their secrets with
them to the grave. Yet a crumbling ruin in an overgrown
wilderness is eloquent of past glories; history, it has been
said, retreats before the bowler hat and the tripper clamour-
ing for his lunch. The Chinese are wise enough to know that
no amount of reinforced concrete, kiosks and turnstiles can
bring back the past. Tung Ch'i-Ch'ang, a prime minister,
art critic and president of the Board of Rites (1555-1636),
wrote: "Northern Sung paintings were rare, T'ang painting
very rare, and pre-T'ang paintings unobtainable" in his
day; and a collector, Hsieh Kun, writing about 1890 of
the pictures he had seen, speaks only of one T'ang painting,
a roll attributed to Ku K'ai-Chih.[2]

Copies of old masters are common to all countries, but
the training of the Chinese artist, which consisted in a
continuous analysis and repetition of old masters, has
fostered the habit of duplication. Since the time of Hsieh
Ho the desire to train the eye and taste along traditional
lines has produced a mass of reproductions, of which many
were legitimate copies not intended to deceive, but which
have since taken their place among deliberate fakes. And
when the Chinese or Japanese set about to fake deliberately
they know of a thousand and one tricks which the European
has never thought of. It is said of the Japanese potter, Suwa
Sojan, that he was struck speechless before his own work
when it was shown to him in the guise of a Sung celadon,[3]
and that Matsumoto Sahei of Kutani bought a vase which

[1] Sirén. *Chinese Paintings in American Collections,* p. 29.
[2] See Waley, A. *Burlington Magazine,* vol. xxx, No. clxxi, June 1917,
pp. 209-217.
[3] *Oriental Ceramics,* vol. i, No. 6, 25, Jan. 1929, p. 2.

when he had brought it home he found to be of his own making. In addition there are a large number of paintings wholly or partially restored, so cleverly in some instances that it is difficult to see where the original ends and the restoration begins. The signature of an artist is easily supplied and the seals of the great collectors Hui Tsung, Ch'ien Lung, and Hsiang Mo-Lin are frequently reproduced. It is an optimistic man who believes that the label on the outside of a Chinese scroll bears any relation to the picture within. Any Chinese picture-dealer will supply you at short notice with paintings by Li Lung-Mien, Ch'iu Ying or Chao Mêng-Fu, all of which have been copied during and ever since their own lifetime. Chien Yung wrote: "The art of forging calligraphy on paintings is an ancient one. In the T'ang dynasty Ch'eng Hsui-chi forged the writing of Wang Hsi Chih. In the Sung dynasty Mi Fei forged the writing of Ch'u Su-Liang. But their forgeries were made for a joke and not for commercial purposes." [1] Mr. Einstein tells us in the *Burlington Magazine* [2] of an American friend, whose collection of Chinese paintings was more conspicuous for its size than quality, who turned down a Ming painting as far too recent, but who later purchased the identical picture from another Chinese dealer who had supplied it with the seal and signature of a Sung artist, at a much higher price. The Chinese have not only a habit of supplying signatures to anonymous paintings but of deleting old signatures to replace them by more famous names. A picture of a horse will be found to carry the name of Han Kan, Li Lung Mien or Chao Mêng-Fu, or a peony that of Yün Shou-Ping. As Mi Fei remarks, "There are many excellent pictures without names, but people of to-day are very liberal in giving names to them; consequently they call all paintings

[1] Waley, A. *An Introduction to the Study of Chinese Painting*, p. 6.
[2] *Burlington Magazine*, No. cxii, vol. xxi, July 1912, pp. 185–192.

14

of oxen by Tai Sung and all paintings of horses by Han Kan." [1] Fortunately many fakes are works of art in themselves. In the absence of large numbers of good reproductions and a knowledge of the language, our European critics are still largely confined "to retailing secondhand accounts and interspersing their remarks with æsthetic vapourizing."

In the January number of the *Burlington Magazine* for 1917,[2] Waley discusses a picture entitled "Going up the River for the Spring Festival," commissioned by Hui Tsung from the artist Chang Tsē-Tuan, *c.* 1126. The spectator is taken up the Pien River along tow-paths, among barges and house-boats and happy holiday crowds, to the capital Pien Chang, which was sacked a year after it was painted. During the sack, Waley tells us, the picture was stolen and a copy (by whom?) substituted. The original passed through the hands of several owners and (*c.* 1352) was copied by Chao Chung-Mu, a son of Chao Mêng-Fu and by Shêng Mou, while in the possession of Yang Chun. In about 1600 it passed from the hands of the Yen family into the Imperial Collection, from which it was stolen by a court official who hid it in a crack in the wall of the royal aqueduct; at the same time a great storm caused the waters to rise and it was badly damaged. About 1890 Hsieh Kun saw a damaged version which he took to be the original, also a copy by the artist Ch'iu Ying. The Museum copy that Waley illustrates is on silk and unsigned. He mentions in the same article the existence of other copies in America and one in the hands of Mr. Chester Beatty and another in the hands of Mr. Eumorfopoulos. Since he wrote, three other copies have been incorporated in the Museum Collections: one from the collection of Sir Valentine Chirol

[1] Sirén, O. *A History of Early Chinese Painting,* vol. ii, p. 31.
[2] *Burlington Magazine,* vol. xxx, No. clxvi, pp. 3–10.

signed Ch'iu Ying in the style of Chang Tsē-Tuan, and another, a very poor affair on paper; the third (from the Eumorfopoulos Collection) is signed by Ch'iu Ying. I have myself seen another copy in the hands of a dealer, a second in the hands of a collector who has recently returned from China, both signed Ch'iu Ying, and heard of a third in the hands of a lady (attribution unknown). Most copies of this picture are attributed to Ch'iu Ying; they seem to date from the nineteenth century and must be copies of his copy, third- and fourth-hand. This is one instance alone in which some small conception can be given of the number of offspring one painting has originated.

The different classes of fakes can be divided into:

(*a*) Crude forms in which the silk has been dyed or hung over a fire to acquire a mellow tint and in which discrepancies of date and subject matter are obvious.

(*b*) Signature and seals added to anonymous paintings, in which the position of the signature or the quality of the writing or the painting may cause suspicion.

(*c*) Signatures that have been washed out or cut away and others supplied, in which the position of the signature does not harmonize with that of the painting or the ink has not sunk so deeply into the silk.

(*d*) Careful copies, made sometimes in all innocence by students, or with the intent to deceive, in which seals, signature and style have all been carefully imitated. Needless to add these are the most difficult to distinguish.

(*e*) "Thinning the second layer," a process only possible with certain paintings on paper, which were not made till the time of Ch'ien Lung, in which the picture is actually split in two and the two impressions sold separately. This process is not feasible except with ink paintings on thick paper.

It is impossible to supply a ready guide to the authenticity of Chinese paintings, which only experience and sensibility can provide. The signatures of the painter, the seals of collectors through whose hands it has passed and the accompanying inscriptions, may confirm or support an attribution, but they are not to be relied upon. Careful practice in calligraphy enabled the Chinese to write in many different styles. It was not until the Yüan dynasty that inscriptions on pictures became fashionable. Landscapes earlier than the Sung should bear their signatures hidden in rocks and plants. Binyon tells us that the seal from orange vermilion came in at the end of the Ming, when it replaced a duller and deeper red that was produced from ruby wood.

It must be remembered that China was the centre of a group of kindred peoples inferior to her in culture, to whom she dispensed the blessings of her civilization. On the northwest lay Tibet, whose independence was recognized only in order that her priests might exercise control over the nomad races of Mongolia for Chinese political ends. To the south and south-west, Malay, Siam, Annam and Burma peopled by Shans kindred to the Cantonese in blood, who paid tribute whenever they felt disposed to cultivate Chinese friendship, or when the Chinese were strong enough to exact it. On the east was Korea, who alone of China's neighbours can be said to have produced a civilization at all comparable, and whose pottery of the Koryŏ period (918–1392) can vie with anything that China has ever made. The little Korean painting that has survived is almost indistinguishable from the Chinese painting that inspired it. Last of all there is Japan, whose relation to China in the world of art has been compared by Binyon to that which has existed between England and Italy. It is no exaggeration to say that Japan owes her entire culture to China as we do to Greece, Rome and Palestine. Although

C

she has developed her institutions along different lines, she has again and again been dominated by Chinese taste: her painting continually reflects the influence of the Chinese art of earlier periods, and in particular the ink painting of the Southern Sung. Her own native schools have an exquisite refinement and a luminosity of colour which is entirely their own, but they do not approach the greatness of Chinese painting at its height; in the craft of lacquer alone the pupil has surpassed the master.

It has been said that a great civilization cannot be born without an antecedent, or die without leaving a heritage. In China the heritage is there, but the antecedents are difficult to find. China had no neighbours upon whose culture she could draw. She was cut off from the contemporary cultures of the world by natural barriers of desert, mountain and sea; unlike the West she was rarely open to the play of foreign influences. Probably the earliest foreign influences were the result of a mission sent in 122 B.C. by the Emperor Wu Ti of the Han to Ferghana (Afghanistan) to find allies against the Hsiung Nu, a market for Chinese silk and a supply of "superior horses." Chang Chien, who headed the mission, is supposed to have introduced on his return the hemp, the walnut and the grape. This mission undoubtedly paved the way for Buddhism, which must have already begun to penetrate the country, although the official date of the introduction is given as A.D. 67, when a mission sent by the Emperor Ming Ti to India to inquire into the tenets of the new religion returned with books and priests. Buddhism brought with it the seeds of Alexander's conquests, and the influence of Greece can be seen in the Buddhist sculptures of Gandhara, Afghanistan and Chinese Turkestan of the second and third centuries B.C. Buddhism was the first and the only really distinctive influence from the outside world until the full impact with the West in the seventeenth century. A great wave from India swept over China during the Han and early T'ang. Everything imported from India was sacred. How Buddhism changed and modified the Chinese view of life we shall consider in another chapter. The aftermath of Buddhism produced the great cosmopolitan culture of the T'ang period when Arabs and Persians, Nestorians and Manicheans, Turks and Mongols met at the Chinese capital. To what extent China in return influenced the painting of the West or that of Persia and the Far East are fascinating problems which do not concern us here. The rôle that Christianity exercised in the life and art of Europe was assigned to Buddhism in the East. Christianity has never exercised more than a fleeting and trivial influence on Chinese art. The Nestorian monument of Hsi An, set up A.D. 781, and a Nestorian manuscript from Tun Huang of about A.D. 800 from the collection of Pelliot (No. 3847 in the *Bibliothèque Nationale,* Paris) stand out as isolated examples of early Christian endeavour.[1] The bronze Ongut plaques containing birds (doves?) and crosses from the Sui Yuan province on the north bank of the Yangtze, dating from the twelfth to the fifteenth century, may also be assigned to Christian influence.

By the end of the Sung the power of Buddhism was spent. China continued to develop her culture in isolation until the coming of the Jesuits heralded the impact with Western civilization. At the request of K'ang Hsi (1662–1722), who was anxious to learn something about contemporary European painting, a missionary by the name of Bouvet proceeded to Paris and returned with two French Jesuits, Gherardini and Belleville, in 1699. Yet in the closing years of this reign the missionaries were persecuted and also during the succeeding reign of Yung Chêng (1723–35).

[1] Moule, A. C. *Christians in China before 1550,* pp. 32 and 52.

During the first part of the reign of Ch'ien Lung a gentler atmosphere prevailed. But Ch'ien Lung never learnt to appreciate the modelling of the face and the projection of shadows, which Western technique displayed, and eventually the Jesuit painters were forced to adopt Chinese methods. Another Jesuit painter, Attiret, wrote to Paris on Nov. 1, 1743, "Il m'a fallu oublier, pour ainsi dire, tout ce que j'avais appris et me faire une nouvelle manière pour me conformer au goût de la nation. . . . Tout ce que nous peignons est ordonné par l'empereur. Nous faisons d'abord les dessins: il les voit, les fait changer, réformer comme bon lui semble. Que la correction soit bien ou mal, il faut passer par là sans oser rien dire." [1] In fact the European technique was never sufficiently popular to displace the native traditional style. For a time K'ang Hsi and Ch'ien Lung amused themselves with portraits drawn in oils. We are told that at the time of MacCartney's embassy (1792–94) some of Castiglione's oil paintings still hung on the walls of the Yüan Ming Yüan. The mandarins in waiting expressed themselves extremely shocked by the shadows of the portraits that the embassy brought as presents from George III, and asked gravely whether the originals really possessed one side of the face darker than the other,[2] although they must have been long familiar with the European style. The superb series of engravings on copper to celebrate the victories of Ch'ien Lung over the Dzoungars and the Mussulmans, engraved in Paris under the direction of Cochin from drawings by Castiglione, Attiret, Sechelbert, and Jesus Damascine, were ordered in 1765 and the last plate finished in 1774.[3] They provoked several Chinese

[1] Bushell, S. W. *Chinese Art,* vol. ii, p. 106.

[2] *Ibid.*, p. 107.

[3] Pelliot, P. *Les Conquêtes de l'empereur de la Chine: T'oung Pao,* ser. ii, vol. 20, pp. 184–274.

copies. In 1786, we learn from a letter of P. Benoit, the Chinese engraved twenty plates with the fortifications of the Yüan Ming Yüan. This was their first attempt at copper-plate engraving. Later engravings included a series of etchings of campaigns against Tibet, Formosa, Nepal, Annam, Yunnan and the Mussulmans of Chinese Turkestan.

There were, however, a small number of Chinese artists who adopted Jesuit Western methods. Among them were Chiao Ping-Chēng, an official of the Royal Astronomical Observatory (where he must have learnt the art from the Jesuits who served in the same department), and his pupil Lêng Mei (popularly called Chi Ch'en).[1] Both were patronized by K'ang Hsi. Ping-Chēng drew at the imperial bidding forty-six pictures of "Farming and Weaving," and in 1666 Lêng Mei took part in depicting the "Grand Cere-mony of the Imperial Birthday." Another artist whose works show Western influence is the painter Wên Tso, also known by the pen-name Ch'u-Chuang. He drew portraits of celebrated military and civil figures in which a Western influence of costume and coiffure is noticeable.[2] Yet another artist who painted in European style was T'ang Tai (T'ang Ching-Yen), a Manchu who collaborated with Joseph Castiglione.[3] During the nineteenth century there arose from time to time other painters who attempted to combine the traditional manner with European principles.

[1] *Kokka*, No. 222, p. 129: "Influence of Western Art upon Chinese Painting," by Kyûshirô Nakamura.

[2] One of the pictures is illustrated in *Kokka*, No. 222, p. 133. It is a portrait of a general Ti Tsing of the Sung dynasty, who is represented dressed in the Chinese manner except for the European tippet that covers the upper part of the chest and the loose flowing hair, reminiscent of the European wigs of the seventeenth century.

[3] There is a "bird and flower" picture produced by their united efforts in *Kokka*, No. 357.

The Irish painter Chinnery, who established himself at Macao, had a number of Chinese followers in Canton, but he never influenced the main stream of Chinese art. The brothers [1] Kao Ch'i Fêng and Kao Chien Fu of Canton and their pupils paint in this style. But this hybrid mixture is no more attractive to many palates than the bastard Græco-Indian Buddhist sculpture of the third century B.C. or the naturalistic painting of the school of Okyo in Japan. There has been a tendency in the last few years among Chinese painters to study European art in Paris. About 1926 Shanghai was full of Chinese versions of Cézanne, and since then there have been Chinese artists who have deserted their native style to plunge into the problems of the most modern European art. But it is to be hoped this is only a temporary adventure of a small number. There is a Chinese proverb that runs "Even a privy is popular when it is new."

It remains to sketch a brief outline of Chinese painting, which can be divided into seven periods for the purpose of our study.

(1) From the age of mythological sovereigns 2852–1766 B.C. to the end of the Ch'in 1766–206 B.C.

(2) The Han period 206 B.C.–A.D. 264, and the period of division that succeeded it 264–618 A.D.

(3) The T'ang dynasty 618–907.

(4) The Sung dynasty 960–1279 (north and south), and the Mongol Yüan dynasty which succeeded it first in the north and then in the south, destroying the remains of the Tartar kingdoms 1206–1358.

(5) The Ming dynasty 1368–1644.

(6) The Ch'ing dynasty 1644–1912.

(7) The Republic 1912.

[1] One of these brothers is dead.

Period 1.—Chinese history opens in 2852 B.C. with the reign of Fu-Hsi, who taught the people hunting, fishing and the rearing of animals; arranged the calendar, ordained marriage, organized clans; invented stringed musical instruments and received the eight trigrams from the back of a dragon horse which arose from the River Lo. These trigrams are composed of whole and broken lines, which can be made up into sixty-four combinations. The Chinese believe they are the basis of an ancient system of philosophy and divination, whose exact meaning has been lost, and also the origin of writing. The Book of Changes is built upon these symbols.[1]

To Lei, the daughter of one of the officials of the mythical Emperor Shun 2256–2208 B.C., legend has credited the invention of painting. The date of the first Chinese painting is a matter of conjecture. Probably the earliest painted forms that have survived are the pottery jars painted in black, terra cotta red spirals that have been excavated in Honan and Kansu and which date from Neolithic times (3000 B.C.). But they appear to belong to a pre-Chinese civilization.[2] On the tortoiseshell and bone finds of Anyang which date from the Shang-Yin dynasty 1766–1122 B.C. we find rough designs of birds and men, while the script is so far developed as to suggest earlier forms of writing which have not come down to us.[3] Tsai Yüan-Pei suggests that painting may have flourished as early as 1324 B.C. if the interpretation of a reference in the Shu King by the commentator Huang Fu-Mi can be trusted.[4] By the Chou dynasty, 1122–249

[1] Mayers, W. F. *Chinese Reader's Manual*, pp. 333–336.
[2] Andersson, J. G. *Preliminary Report on Archæological Research in Kansu.*
[3] Hopkins, L. C. "The Honan Relics: a New Investigation and Some Results," *Journal of the Royal Asiatic Society,* Jan. 1921.
[4] Zen, S. H. C. *Symposium of Chinese Culture,* p. 62: "Painting and Calligraphy," by Tsai Yüan-Pei.

B.C., a bronze technique was fully developed which supplied decorations in cloud and thunder pattern and in conventionalized animal and plant designs. Towards the end of the Ch'in, references appear to pictures of the sun, moon and stars, dragons, tortoises, eagles and other monsters. The first paintings were devoted to the worship of nature and the cult of the ancestor. The *K'ung-tzŭ-chia-yü* says Confucius once visited a Ming tang (official temple) whose four walls were decorated with paintings of the great monarchs of antiquity, Yao and Shun, and the tyrants at the close of the Shang-Yin and Chou dynasties.[1] Wang Yi, a commentator of the Odes of Ch'in, states that in the Ch'in kingdom the ancestral temples of early kings and ministers were painted with pictures of mountains, spirits, sages and monsters. Probably they were very similar to the designs that have survived in the early Korean tombs, which date from the third to sixth century.[2] No such important mural paintings from this period have survived either in China or Japan.

The Chinese do not date the invention of the brush till the time of Mêng T'ien who died in 209 B.C., although we have reason to believe that the inscriptions on bronzes show a calligraphic dexterity at a much earlier date.[3] According to Sirén silk is not definitely mentioned till the reign of Ho Ti (81–106); the earliest paintings must have been made entirely on wood or plaster walls. It was not until the invention of paper, attributed by the Chinese to Ts'ai lun A.D. 103,[4] that the materials became cheap enough

[1] Zen, S. H. C. *Symposium of Chinese Culture,* p. 64: "Painting and Calligraphy," by Tsai Yuan-Pei.

[2] Eckhardt, A. *History of Korean Art,* pp. 122 *et seq.*

[3] Yetts. *Catalogue of the George Eumorfopoulos Collection of Chinese and Corean Bronzes, etc.,* vol. ii, p. 43.

[4] Clapperton, R. A. *Paper-Making by Hand: An Historical Account,* pp. 1–26.

to allow a wide use. No paintings as early as this period other than those on Neolithic pottery have survived.

Period 2.—We have a good idea of what the paintings of the Han dynasty were like as more or less faithful translations of them engraved upon wood and stone have survived, and some fragments of painted pottery. Chavannes has illustrated the engravings from the stone slabs of the famous Han mortuary chambers at Hsiao T'ang Shan and Wu Liang in Shantung.[1] The painted pottery and stamped bricks of the Han provide us with pictures of hunting scenes, court ceremonies, processions and war chariots in battle: the animal fight painted on the pottery tiles of the Boston Museum is one of the most famous relics that has survived.[2] We are left with an impression of linear design without shadow or perspective, drawn in profile, not unlike the stone engravings of early Egyptian art. The Han period has been considered the great age of figure painting. We know of the portraits of famous ministers that were painted on the walls of the Ch'i Lin Tower by the order of Han Hsuan Ti. Han Ch'eng Ti (32–7 B.C.) caused a portrait of a queen of the Hsiung Nu to be painted on his palace walls.[3] The painting of the thirteen emperors, attributed to Yên Li-Pen, in the Boston Museum must be a relic of this tradition.[4]

The next development was the painting of narrative, and the illustration of poems and legends is associated with the six dynasties. We know of paintings illustrating the "Classic of Filial Piety," the "Poem of the North Wind"

[1] Chavannes. *Sculpture sur pierre en Chine.*
[2] Tomita, K. Museum of Fine Arts, Boston: *Chinese Paintings.* Plate I (A).
[3] Zen, S. H. C. *Symposium of Chinese Culture*: "Painting and Calligraphy," by Tsai Yuan-Pei, p. 69.
[4] Tomita, K. *Bulletin* of Museum of Fine Arts, Boston, Feb. 1932, pp. 2–8: "Chinese Paintings."

and the "Poem Shu Li" in the *Shu King* [1] (the book of poetry); the painting entitled "The Admonitions of the Instructress," attributed to Ku K'ai-Chih, may well be a genuine survival from this period, but the general trend of expert opinion is to place it as a T'ang copy. This famous and important relic has been described by Binyon [2] and Waley,[3] so that I need do no more than mention it here. Ku K'ai-Chih seems to have been one of the first painters of landscape. There is a hill landscape in one portion of the "Admonitions of the Instructress," and we know of other probable landscapes of his, which have perished, entitled "Rivers, Hills, Cities and Houses in Wu" and "Looking at the Wu La Mountains in Snow." By the Sui dynasty (589–618) there were several artists who excelled in painting houses and palaces, but bird and flower painting does not seem to have been fully developed till the T'ang. Hui Tsung's collection contained no pre-T'ang examples of this genre.[4] It is doubtful whether any actual paintings on silk or paper have survived which can be safely attributed to this period.

Period 3.—It has been said that if dynasties are to be measured in terms of hills and valleys, sunshine and shadow, then the T'ang period is a peak that basks in almost tropical sunshine. Under the T'angs China acquired stable government, thus ensuring the wealth and leisure which provide the soil in which art can grow, though they cannot supply the seed. The T'ang period was an age of cosmopolitanism, when China was open to foreign influences. The borders of China reached beyond the Palmirs; Kashmir and Gandhara were vassals, even the king of Samarkand paid tribute.

[1] Zen, S. H. C. *Symposium of Chinese Culture,* p. 70.
[2] Binyon, L. *Painting in the Far East,* pp. 43–54.
[3] Waley, A. *Introduction to Chinese Painting,* pp. 45–66.
[4] Hirth, F. *Native Sources for the History of Chinese Pictorial Art,* p. 18.

III. SCENE FROM THE ADMONITIONS OF THE INSTRUCTRESS

Signed Ku K'ai-Chih (*b. c.* 344, *d. c.* 406).

(1′ 3″ × 10″)

The British Museum.

"At that period Ch'ang-an was the capital of the world, as Rome was in the Middle Ages and Paris is to-day. Later China was to become not the centre of the great world, but a world by herself apart."[1]

The mild and delicate lines of T'ang silver mirrors, the graciousness of T'ang pottery figures and the clinging draperies of T'ang Buddhist paintings are far removed from the austere rugged designs of the Chou, and the semi-conventionalized patterns of the Han. The ruthlessness of the civil wars of Chou and Han were memories. Struggle and turmoil had given way to wealth and peace. The soil was ready for Buddha's message. Buddhism was officially introduced during the Han period (A.D. 67), but it must have begun to penetrate some time before that date, though it was not until the T'ang that the fertilization bore fruit. For probably the first time China was shaken to the core by an alien influence and the whole direction of her culture changed. To thousands of common people Buddhism offered the novel beauty of a lotus paradise. The worship of a cruel and indifferent nature was exchanged for the gentle compassion of Buddha's smile. Thousands deserted their homes to become priests. Enormous numbers of Indian monks flocked into the country. Buddhist influences were so far-reaching that they invaded every department of life. The sculpture, the poetry, the painting of the T'ang dynasty all acquired a graciousness which can be traced to the same source. What little Chinese painting of this period has survived is strongly influenced by India. We are told Chang Sêng-Yu (whose works have perished) painted in rich pigments in a method of vermilion and verdigris he had learnt from that country. But as the dynasty drew to its close persecutions succeeded each other, and in 845 Buddhism experienced a set-back from which it

[1] Waley, A. *Introduction to Chinese Painting*, p. 97.

never recovered. Most of the Buddhist paintings were frescoes, painted on the walls of temples, and time and persecutions have obliterated them. Of the hundreds of frescoes with which Wu Tao-Tzŭ and Yen Li-Pĕn adorned the temples of Loyang and Ch'ang-an not one remains. Fortunately, owing to the valuable work of Stein and to the dryness of the atmosphere of the Gobi Desert, a large collection of paintings of the T'ang period was discovered in recent years hidden away in a cave monastery at Tun Huang, the last halting place on the frontier of China on the road that the pilgrims took overland on their way to India. They are probably only provincial and archaic fragments [1] of a great tradition, but they form, as far as we know, the only large body of material in existence that reflects the spirit of T'ang painting, and their importance cannot be over-emphasized.

Before the end of the T'ang dynasty, Chinese books tell us that landscape was divided into the Northern and Southern schools. The style of the north was typified by vigorous brush strokes and detail, that of the south by delicacy and chiaroscuro. Ch'ên Chieh-Chou of the Ch'ing period makes the following remarks in his Hsiao-hua-p'ien (*A Study of Painting*): " Meteorological phenomena differ according to localities; so in like manner man's nature differs according to places of habitation. Consequently men born in the south, with its mild and graceful scenery, are subject to influences either good or bad, being liable to become either genteel and refined, or light-hearted and insincere. On the other hand, they who are reared amidst the grand and majestic landscapes of the north will, if rightly directed, become manly and powerful, but otherwise they are apt to turn rude and unbridled. Such is the natural order of things, and it is nothing strange that art

[1] Pelliot and Waley differ here.

晉武帝司馬炎

IV. SECTION FROM 'PORTRAITS OF THE EMPERORS'
Attributed to Yen Li-Pen (c. 640-80).
The Museum of Fine Arts, Boston.   (*Ht. approx.* 1' 8¾")

itself is divided into the two separate schools of the North and South, according as pictures are done in conformity with the characteristic nature of the Southerners or with that of the Northerners." [1] The Northern school enjoyed the special patronage of the Court. It became the father of the Kano school in Japan. The Southern school is easily confused with Zen Buddhism, and the "literary school" which it engendered under the auspices of Confucianism, was at its height in the Ming and early Ch'ing, and is still in fashion to-day. It is in turn the father of a school of early nineteenth-century painters in Japan. The names of Li Ssŭ-Hsün and his son Li Chao-Tao are given as originators of the Northern style, Wang Wei of the Southern. In the T'ang period painters first began to specialize in paintings of animals, birds and flowers. The name of Han Kan is associated with horses, Tai Sung with buffaloes, Pien Luan and Chou Hüang with flowers. The T'ang painters, Chang Hsuan and Chou Fang, were famous for their beautiful women.

Period 4.—The vigour of the T'ang dynasty was succeeded by the delicate beauty of the Sung, which numbered at least a dozen painters among the imperial clan. It was an age of austere simplicity, extreme sophistication and great scholarship. It was probably one of the most cultivated periods that China has ever known. It produced famous historians, brilliant essayists, and a long list of poets and painters. Its paintings were perhaps too soft and sweet and tender to be healthy. Its idealism was too full of dreams. The great empire that the T'ang had built was crumbling before its close. The Tartars were nibbling its flanks. All that gentleness that Buddhism had inoculated, all the beauty and refinement that a cosmopolitan culture had bestowed, all the riches and luxuries that a far-reaching overland trade

[1] *Kokka,* No. 196, p. 424: Sei-ichi Taki.

routes and a great sea-borne commerce had gathered, could not keep them at bay. A wistful resignation enters into the Sung paintings. It is as if they knew but dared not see that their beautiful world was drifting on the rocks. There comes a time in all civilizations when the peak has been reached and passed for the slopes on the other side. It seems that as soon as certain naturally defined standards of culture have been exceeded the shadows begin to fall. The beauty of Sung painting is the beauty of consumption, for its loveliness is heavy with the seeds of incipient decay.

The Sung period was above all the age of landscape. In despair of establishing a Nirvana on earth, it is to nature that their poets and artists turn. In the leaning stems and knotted roots of blasted pines, in the crumbling rocks and dissolving mists of their landscapes, the Sung painters have mirrored their haunting visions. Their fears were soon realized. In 1127 the Northern Sung fell before the Tartars and in 1276 the Mongols captured Hangchow. The Mongols who established themselves on the throne of China as the Yüan dynasty were of the same stock as the Huns that invaded Europe. They were ruthless nomads of the desert who had no use for tilled fields or the culture and luxuries of Chinese life. They contributed nothing to Chinese painting but a passion for pictures of horses and falcons. They soon adopted the manners and way of life of those they conquered. In a generation they had abandoned the healthy simplicity of their life of the steppes for the silks and rich foods of palace life; but they had not the stamina to endure Chinese civilization, and their fall was as swift as their rise. In 1308 "Ashapuhua, observing that the emperor (Wu Tsung) looked worn from day to day, remarked that not controlling the appetite in eating and drinking and the love of harem ladies was like cutting a solitary tree with axes; it was sure to fall. The emperor made him his minister, but continued to love wine and women as before," [1] and in 1353 "Two Buddhists instructed the emperor (Shun Ti) in the art behind the curtain; each of the monks took three or four women under pretence of maintaining them. They used to tell the emperor human life is short, why not enjoy the secret pleasures of entrancement!" [2] In 1355 Chu Yüan Chang (the founder of the Ming dynasty) raised soldiers and by 1368 the Yüan dynasty had expired.

Period 5.—The Ming dynasty was a Chinese dynasty but it produced none of the lofty idealism and austerity of the Sung. To the followers of Confucius who came to control the destinies of China, the romantic fir trees and moonlight of the Sung artists Hsia Kuei and Ma Yüan were anathema. Kuo Shun, a fifteenth-century painter, on being shown a picture of the Sung period is said to have exclaimed, "What have I to do with the tail ends of mountains and truncated streams, the production of ignoble refugees?" [3] or as Giles has translated it, "Rotten rocks and dirty water; away with these sweepings of the Sung dynasty." [4] The glowing colours of the Ming cloisonné vases, the bold designs of its porcelain enamels, speak another language from the green and white monochrome glazes of the Sung; they lack their contemplative beauty and their high ideals, but they possess a vitality that the Sung never possessed; for although the founder of the new dynasty was a pock-marked Buddhist monk, the influence of Buddhism was spent. The chief achievement of the Ming painters is the Literary school, which arose in reaction to the Academic school of bird and flower painting (of the Sung) inspired by Hui Tsung which had fallen into decay. The Literary

[1] Faber, *Chronological Handbook of the History of China*, p. 184.
[2] *Ibid.*, p. 187.
[3] Waley, A. *Introduction to Chinese Painting*, p. 210.
[4] Giles, H. A. *Chinese Pictorial Art*, p. 144.

painters were amateurs, they despised technique and they specialized in landscape in ink without colours. In due course the Ming went the same way as the Yüan. In 1644 "The rebel Ch'ang had success in Szechuan. Chungking was valiantly defended, but he undermined the city wall and blew it up, captured the commander and others whom he executed. As it thundered and the sky darkened with rain at that time he had all his big guns trained and discharged towards heaven, saying it was no business of heaven that he killed men." [1] Meanwhile, the account continues, King Fuh, grandson of Shu Tsung, the last representative of the Mings, established at Nanking, "felt unhappy that his furniture and utensils were not equal to the imperial standard; he wanted several hundred thousand taels for that purpose, to which some ministers objected." But by 1645 he sighed no longer for these amenities for he had been captured and executed by the Manchus.

Period 6.—The Ch'ing dynasty, like the Yüan dynasty and the Sui and Wei dynasties before it, was a nomad dynasty from the northern steppes. But if it did not, like them, contribute any new tradition, it produced several very able rulers under which China achieved a stability she had never known since the T'ang. The reigns of K'ang Hsi (1662–1722) and Ch'ien Lung (1736–95) were both famous. In the reign of Ch'ien Lung China experienced another period of expansion and tremendous prosperity. She occupied Tibet, the Gurkas were defeated, Burma was invaded and paid tribute, Annam submitted. The emperor himself was a scholar, painter, poet and connoisseur as well as a great administrator. The land was so wealthy that he was able to remit the land taxes for several years in succession. But the Ch'ing dynasty did little but carry on the

[1] Faber. *Chronological Handbook of the History of China,* p. 228.

traditional painting of the Ming. There was no break with the past, and no fresh inspiration. The Literary school and the academic painting of flower and bird both continued as before.

Period 7.—The collapse of the Manchu empire is too recent to be viewed in detail. The present incursions of the Japanese have their historical parallels in Chinese history. Are they fated to play the rôle of the Yüan and Manchu dynasties over again? But the impact of the West is something the like of which China has never experienced since the arrival of Buddhism and of which it is as yet impossible to see the ultimate consequences. China has often been invaded and conquered but she has always imposed her culture on her conquerors. She has rarely come up against a culture in any way equal to her own. To-day she is shaken to the roots; all the traditional habits of thought and life are out of fashion. The poverty, the foreign encroachments, the misgovernment of the last years of the Ch'ing dynasty and the turmoil of the first years of the Republic have eaten into the vitality of Chinese national life. Chinese painting must languish while she is in travail. Her young men have other and more important problems to attend to. But when the dust of the present storm has settled China will without question emerge ultimately victorious, as she has done so many times before. But along what lines her new painting will develop and how she will adapt Western influences to shape a new tradition it is too early as yet to know.

Is there, it may be asked, a logical progressive development in Chinese painting? I cannot say that there is. It is not easy for the student of Chinese history to believe in progress. The same tale is told over and over again. Dynasty after dynasty arises, blossoms and decays. The

D   33

vigour of youth, the splendour of full-blown maturity, the tragedy of decay follow each other in relentless sequence. In art the rise and fall of great traditional schools follows the same lines. The later history of Chinese painting follows that of England. The earliest painting is religious; in the eighteenth century the art of both countries went to court, but in China it had been there already and it stayed there much longer. China never experienced the reign of the middle-class taste which England experienced under the Victorians when art was dictated by the purses of the newly rich industrialists. In China the tradition of the eighteenth century languished on into the twentieth century until the collapse of the Manchu monarchy, when it had long out-lived its day. Painting must be the expression of contemporary civilization and ideals, and as civilization changes it must change with it. No art that has lived so long on its past can be a living force, as no nation that lives on its past has a future. The care that the Victorian artists lavished on photographic representations and plastic ingenuity the academic painter of China lavished on delicacy and the virtuosity of calligraphic technique. The rebellion of the literary painters of the Ming heralded unconsciously the revolt of the post-impressionists in Europe towards the end of the nineteenth century. In both countries the old traditions are openly questioned to-day. Our painters and their painters wander in the wilderness; they linger between two worlds, one dead and the other to be born.

2

The Influence of Religion

IN all ancient civilizations the earliest painting is subordinated to the interests of religion. China is no exception. Gregory the Great wrote, "Painting is admissible in churches in order that those who are unlettered may yet see by gazing at the walls what they cannot read in books." [1] A life of Confucius, attributed to one of his disciples, describes a visit of the sage in the year 517 B.C. to the palace of Ching Wang of the Chou dynasty at Loyang, where he saw on the walls of the audience hall portraits of the heroes and sages, the tyrants and degenerates of Shang Yin and Chou dynasties. Confucius, we are told, viewed it all with silent delight, and then turning to his followers exclaimed, "Here you see how the house of Chou became so great. As we use a bronze mirror to reflect a recent scene, so antiquity may be pictured as a lesson for posterity." [2] The whole spirit of early Chinese painting ministered to the need of the religious and social order; its ambition was to encourage good and discourage evil. Artists conceived it their duty to warn the dissipated and admonish the extravagant, and above all to transmit the values of earlier and better days. The very earliest painting has completely perished, but we know it was dedicated to the worship of nature and the cult of the ancestor. The emperor was the link between his people and the heavens. Their prosperity directly depended on his moral qualities. The abundance of harvests or their failure, drought, flood,

[1] Roger Hinks. *Carolingian Art,* p. 97.
[2] Bushell, S.W. *Chinese Art,* vol. ii, p. 118.

civil war, the appearance of strange animals, were all to be interpreted as the pleasure or displeasure of the heavens at his behaviour. Chinese records are full of royal backslidings and consequent visitations.[1] An elaborate ritual arose around the person of the emperor to protect him and indirectly his people against conduct which entailed these misfortunes. The colour of his clothes, the shape of his dishes, the very food he ate was carefully prescribed for each season of the year.[2] By divination with tortoiseshell and artemisia, by music and elaborate etiquette, he strove to consult and to pacify the powers of nature. Every action must run in

[1] In 194 B.C. Empress Lü murdered her son's (the emperor age 11) step-brother and his mother, the Lady Ts'i (Faber. *Chronological Handbook of the History of China*, p. 40). Next year there was an earthquake in Shensi and the year after flowers and fruit in winter, also thunder and drought. (The appearance of anything unnatural is a sure portent of heaven's displeasure.)

"A.D. 96 a palace lady, Yin, was raised to the rank of empress. Locusts in the summer." (*Ibid.*, p. 58.)

"A.D. 133. The emperor ennobled his wet nurse. Earthquake at the capital. The ground split eighty-five *chang* (a chang is about 10 feet). The emperor at the head of high officials and honest scholars went there. As he charged them to speak openly Li Ku declared that the wet nurse and relations from the female side ought not to be put in power, neither should eunuchs." (*Ibid.*, pp. 60, 61.)

"A.D. 972. Great rain burst through the embankments of the Ho. The emperor dismissed from the 380 and more inmates of the harem one hundred with rich presents." (*Ibid.*, p. 144.)

Lastly, "A.D. 1124. Earthquake at Ho-tung, Shensi and the capital. Rebellions broke out in several places. . . . The daughter of a wine merchant at the capital suddenly grew a moustache seven to eight inches long; she looked very much like a gentleman; she was made a Taoist priest by imperial rescript. It was also said that a male person, a seller of fruit, gave birth to a child." (*Ibid.* p. 162.) The next year the Emperor Hui Tsung of the Sung dynasty abdicated in favour of his son. He had given the country to the care of rapacious officials, whilst he spent his days in collecting pictures or immersed in Taoist mysteries. In 1127 both he and his sons were carried off by the Kins into Siberia, and the Northern Sung dynasty came to an end.

[2] Grantham, A. E. *Hills of Blue*, pp. 11, 12.

harmony with the waxing and waning powers of the seasons. To the Chinese all creation was divided into male and female elements—the *yang* and the *yin*. The *yang* was the male principle, the origin of life and light and heat, and the *yin* the female principle, the origin of darkness and cold. The seasons of the year, bird, plant and animal life were all governed by one or the other. The appropriate duties of the emperor and the empress in each month of the year were worked out accordingly. Failure to act in sympathy ended in disaster.

Although no pictures of the earliest historical periods, the Shang and the Chou (1122–249 B.C.), have survived, bronzes of the same period have come down to us. Their decoration dwelt continuously on the moral issue, so that their user might be constantly reminded of his duties. The *t'ao t'ieh* animal masks, which are the commonest motive of decoration on the Chou bronze ritual vessels, are an embodiment of the principle of avarice and sensuality. A humbler successor, the *t'an,* was often painted on the walls of magistrates' *yamens* up to the time of the revolution to convey a warning to officials. Professor Yetts has explained that the word *chüeh* (used to denote a certain kind of libation cup) is, according to the *Shuo wên,* the pictogram of a bird. The vessel derives its name from the note of the bird *chieh chieh, tsu-tsu,* "sparingly sparingly, enough-enough." [1] The pages of the *Po ku t'u lu* (Illustrated Descriptions of Antiquities) are full of similar attempts to explain ancient bronze designs. They are not in any sense reliable, but they show us how the Chinese have interpreted the spirit behind these motives. We are told that Wu Wang of the Chou dynasty had moral precepts inscribed on all his cups, the pillars of his hall, his stick, his

[1] Professor W. P. Yetts. *Catalogue of the George Eumorfopoulos Collection of Chinese and Corean Bronzes, etc.,* vol. i, p. 23.

sword, his windows. On his cups were inscribed the words: "Drink only to fortify your body; eat only to preserve your life, scorn a quantity of dishes, prevent their being set before you." And on his stick: "How dangerous it is to hate and give way to anger. How far violent passions lead from the right way. How readily the rich and mighty forsake justice." [1] This habit of decorating the home with moral maxims has survived to-day. Every Chinese restaurant and many houses of business are hung with scrolls full of lofty sentiments. Most early pictures must have been painted in the same vein. Giles mentions that a picture illustrating the drunken orgies of Chou Hsin, the last tyrant of the Yin dynasty who died 1122 B.C., was hung in the rooms of the Emperor Chêng Tê who was too fond of women and wine. [2]

Alongside the worship of nature flourished the cult of the ancestors. This is the oldest religion of the Chinese;— from it sprang the worship of the family and the filial piety, which Confucianism at a later date incorporated, while its rival, Taoism, was based on the ancient worship of nature. These two are the roots from which spring the chief religious practices of the race. They are to-day the worship of the bulk of the unlettered masses of China, who number three-quarters of the population. To these humble folk all nature is animate. The bad spirits (*kuei*) are warded off by propitiation, by magical drugs, incantation and amulets, by charms and music. To placate the spirits of mountain, tree and river a special pseudo-religious science, geomancy, called *fêng shui*, has come into existence. The old-fashioned Chinese would never build a house without consulting the professors of this science before he chose his site. This worship of hill spirits was later borrowed by the Buddhists and put to different ends. To-day the peasants in many

[1] Grantham, A. E. *Hills of Blue*, pp. 31, 32.
[2] Giles, H. A. *Chinese Pictorial Art*, p. 5.

parts of China believe in were-tigers; and in Shensi shrines to the fox-god still exist. The souls of the departed were believed to exist after death and to have power to help or hinder those that were left behind. Hence the elaborate ceremonies connected with the burial of the dead and worship at the family tombs. The ancestors must be worshipped, fed and consulted at regular intervals, and informed on every solemn occasion of the course of events, if they are not to take offence. Paper money,[1] paper models of sedan chairs and bearers (to-day paper motor cars), paper pigs, chickens, concubines, servants and horses are burnt in profusion at a funeral to provide the spirits with these articles in the next world. This is the origin of the Han and T'ang pottery figures which are so sought after by collectors. In the earliest times cattle were slaughtered and women buried alive in the tombs of the deceased. Worship at the family graves takes place at the Ch'ing Ming Festival. At the New Year the tablets of the dead are brought out and their pictures hung on the wall. The worship of ancient sages, national heroes and dutiful women has been perpetuated in this way. Chang Yen-Yüan of the T'ang dynasty, writing in the middle of the ninth century, remarks on the great moral influence attributed by earlier writers to paintings :"Those who had distinguished themselves by loyalty or filial piety were portrayed in the Cloud Terrace Museum ; those whose heroism had been conspicuous found their way to the galleries of the Unicorn Tower. The sight of good is in itself a warning against evil, the sight of evil arouses thoughts of virtue. . . ." Ts'ao Chih says: "There is none who in front of a picture of the Three Kings and Five Emperors (the mystical paragons of Confucianism) would not raise his head in thankfulness, nor any that before a painting of the depraved monarchs of

[1] Not banknotes, but make-believe currency.

39

the decadence would not heave a sigh. There is none who contemplating the picture of a good and honest man would not forget his meals: nor any that coming on the image of a licentious husband or abandoned wife would not avert his gaze." [1] The Chinese have at all times attached an immense importance to the moral life of the artist. Kuo Jo-Hsü of the Sung dynasty wrote that painting was a sport fit only for high-minded personages who shut their eyes to fame and wealth and who lived in retirement from the world. [2] He expressed the view that if their characters were noble their pictures would reflect their sentiments. Painters who were devoid of these qualities, however skilful or elaborate, were mere craftsmen. The secret of great art sprang from the character of the artist himself; he could neither give it to others nor transmit it to descendants. Painting was the external manifestation of the mind; the "seal of the mind" Kuo Jo-Hsü calls it, comparing the relation of the personality to painting as that which exists between the seal and its impression. It is not surprising, he adds, that painting should become high or low according to the personality of the painter, for it declares unerringly whether the painter is a lofty minded individual or a man of low character.

The bulk of Chinese painting was executed in the same fashion as in the Middle Ages in Europe. That is to say, painting was a craft among crafts, handed from father to son, its secrets jealously guarded. The same ideas and the same designs were handed down from generation to generation. A great many paintings, particularly Buddhist works, were anonymous, just as the cathedrals of the Middle Ages

[1] Waley, A. *Burlington Magazine*, vol. xxx, No. ccxiv, Jan. 1921, p. 32 : "Chinese Philosophy of Art"; *Introduction to Study of Chinese Painting*, p. 162.

[2] *Kokka*, No. 244, p. 69: Sei-ichi Taki.

were anonymous. The personality of the artist who executed them did not count at all. He received a certain understood remuneration for his activities, with which he was quite content. The idea of the fashionable portrait painter, in search of distinction and wealth, would have been abhorrent to both ancient China and mediæval Europe. This outlook bred both disadvantages and advantages. Chinese painting in the hands of small men was apt to become dead and conventional. There was no room for invention or "progress"; the same language was repeated again and again when the conditions for which it was appropriate had long passed away. New problems were smothered by the tenacity of the old traditions. But at the same time the beauty of the old designs was preserved, and while the big men were capable of breaking through the tradition, the smaller painters were saved from disintegration. That is why the painting of the most insignificant Chinese artists is always pleasant and interesting when it is not great. The design is invariably a faint echo of some great traditional theme. Apart from the artisan class there lived a handful of priests, eccentrics, and aristocrats who had the leisure to cultivate painting as a hobby. It was from the ranks of these men that the great masters were recruited. The Chinese insist that a great painter should also be a man of letters. Scholarship enabled the painter to enter realms of thought and to entertain subtleties of expression lost to the illiterate. Têng Ch'un of the Sung dynasty wrote: "Painting is the consummation of letters. . . . Some one may ask 'Why then have not all gifted men of letters shown a taste for art?' True, there may be some exceptions, in most cases the votary of letters is also the votary of art: and rarely are true artists to be found who are not deeply versed in learning." [1] The connection between letters and painting,

[1] *Kokka*, No. 216, p. 291.

and in particular poetry and painting, has been continually dwelt upon by Chinese critics. In theory painting in China existed only as the diversion of the sage, the priest and the scholar (the artisan catered for the simple Taoist and Buddhist paintings in demand among the people). "From ancient times (says Kuo Jo Hsü) most masterly paintings have been the products of the leisure hours either of noble souled patriots or high-minded personages, who in disgust at the corrupt government took to the secluded life and devoted themselves to the study of the eternal laws of justice. Because they conveyed their lofty sentiments when they painted, their productions are full of life and spirit." [1] Calligraphy, poetry, painting were all natural activities of the elevated mind. Many Chinese artists were also poets (Wang Wei is a notable example), all of them calligraphists.[2] The higher tradition of Chinese painting is essentially amateur and aristocratic: the poor had not the leisure nor the scholarship to compete with the men of letters unless they could attract the patronage of some man of wealth.

Chinese society is often portrayed as a tripod whose three legs are Confucianism, Buddhism and Taoism. These are the three great religions of China, and each in turn has impressed its influence on Chinese art. It is curious that the founders of these three religions were contemporaries. Confucius lived from 551 to 479 B.C., and Lao Tzŭ is supposed to have been his contemporary, for there is an account of their meeting while Buddha was preaching his gospel in India between 563 and 483 B.C. Confucianism and Taoism were natural growths, but Buddhism was an importation from India. There have been two other imported religions, Christianity and Islam, but neither of them has to any lasting extent influenced the course of Chinese painting.

[1] *Kokka,* No. 216, p. 290.
[2] Ch'iu Ying is quoted as an exception.

No satisfactory estimate of the Mohammedan population of China exists. Their arrival in China must date at least from T'ang times. In 757 the Caliph sent soldiers to the aid of a T'ang emperor and there is a Mohammedan monument in Sianfu which dates from 742. There is also the record of an embassy from the Caliph in 651. "The Min Shu, compiled at the end of the sixteenth century or at the beginning of the seventeenth century from older sources by Ho Ch'iao-Yüan, says that some time between 618 and 626 four disciples of Mohammed brought Islam to China. The *P'an-yu-hsien chih*, ch. 53, p. 7a, says: 'When sea trade was opened in the T'ang dynasty, Mohammed, the moslem king of Medina, sent his maternal uncle the priest Su Ha-Pai Sai to China to trade. He built the Kuang tower and the Huai Sheng mosque. He died soon after the tower and mosque were completed."[1] This must refer to Mohammed's uncle whom de Thiersant states came to China (Canton) 628-629. By the Yüan period (1206-1358) they must have settled in great numbers to trade. Marco Polo remarks that Yunnan was a Mohammedan province. Persian music and textiles were popular at the Yüan Court; and it is probable that the Mohammedans may have contributed more than any other factor to the creation of the technique of Chinese porcelain with underglaze blue, which it is suggested was derived from Persia.[2] The Chinese Mohammedans have never been completely sinicized, although they speak and write Chinese and have little knowledge of Arabic. Kansu and Shensi are the two provinces in which they are most numerous, but they are widely scattered the length and breadth of the country. Laufer remarks that they still do not eat with their neighbours. A Chinese proverb

---

[1] T'ien-Tsê Chang. *Sino Portuguese Trade from 1514-1644*, pp. 7, 8.
[2] Leigh Ashton. *Connoisseur*, May 1933, vol. xci, No. 381: "Dating Ming Blue and White," pp. 283-293.

gives them a reputation for wrangling and pugnacity, which their history supports. The Mohammedan insurrections of the seventeenth and eighteenth centuries (1648–49 and 1781–83) were followed by the terrible rebellions of the nineteenth century (1855–73 and 1861–77). Islam has left little influence on painting because paintings were not permitted in its mosques. But the Arabic script was immediately appreciated by the Chinese for its ornamental qualities and it is often found as a motive on Chinese blue and white porcelain and bronzes of the Ming period. It was during the Ming dynasty (1368–1643) that they reached the height of their power. As early as 1392 the first emperor of the dynasty issued an edict in favour of Islam, granting permission to found two mosques, one at Nanking and the other at Sianfu (the capital of Shensi); and gave his permission to settle, travel and trade in all parts of the empire. The Emperor Ch'êng Tê (1506–21) is even credited with having adopted the faith.[1]

Confucius was born in 551 B.C. He did not originate, but collected, arranged and transmitted the philosophy and folk-lore of those that came before him, and purged it of what he considered unsuitable. The material that he handled was the anonymous accretion of centuries, handed down from father to son, by word of mouth. The *Ballads of the Book of Poetry* and the *Observances of the Book of Rites* which he edited might have passed into oblivion but for his care. He seems to have been a drastic editor. All the songs which centred round the fecundity rites of the spring ceremonies, which the worship of nature enjoined, he rigorously suppressed. From the customs of the ancients he elaborated an ethical code, and the rest of his life was spent in travelling from state to state in his fruitless search of an ideal prince

[1] Laufer, B. *Ars Islamica,* vol. i, pt. ii, mcmxxxiv, p. 135 : "Chinese Muhammedan Bronzes."

who would put his principles into practice. Confucianism, it has been argued, is a code of ethics and not a religion. There are Confucian temples, but Confucius is reverenced as a sage, not worshipped as a god. There is no priesthood, for his rites are celebrated by officials. Confucius showed no curiosity about the world of the spirit. The emphasis of his teaching lay upon the leading of a good life in this world. He was not concerned greatly about an existence in the next. Others have replied with equal vigour that the worship of Confucius was celebrated with the ritual and sacrificial significance that is associated with a religion in which music, incense and burnt offerings all played their part, and that the code of ethics he transmitted recognized a divine order in the cult of the ancestor.[1] In practice his code of ethics centred in the doctrine of filial piety, on which the whole state was built. The relation of father and child was the secret of all other relationships. The relation of teacher and pupil, of ruler and subject, and of brothers and of friends were built on the same foundation. The State began and ended in the family. The *Analects* [2] and the *Hsiao Ching* (Classic of Filial Piety) contain the kernel of this teaching. Confucius believed that the nature of man was good. It was the small man who failing to develop the possibilities dormant in his character, because he neglected to observe the proper rules of conduct or to make friends with superior people, forfeited his own good nature. It is the superior man or *shêng jên* to whom he continuously refers in his teachings. This man is upright, benevolent, tolerant, sincere, loyal and scholarly. His life is governed by consideration for others, by restraint, moderation, courtesy, and above all by filial piety. It was a life regulated by harmony of music and dignity of ceremony.

[1] Sir Reginald Johnston. *Confucianism and Modern China*, ch. vii.
[2] For study in translations, see Dr. Legge, Chinese Classics Series.

45

There was a temple to Confucius in every district and departmental city. These temples were empty except for an altar carrying a solitary tablet inscribed with the name of the sage. The simplicity of their architecture and their furniture and the quiet groves of trees which line their courts give them an air of tranquillity and austerity. Here at the four seasons of the year the leading officials under their most senior representative gathered to observe his ceremonies. It has been pointed out that Confucianism supplied at once the advantage of a political order and an established church. Buddhism and Taoism were to the Confucian the diversion of small people, harmless enough as long as they were not sufficiently strong to threaten the established order. It is difficult not to admit a tinge of atheism. "Religions are many, reason is one," runs a Chinese proverb. "If you have not learned how to fulfil your duties to living men, how can you hope to fulfil them when you are dead? If you do not know about life what can you know about death?" is a passage from the *Anaelects* cited by Wade to support the view that Confucius was an agnostic.[1] Yet there is nothing in Confucianism incompatible with the existence of the spiritual world, but there is an appeal to reason against superstition.

The opponents of Confucianism have complained that its conservative outlook contributed more than any other factor to the tardiness with which China has adapted herself to the new individual era. The most serious criticism levelled by young China is that the loyalty to the throne, which it maintained unswervingly, retarded a democratic outlook; but Confucius only extolled loyalty when the responsibility of the royal mandate was observed, and

[1] Sir Reginald Johnston. *Confucianism and Modern China,* p. 89. Sir Reginald Johnston points out that the authenticity of the passage is doubtful.

directly it was abused to the detriment of the people it was withdrawn. Another criticism was that the loyalty and devotion to the family, which is encouraged at the expense of any other relationship, suffocated the growth of patriotism and the formation of public opinion.

The old China was in the grand sense cosmopolitan. She represented a civilization, not a country. "Among the truly educated there is no distinction of class." Moreover, it was a way of life responsible for the quiet dignity, courtesy and tolerance of the older generation of Chinese. To those who have moved among them they seem to have been the most civilized of all peoples. Like the other religions of China, Confucianism has endured alternate favour and disgrace. In the reign of Shih Huang Ti (246-209 B.C.), who assembled all China under the rule of one man, Taoism was in favour and Confucianism under a ban. Confucianism had favoured the appeal to ancient histories which Shih Huang Ti was anxious to eliminate, for they fostered the survival of feudalism. In 213 B.C. all books except those dealing with medicine, divination and agriculture were destroyed. During the T'ang dynasty Buddhism was at the height of its power. The Sung Emperor T'ai Tsung (A.D. 977–998) bestowed posthumous honours on forty-four generations of the sage's descendants and exempted all of them from taxation. In 1233 the title of Holy Duke was bestowed upon his heir, and in 1294 Kublai Khan of the Yüan dynasty (1206–1358) gave his descendants estates on the borders of Kiangsi and Shantung. His heirs ranked immediately below the imperial princes. Since Ming days, except for a mild patronage extended to Buddhism or Taoism from an occasional emperor, Confucianism has been the religion of Chinese society. In the early days of the Republic Confucianism was identified with the monarchy; its temples were turned into barracks or hospitals. On January 1, 1935, a mandate appointed the lineal descendant of Confucius to be an official of the first grade with the title of Officer in Charge of the Sacrifice to the Superior Excellence the Most Holy senior teacher of Confucius. It would seem that a restoration is already under way.

The temples of Confucius, like those of Islam, were not hung with paintings, but the Confucian influence on painting was very strong nevertheless. The Confucians set up a literary ideal. The scholar, not the soldier, was their model. China emerged from the feudal period so early that feudalism has left no mark on the national character. By the Ming dynasty the population was divided into farmers, artisans and officials. There were few big cities and no landed aristocracy except in the north, where the Mongolian princes had established themselves. The bulk of the country was owned by village clans as it is still for the most part to-day. The officials were recruited by a competitive examination.[1] This examination was the avenue to official life. Except for certain elements (the actor, the barber, the boatman and the soldier), whose professions put them beyond the pale, the examinations were open to all. A literary career was the open sesame for every ambitious man, just as the priesthood had been in mediæval Europe. It has been aptly said that life was dictated by the outlook of the library. The Ch'ing dynasty which the Manchus carried to the throne perpetuated the same traditions. This worship of letters led to the literary control of art, which was manifest in the Wên-jen-hua (Japanese Bunjingwa) or literary school. This literary school painted in ink. They were amateurs, not professionals, who thought more of fine sentiments than skilful technique, and worked in reaction to the academic

[1] The subject was taken from the Four Books or the Five Classics of the Confucian Canon.

V. LANDSCAPE
By Wang Yüan-Ch'i (b. 1642, d. 1715)
The British Museum (Eumorfopoulos Collection). $(2' 5\frac{3}{4}'' \times 1' 9\frac{1}{2}'')$

school which by Ming times had degenerated into a futile and delicate prettiness. Their rebellion was not effectively launched until the Ming period and it must have been directly sponsored by the growing power of the Confucian party. The literary school one would have expected to have been calligraphic in feeling, but although its sentiments were literary, it discouraged the rhythmic calligraphic qualities of the brush which it associated with the academic school. Literary association took the place of line. Many of these pictures are decorated with poems or quotations from the classics. The literary painters were essentially amateurs. Many of them were scholars who had failed to qualify, or politicians who had retired from the service of the State. At the fall of the Ming dynasty a great number of officials joined the priesthood and devoted themselves to the study of art instead of politics.

Enormous numbers of these literary pictures have survived and they have been particularly popular in Japan, where they produced a renaissance in the early nineteenth century. At that time the Japanese were tired of the bright colours and elaborate technique of the Tosa and Kano schools and the vulgarity of the Ukiyoyé painters. Men like Watanabe Kwazan and Chikuden, and Buncho headed this movement. Most of them identified their pursuit with the improvement of the mind. "I do not know what to say of those who handle landscapes only for the sake of amusements," writes Watanabe Kwazan.[1] These literary paintings have been misunderstood by the West up to very recent years. Fenollosa calls them formless and woolly, adding, "The whole mass of what at least Bunjingwa critics have to say is mostly rot." [2] Mr. Sei-ichi Taki in the *Kokka* points out that the most common misunderstanding is

[1] *Kokka,* No. 210, p. 114.
[2] Fenollosa, E. *Epochs of Chinese and Japanese Art,* vol. ii, p. 148.

to confuse the "literary" paintings with those of the Southern school.[1] The tendency to divide all Chinese landscape painting later than the T'ang into that of the Northern and Southern schools is an unsatisfactory one. Many artists painted at the same time in two styles one of which is associated with the north the other with the south. The work of other artists contained the qualities of both. This distinction of style is in fact a very loose term, which can only be used in a broad sense: in a general way simplicity, powerful composition and calligraphic dexterity is characteristic of the paintings of the north, just as those of the south are remarkable for delicacy and suggestion. Bunjingwa paintings have a general affinity to the Southern school, but all the productions of that school are not necessarily Bunjingwa. It is generally presumed that the literary label is only applicable to the products of Ming and Ch'ing artists, but Sei-ichi Taki tells us that the term was in use in Japan before Ming times, nor can it be said that literary painters were the only ones who confined themselves to ink monochrome. The artists Ma Yüan and Hsia Kuei of the Sung, who are essentially romantic and calligraphic in style and who are to be associated with the north rather than with the south (if the term is to be extended to Sung), confined themselves to ink, while some of the Bunjingwa school tinted their paintings with colours. The term Wên-jen-hua simply means " painting by men of letters." It is a misleading caption, for as I have already shown scholarship has always been one of the fundamental qualities attributed to a great painter of any school.

The professional painter had crept into Chinese life just as he had done in Europe: Fashion did not permit him to blossom into a fashionable portrait painter, but he set himself to capture the court and the official world with elegant

[1] *Kokka,* No. 216, p. 289.

VI. LANDSCAPE

By Professor Liu Hai-Su, a distinguished contemporary painter who
has given new life to the traditions of the literary school.

By his permission.   (*Ht. approx.* 4′ *to* 5′)

pictures of birds and flowers, green and gold landscapes in seductive detail, and to undermine the lofty conceptions of the literary mind by the brilliancy of his professional execution and delicacy of his colours. The so-called literary school of the Ming and Ch'ing were a revolt against this technique. The revolt that Cézanne inaugurated and Gauguin and Van Gogh continued against the academies of the West rises to the mind. But whereas the rebellion against technique in the West was combined with a revolt against any literary or religious sentiment, it was otherwise in China. A literary sentiment, entirely moral and almost religious in origin, continued to invest paintings; instead of breaking away from tradition they returned to it, just as there is an attempt among modern painters in the West to recapture the simplicity and sincerity of mediæval times.

The Ming artists Wēn Chēng-Ming and Tung Ch'i Ch'ang are generally considered to be the founders of the Bunjingwa school. Wang Shih-Min was an able exponent under the Ch'ing. But by the middle of the Ch'ing dynasty the literary school had begun to degenerate. Strange dashes and blots passed for a nobility of sentiment. Indifference to technique alone is even more foolish than a pursuit of skill with nothing to say. "If nature" wrote Watanabe Kwazan, "is too closely followed, painting is apt to become vulgar. This is the first thing to be avoided. The same idea was expressed by Tung-p'o who said: 'It is puerile to make the representation of form the sole aim of art. But to think only of tone and spirit is surely to fall into the error of studying a landscape science of extreme grotesquery. One who is so misguided is liable to mistake clumsiness for tastefulness, the expression of violent emotions for sentiment. This point is so subtle and delicate that I cannot explain it all in words.' " [1]

[1] *Kokka,* No. 210, p. 130.

Buddhism was also a foreign religion. Siddhartha, the founder of Buddhism, was a son of an Indian chief of the tribe of Sakya who belonged to the clan Gautama, hence the terms Gautama Buddha and Sakya-muni (*muni*=saint). His life was divided into various acts which are frequently depicted in Buddhist paintings. In the Stein paintings from Tun Huang at the British Museum these motives are repeated over and over again. Buddha descends from heaven in the form of a white elephant: he enters his mother's side without causing pain; he is born from his mother's side in human form; he is educated by his aunt; he marries; at the age of twenty-nine he exchanges the palace for an ascetic life; he receives a vision under the Bodhi tree; he is tempted; he preaches his new gospel; he lays the foundation of his teaching; he dies in 483 B.C. The gospel of Sakyamuni was an interpretation of Hindu Brahmanism. In China, as in all Buddhist countries, the principal Buddha is Sakyamuni. He is invariably represented sitting cross-legged on a lotus throne with eyes half closed in contemplation. He is represented as an all-wise and all-compassionate being, but it rests within the possibility of all human beings to achieve the same perfection. The *lohan* and the *pusa* (Buddhist saints who have in fact achieved enlightenment) are steps along this road. To Sakyamuni and his followers the pleasures of this world produced desires which in their turn produce suffering. It was only after countless reincarnations, filled with meditation, careful living and good works, that escape from reincarnation (the wheel of life) was possible. Buddhism provided a road along which any one might travel to a higher existence if he was prepared to combat the six senses and to eliminate the seven passions (pleasure, anger, sorrow, fear, love, hate, desire). Sakyamuni left no scriptures, and it was not until after his death that five hundred

Arhats met at Rājagriha and laid down the *vinaya* (statutes and rules of his community) and *sutras* (expositions of the doctrine).[1] At the end of the second century, as the result of a grand schism, the monk Nāgārjuna founded the Mahayana sect (Greater Vehicle) as opposed to the Hinayana (or Lesser Vehicle) in which the original traditions were embodied. Both these forms were transmitted via Gandhara to Chinese Turkestan. By the third century B.C. Buddhism had become a missionary religion; by the eighth century it was toppling in India; and by the thirteenth it had become moribund. The ideal of the Buddhist was Nirvana—the sinless existence, which could only be achieved by extinction of all desires. The soul of every individual passed through innumerable reincarnations, until it reached this goal. The wheel of life to which Buddhist texts continually return is the wheel of reincarnation. Beast, bird and insect alternate with man and woman. Each soul was born into a higher or lower sphere according to the life it had lived in a former existence. The Buddhist monk shaved off his hair and went about in a coarse robe. If he was an itinerant monk he lived by alms. He was supposed to possess no more luggage than a begging bowl, a razor, a staff, and a sieve to strain living things from his food. He was not to steal or to take any form of life. He forswore sexual intercourse, intoxicating liquors and any but the plainest food, and even this he could eat only at certain times. He was forbidden to acquire gold or silver, to listen to dancing or music or to anoint the person with unguents or deck his dress with flowers. He was not to sleep in a wide or high bed.[2] His life was passed in meditation, begging and the chanting of the *sutras*. These wandering priests must have led very similar lives to the mendicant orders of the

[1] Getty, A. *Gods of Northern Buddhism,* p. xxv.
[2] Plopper, C. H. *Chinese Religion seen through the Proverb,* pp. 203, *seq.*

Church of Rome. The whole Buddhist ceremonial has a distinct flavour of Roman Catholicism. The high altar and smaller shrines of the Buddhist temple, the intoned prayers, the pictures and images, the genuflections and prostrations, the elevation of the holy rice, the processions and ejaculations of prayers to Buddha, the masses for the dead, the fasts, the canonization of saints, the belief in miracles and the worship of relics, might have been modelled on Catholic observance. Well might a French missionary write, "the devil has mimicked the Holy Mother Church in order to scandalize her."

It is difficult for us to understand how easily China was dazzled and conquered by this new religion, whose celibacy was directly opposed to her own ancestor worship and whose monks preached a life of asceticism and self-sacrifice antagonistic to the Confucian tradition. The interminable civil wars of the Chou dynasty had been ruthless and bloody, and by the Han China was weary and disillusioned. The magic of Taoism was too remote, the code of Confucianism was too intellectual, for common consumption. Then came Buddhism, offering tenderness, pity, kindness and charity and deliverance for all human beings and a consideration for all living things. This was a different message from anything that China had hitherto experienced. The appeal to a life of faith and service, the promise of a future existence in a lotus paradise, evoked an enthusiasm that swept all before it.

The official introduction of Buddhism into China dates from A.D. 67, when the envoys whom the Emperor Ming Ti of the Eastern Han (A.D. 58–76) had sent in A.D. 63 to India to enquire into the origins of Buddhism, returned with images, scriptures, and two Indian monks, but it must have leaked into China many years before that date. The *Fa Yuan Chu*

Lin, by a Buddhist priest Tao Shih, says that as early as 237 B.C. a native of India, Li Fang, arrived at Sianfu with seventeen companions and was imprisoned but miraculously escaped; but there is no mention of Buddhism by Ssŭ Ma Chien in the *Historical Records*. The whole question of the date of its arrival is exhaustively discussed by Professor Yetts.[1] Whatever differences of opinion exist, it is commonly agreed that it did not make much headway for several centuries. It is not until A.D. 335 that a decree removed all obstacles placed in the way of Chinese entering the Buddhist priesthood. In 399 the famous Chinese pilgrim Fa Hsien left for India. He returned in 414 with Buddhist scriptures and devoted the rest of his life to their translation. Then began a flow of missions and missionaries to and from India that went on for the next six or seven hundred years, for the Indian persecutions of the sixth century made China into an asylum for Buddhist refugees. In 405 there arrived from India the great Buddhist teacher Kumārajīva. He settled at Ch'ang-an, which became the centre of the Buddhist zeal. At the end of the third century the Wei Tartars invaded China from the north. Their home was Siberia. In 398 they selected their capital at P'ing-ch'eng and by the first part of the fifth century Ch'ang-an had fallen. Buddhism established an ascendancy over this Mongol people. "So numerous had the monks become in 438 that the Wei emperors' armies were depleted, and an edict was issued forbidding men under fifty to enter the monasteries. There was a more drastic persecution of Buddhism in 466, following upon an unpleasant shock which the emperor had one day sustained at Ch'ang-an, where strolling into a monastery he had discovered not only a secret store of arms and

[1] Prof. W. P. Yetts. *Catalogue of the George Eumorfopoulos Collection of Chinese and Corean Bronzes, etc.*, vol. iii: Introduction.

ammunition, but also a hidden distillery and a subterranean harem." [1]

It was to the Weis that we owe the Buddhist sculptures in the rock temples of Yün-kang near their capital at P'ing ch'eng, and when in 494 they removed their capital to Loyang their industry was continued in the carvings at Lung-mên caves. But it was in the reign of Liang Wu Ti and his contemporary the Empress Hu of the Northern Weis, that the high-water mark was reached. In 517 he made the Buddhist prohibition against the taking of life into laws binding upon all; while to obtain the enormous sums lavished on Buddhist temples she cut down the salaries of her officials. Together they vied with each other in their lavishness to the Buddhist cause. "While she built the Monastery of Eternal Peace close to her palace and a pagoda nearly 1000 feet high, he erected one of twelve storeys and himself held public dissertations on the Buddhist sculptures there; while she turned thousands of workmen into the caves near Loyang to hew prophets, gods and angels out of the rock, he tried to carve the precepts of Buddha into what was harder still, the human heart. While she dispatched Sung Yüan to India to collect Buddhist writings, he summoned the founder of the famous Zen school of Buddhism, the famous patriarch Bodhidharma, freshly landed in Canton to visit him in his capital." [2] In 527 and on two later occasions he renounced the world for a monastery and had to be handsomely ransomed on each occasion before he would return to secular life. She retired into a nunnery in 528, from which she was extracted to be assassinated by the order of the rebel Erh-Chu-Jung. Liang Wu-Ti ended his life in a similar manner, at the hands of another rebel, Hou Ching. The death of each was directly

[1] Waley, A. Introduction to Chinese Painting, p. 79.
[2] Grantham, A. E. Hills of Blue, p. 210.

due to the opposition that the extravagance of their patronage of Buddhism had instigated.

The devotion of the T'ang emperors to Buddhism was renowned. The piety of the Empress Wu Chao was particularly celebrated. Originally a concubine of T'ai Tsung, the second emperor of the T'ang, this woman was retired into a Buddhist monastery on her husband's death, but she was brought out by the empress of his son Kao Tsung to oust a popular favourite, Hsiao Shu. She did her work only too well; not only Hsiao Shu, but also the empress herself, were put out of the way by her creatures and she assumed complete control of Kao Tsung and his kingdom. When he died she replaced him in turn by her three sons, one of whom was murdered and another banished because they were not amenable to her wishes. But she filled the land with carvings and temples and enormous copper statues of Buddha. When the monk I Ching returned from India after a pilgrimage of twenty-four years, she welcomed him in person with chants, gongs and banners, had him installed in a special temple and provided him with a translator of Sanskrit whom she had obtained in Khotan. "The dowager had in the year 688 the Hall of Heaven built by Huai I (her favourite Buddhist monk), for which 10,000 men worked daily, the expense mounting to hundreds of thousands. Hwai I had a bull killed and used the blood to paint a picture two hundred feet high, pretending he did it with the blood of his knee. As now (694) the palace physician came into favour, he secretly put fire to the building which was consumed, and the picture he had hung outside was torn into several hundreds of pieces by the wind. The dowager took it quietly and ordered him to build another hall, at which he felt uneasy and used wild expressions, so the dowager then had him murdered in a quiet way." [1] We

[1] Faber, E., *Chronological Handbook of the History of China,* p. 117.

57

are told that the next Ming T'ang (Hall) which she erected with the advice of her new favourite, a doctor, was 45 feet higher than the one the dead favourite had built and burnt. "Being of a pious disposition she called it the Palace of Celestial Communications." She was very fond of high-sounding titles. In 690 she caused a new translation to be made of the Great Cloud *sutra* in which passages were inserted which foretold that Maitreya would come to earth again in the guise of a woman.[1] The inference delighted her vanity and copies were judiciously circulated. Unlike her predecessors, Liang Wu Ti and the Empress Hu, she did not allow her piety to interfere with the efficiency with which she governed.   Another T'ang emperor to favour Buddhism was Hsien Tsung (806–825). In 819 he caused a bone relic of Buddha to be received by a superior officer and kept for three days in the palace; then it passed in procession through all the Buddhist temples of the land. It was on this occasion that the Minister of Justice, Han Yu, presented a petition against the worship of Buddha which has since become famous. He was degraded and sent as Governor to Ch'ao chou in Kwangtung; later he was be-headed[2] with his two sons. But Han Yu's petition was to bear fruit twenty-six years later. For in 845 there was a terrible persecution of the Buddhist monasteries by an imperial decree instigated by the Taoists. Four thousand six hundred temples were broken up and 260,500 monks and nuns sent back into secular life; 40,000 private shrines were removed and much land was confiscated.[3] All bronze images and bells were coined into cash. This was the last and most severe of the three persecutions which Buddhists

[1] Waley, A. *A Catalogue of Paintings recovered from Tun Huang by Sir Aurel Stein*, p. xxxix.

[2] Another account says he died in his bed.

[3] Faber. *Chronological Handbook of the History of China*, p. 132.

VII. AMITĀBHA BUDDHA

T'ang dynasty (618–906). Brought by Sir Aurel Stein from Tun
Huang.

The British Museum. $(1' \ 10\frac{1}{2}'' \times 1' \ 3\frac{1}{2}'')$

speak of as the calamity of the three Wu's (Tao Wu Ti of the Wei dynasty, Wu Ti of the Northern Chou and Wu Tsung of the T'ang).

Buddhism reached China in two forms, Hinayana and Mahayana, but it was the latter sect that prevailed. It was from these two sects that the conception of the Arhat (Chinese Lohan) and Bodhisattva (Chinese Pusa), which play such a big part in Buddhist painting of China, arose. The ideal of the Lohan came from the Hinayana sect, and was the purer and more primitive. The Lohan was a being who had emancipated himself from the doubts and delusions of the world. By his own efforts he had reached the perfect tranquillity and passionless harmony which Nirvana offered. He had passed to the other shore, to the "clear pool beyond the jungle," to "the island amid raging waters." His message to the world was a call to follow his example. The complaint of the Mahayanists was that the Lohan were too occupied with the salvation of their own souls to help the world. They blazed a trail but did not extend a helping hand. Instead the Mahayana substituted the conception of the Pusa. These benevolent and beautiful beings, so long as a soul is left in pain and sorrow, refused the fruits of Nirvana. It was an ideal likely to appeal tremendously to the popular imagination, which found the road of Arhatship too hard to climb. Unfortunately, as Sir Reginald Johnston has remarked, in the course of centuries the Pusas became objects of worship rather than examples to be imitated. Pictures of Lohan and Pusa have at all times been much in vogue. The Lohan appear in pottery, plaster and paintings, generally in numbers of sixteen, but groups of five hundred and even more are known.[1] The first mention of the sixteen Lohan is found in a book written by a

[1] Doré. *Recherches sur les superstitiones enc hine, IIème Partie Tome VIII*, p. 387 *and sequitur.*

Singhalese priest, Nardîmitra, who lived about eight hundred years after Sakyamuni's death.[1] The Chinese painting of Lohan reached its height during the T'ang dynasty. Perhaps the most distinguished of all Lohan painters was the priest Chang Yüeh of the five dynasties. Li Lung-Mien and Liu Hsü-Chung made themselves famous on these same themes. Later Chodensu took up the subject in Japan. The Japanese have divided Lohan into two schools according to the paintings of Li Lung-Mien and Chang Yüeh. The Lohan of Li Lung-Mien, they say, are natural human figures, but those of Chang Yüeh are almost demoniacal. Chinese artists have delighted to depict them as the most extraordinary grotesque creatures. They seem to have provided material for caricature of strange foreigners —Indian, Tibetan and Turkish types are in evidence in every group—nor did the Chinese artists confine themselves to Buddhist sages, but absorbed many distinguished figures who had no particular connection with Buddhism. In a large group of five hundred plaster Lohan, almost life-size, which can be seen in the temple of the Five Hundred Lohan, in Canton, one is pointed out as a figure of Marco Polo. Whether this figure actually represents Marco Polo is immaterial; it exhibits an example of the tendency to exalt any distinguished civil or military figure to their ranks. There is considerable Taoist feeling in some of these groups, which reminds one of the grouping of the Eight Taoist Immortals. Lohan are found consorting with dragons and tigers and cranes, which are the Taoist emblems of longevity. Chinese painters depict them sitting amid fantastic rocks and gnarled pines in every conceivable posture and expression awaiting transformation to Buddhahood. They are oblivious of personal appearance and their ragged clothes hang about their persons in wild disarray, disclosing

[1] *Kokka*, No. 377, note to Plate iii.

VIII. PART OF A SCROLL OF SIXTEEN LOHAN
Attributed to Wu Wei (*b.* 1458, *d.* 1508).

(1′ 11″ × 1′ 1½″)

scraggy limbs and hairy chests. Their heads are generally represented as out of all proportion to their bodies. Their high, bald skulls are studded with strange swellings, and from under bushy eyebrows their eyes are sunk in sagging cheeks. In their knotted hands they clasp fly-whisks, rugged staves, or copies of the sutras. Their feet are shod in coarse sandals, and the lobes of their ears hang down their necks. Their expression, if not wrapt in contemplation, is often severe, and they greet each other with angry ejaculations and abrupt gestures. Yet in most of these paintings there is a delightfully humorous and whimsical element, which eludes description. They are a far cry from the blood-stained erotic divinities of Thibet. Among these Lohan is to be found Mi Lieh Fu or Maitreya, who was once an Indian prince, and who has been appointed to appear as the successor of Buddha after this world has passed through 5000 years of sin. But he is a familiar figure with a large bare stomach and a cheerful smile.

The Pusa were very different people. Many legends are told of their expeditions into hell to succour suffering sinners. There were thousands of them, but very few had a definite personality. The four most important were Kuanyin (Avalokitesvara), Wên Shu (Manjusri), Ti-Ts'ang (Kshitigarbha), P'u Hsien (Samantabhadra). They were worshipped respectively on the four mountains *P'u to shan* near Ningpo, *Wu t'ai shan* in Shansi, *Chiu hua shan* in Wu hu and *Omei shan* in Szechuan. These are called the four sacred hills of Buddhism. The most important figure was Avalokitesvara, who in the form of Kuanyin, the Goddess of Mercy, is the most popular deity in China. Avalokitesvara was a male deity in India, and the change of sex has never been explained. Her features must be familiar to all collectors of Oriental china in the white porcelain figures of Fukien. She wears floating scarves, and her face is slightly

61

reminiscent of Queen Victoria. Her emblems were a narrow-necked phial from which she sprinkled the world with her comforting dew, and a spray of willow, the symbol of compassion. To all who approach her in trouble she extends her willow wand.[1] Chinese mythology tells us that she was the daughter of a legendary king of Chou by whom she was executed because she would not marry the suitor of his choice. On her arrival in the next world a shower of lotus petals shook the very foundations of hell, and imprisoned penitents escaped. To prevent further embarrassment she was sent to Pu to shan. In the words of a Buddhist hymn "she is for ever ferrying the souls of men safely across the ocean of misery, prayed to in a thousand places and in a thousand places responding to the call."[2] The waters round Pu to shan are called the sea of water-lilies and are supposed to be closed to fishermen. Actually her shrine does not date back to earlier than the ninth century. In the fairyland of the Western Heaven in Buddha's paradise which Amitābha governs, all are reborn inside the petals of lotus flowers in the sacred lake, to which they have been wafted by the grace of Kuanyin. But only the petals of those flowers which entertain the souls of the righteous open immediately, so that they can bask in the golden radiance of Buddha's smile. The petals of those flowers which contain the souls of those who have committed the five deadly sins do not open before the lapse of twelve greater *kalpas*, "a period of time so vast as to be almost beyond the reach of human thought." [3] Within the painless purgatory of their lotus

[1] A copy of a beautiful Japanese wooden figure of this goddess, probably of Korean workmanship and dating from the seventh century, can be seen in the Gallery of the Oriental Prints and Drawings in the British Museum. The original was discovered by Fenollosa in the Horiuji Temple (in 1884).

[2] Sir Reginald Johnston. *Buddhist China*, ch. xi.

[3] *Ibid.*, p. 107.

IX. KUANYIN, THE GODDESS OF MERCY
Painter unknown, but signed 'Wu Tao-Tžu.'
Ch'ing dynasty (1644–1912)
$(4'\ 8\frac{1}{2}'' \times 2'\ 1\frac{1}{2}'')$

petals they are withheld from the joys of paradise. The name Avalokitesvara comes from the Sanskrit and means the "looking down lord." She is also addressed as the "all pitying one." Sometimes she is called "the Kuanyin who came across the sea." In one sense she is worshipped as the giver of sons and in this rôle is attended by a dove or a fish, the symbols of fecundity, or she appears carrying a small child. E. J. Dukes, writing *c.* 1880, mentions a white earthenware figure of Kuanyin holding a child placed in a "Romish chapel" at Foochow in the place of the Virgin Mother and Child. A Chinese term for a beautiful girl is a "living Kuanyin," and in yet another guise she is the patron saint of sailors and the sea. Many a pirate must have invoked her special protection at her island shrine in the Chinese archipelago. But although she taught that sinners could escape to the portals of her painless purgatory, Buddhism like Christianity possessed a hell. Waley points out that before the arrival of Buddhism China knew nothing of life after death.[1] It was not until A.D. 650 that T'ang Lin invented the underworld.

The Chinese hell is presided over by Yama, sometimes attended by a female consort and assisted by his ten kings, through each of whose courts the soul must pass on its way to salvation. Chinese paintings of hell represent magistrates sitting at their desks attended by lictors; before them is an open book and in their hands they hold a pen. They stroke their beards with grave gestures, while they contemplate the accused, listen to witnesses and pronounce sentence. Below them ox-headed, horse-headed and green-faced demons with smiling faces hurry off bedraggled victims, who sob and supplicate as they go. The base of these pictures concludes with a presentation of the forest of knives, cauldrons of boiling oil and the other pleasures that await them.

[1] Waley, A. *Catalogue of Paintings recovered from Tuan Huang*, p. xxvi.

The list of sins and their appropriate tortures is very gruesome reading.[1] It is related that the agonies of hell depicted
by the painter Chang Hsiao-Shih were so realistic that the
people declared he must have been there himself.[2] Those
of Wu Tao-Tzŭ inspired the butchers and fishmongers of
the capital with such terror (Buddhism forbade the taking
of animal life) that they forsook their trades and took up
honest employment. The inferno he painted in the Chao
Kŭng Ssu monastery in the capital Ch'ang-an was so hor-
rible as to make the hair of every one who saw it stand on
end.[3]

The T'ang times in which Buddhism flourished were an
age of cosmopolitanism. Buddhism broke down the isolation in which Chinese civilization had been cradled. It
brought with it influences from the outside world. These
contacts were mostly Indian, but there was also a faint echo
of Greek civilization. With the collapse of Buddhism, China
shrinks into itself. Henceforward she develops her civilization in complete isolation. By the Sung dynasty Buddhism
had split into many sects of which the most important were
those of Ch'an (Japanese Zen) and the "Pure Land Sect"
(the worship of Amitābha). The appearance of Ch'an or
Zen, the contemplative school of Buddhism, is attributed
to the arrival of Bodhidharma from India in the year
520 A.D. (? 526), but treatises of Zen philosophy form part
of the earliest Buddhist translations. It was a mystical revolt
against institutionalism, which took the form of a reaction
against the worship of relics and observance of dogmas.
Zen patriarchs are frequently represented tearing up the
sutras or as burning idols to warm themselves. "I have come
from India to teach you that Buddha is thought. I care

[1] Wieger. *Moral Tenets and Customs in China,* ch. 11, pp. 345-391.
[2] Giles, H. A. *Chinese Pictorial Art,* p. 44.
[3] *Kokka,* No. 320, p. 157.

X. THE SIXTH CH'AN PATRIARCH, THE
PRIEST HUI NING (637-712) TEARING UP
THE SUTRAS
By Liang K'ai (c. 1203).
The Collection of Count Matsudaira, Tokyo.

(*Ht.* 2′ 9½″)

nothing for monastic rules or ascetic practices. As for walk-ing on water and through fire, climbing sword wheels, sit-ting upright for hours without rest and such practices; they belong to the world of being. . . . Thought! Thought! Thought! . . . It is hard to seek, expanding it covers the whole world, shrinking it is too small to lodge a pin. . . . I seek the heart, I do not seek Buddha. For I have learnt to know that the outer world is empty and untenanted." [1] Waley remarks that the nearest English parallel to Zen would be the religion of the Quakers. The Zen patriarchs taught religion as an individual and mystical experience. Students of Zen despised the priesthood and held scripture and learning in contempt. The sixth Zen patriarch, who died in 712, could neither read nor write. On his arrival Bodhi-dharma was welcomed to the court of Liang Wu Ti, but his doctrines must have appeared most unpalatable to that monarch, whose pride in his pagodas and temples, his crowds of monks and his pile of books, was only equalled by his belief in the efficacy of relics. It can scarcely have been more popular with the vested interests of Buddhism who tried in vain to poison him. Bodhidharma soon offended Liang Wu Ti and retired to Loyang. (He is often represented in Chinese paintings as crossing the Yangtze on a reed.) There he lived for nine years in Shao ling monas-tery in the Shao shih mountains (Sung chou in Honan) in contemplation before a wall. His wish to return to India was never granted, and after his death he is reputed to have been seen wandering over the hills shod in one sandal; the other was all that they found in his otherwise empty coffin.

The Ch'an school was at its height during the Sung, and the school of painting which it inspired flourished during the thirteenth and fourteenth centuries. They chose bird,

[1] Waley, A. *An Introduction to the Study of Chinese Painting,* pp. 216, 217; *Zen Buddhism and its Relation to Art,* p. 10.

flower and religious motives. They painted simply in ink and their works are continually confused with the later Bunjingwa paintings. Most of these painters were priests. The priest Mu Ch'i was one of the most famous but his pictures have found less favour in China than in Japan.[1] The Ryû Ko Temple in Kyoto possesses several pictures from his brush. He was an eccentric character fond of music and poetry. He led the life of a vagabond; although his pictures have been considered coarse and eccentric by the Chinese, he is venerated in Japan, where the Zen tradition is still alive to-day. Zen was introduced into China during the sixth century, grew in the Sui and T'ang and achieved great popularity under the Sung. It was introduced into Japan in 1191 and became the foundation of the code of the Samurai. A study of Zen is the best introduction to the study of Japanese art, and the best books on Zen have been written by Japanese. From Zen sprang the Cha-no-yu or tea cere-mony, which has a very close bearing on the arts of Japan, because it provided a yard-stick by which all pottery, painting and bronzes have been measured. The Japanese have been indifferent in the past to all objects of art which did not adapt themselves to this ceremony. It was at once an æsthetic communion and a political and religious philo-sophy. It is the great tea-masters who have dictated the lines of Japanese taste. All that love of cold and austere glazes, which manifests itself in porcelains of the Sung dynasty, and delights in the rough blue and white porcelains of the Ming is the fruit of their teaching. They taught that the insufficient is better than the superfluous. Their emphasis was placed on austerity and restraint. The Zen pictures of China are painted in the same vein. Zen sages are continually repre-sented. There is Yu Shan-Chu on his donkey and Chen Huan on his bullock, and the strange pair of scullions Han

[1] See plate facing page 76.

XI. THE LOHAN PU TAI

By Chang Hung, Ming dynasty (1368–1643)

The National Collection, Peiping.   (5′ 9″ × 1′ 4″)

Shan and Shih Tê; and, most famous of all, the uncouth priest Pu Tai, with his jolly face and prominent stomach. He was said to carry his food in a bag on a stick. If given a fish he would shove it among his clothes, for he was indifferent to ridicule. He lived a wandering life in rebellion to all authority, and he is generally portrayed asleep against his sack or romping with children. His picture is a particularly common motive in Japanese painting.

The Zen search for naturalness led eventually to the neglect of learning and to the cultivation of absurd gestures and paradoxes. Contemplation became a business. The correct postures and attitudes were as complicated as any physical exercise. "Secure a quiet room neither extremely light nor extremely dark, neither very warm nor very cold, a room, if you can, in a Buddhist temple located in a beautiful mountainous district. You should not practise Zazon in a place where a conflagration or a flood or robbers may be likely to disturb you, nor should you sit in a place close by the sea or drinking-shops or brothel-houses, or the houses of widows and of maidens, or buildings for music; nor should you live in close proximity to the place frequented by kings, ministers, powerful statesmen, ambitious or insincere persons. You must not sit in Meditation in a windy or very high place lest you should get ill. Be sure not to let the wind or smoke get into your room, nor to expose it to rain and storm. Keep your room clean. Keep it not too light by day nor too dark by night. Keep it warm in winter and cool in summer. Do not sit leaning against a wall, or a chair or a screen. You must not wear soiled clothes or beautiful clothes, for the former are the cause of illness, while the latter are the cause of attachment. Avoid the Three Insufficiencies—that is to say, insufficient clothes, insufficient food, and insufficient sleep. Abstain from all sorts of uncooked or hard or spoiled or unclean food, and also from very delicious dishes, because the former cause troubles in your alimentary canal, while the latter cause you to covet after diet. Eat and drink just to appease your hunger and your thirst, never mind whether the food be tasty or not. Take your meals regularly and punctually, and never sit in Meditation immediately after any meal. Do not practise Dhyana (Zen) soon after you have taken a heavy dinner, lest you should get sick thereby. Sesame, barley, corn, potatoes, milk, and the like are the best material for your food. Frequently wash your eyes, face, hands and feet, and keep them cool and clean." [1] Later Zen seems to have borrowed from Taoism. In their search for naturalness its priests became drunk and ribald. If its exponents were devoid of personal ambition they were equally devoid of social duty. In the tenth century it decayed and to-day its monasteries are almost indistinguishable from those of popular Buddhism.

The last and most popular form of Buddhism was the worship of Amitābha,[2] who was supposed to have been an Indian ruler, Dharmakera, who forsook his throne to become a monk. In due course he became a Buddha, upon the condition that he was allowed to establish a paradise in the Western Heaven to which all mortals might go who called upon his name. Mere faith in Amitābha and a repetition of his name was sufficient to secure deliverance. It was a doctrine of faith but not of works.[3] The sutra of the Precious Lotus informs us that "one who with steadfast faith and a quiet mind calls upon that name for a period of a week or even a single day may face death with security." To the "Pure Land School" psalm-singing became a

[1] Kaiten Nukariya. *The Religion of the Samurai* (A Study of Zen Philosophy and Discipline in China and Japan), pp. 188-190.

[2] Reichelt, K. L. *Truth and Tradition in Chinese Buddhism*, pp. 127-170.

[3] Plopper, C. H. *Chinese Religion seen through the Proverb*, p. 361.

mechanical dispensation for sin. The land resounded with *Na Mo O Mi To Fu* (Praise to Amitābha) and every rock and cliff was engraved with *Om Mani Padme Hum* (O! the jewel in the lotus), a reference to his famous sutra, but it was also filled with bands of lazy useless monks, whose greed and immorality became a byword. Their ranks were recruited from the children of the very poor. They were dirty and illiterate. The spread of popular education under the Republic is threatening to remove the sources from which the priests have been recruited. Unless there is a popular revival Buddhism is in a fair way to survive only as a lay philosophy.

The Buddhists built their monasteries in distant and beautiful situations among the hills and forests. They were not so much concerned with the reform of this world as with existence in the next. The cultivation of the individual soul in contemplation among the hills appealed to them more than work in the cities. These monasteries became places of pilgrimage for the poor, and a refuge for artists and philosophers in times of trouble. It is difficult to assess their immense contribution to art. The appearance of Buddhism marks the first important popular movement in Chinese art. There is much that is crude and mediocre in the countless Buddhist images and pictures that have survived; they were largely the work of the people and they are only the fragments of a great tradition. The great Buddhist masterpieces have perished and we are unable to obtain a clear conception of their magnificence to-day. So far as we know no Buddhist wall-paintings of the T'ang dynasty or earlier are in existence. The oldest that have survived are in Nara, Japan, and they date from the seventh century. None of the great works of Wu Tao-Tzŭ, who is recorded to have painted three hundred frescoes on the walls of Ch'ang-an and Loyang, have come down to us. The majority of

Buddhist paintings decorated the walls of the monasteries. Most of these must have fallen into ruin, if they were not deliberately destroyed during the persecutions of the middle of the ninth century.[1]

The pictures that were recovered by Sir Aurel Stein from the walled-up chapel of the caves of the Thousand Buddhas near Tun Huang on the western frontier of China in 1906–8 —now divided between the British Museum and the Museum of Central Asian Antiquities, Delhi—form the most important collection of this tradition that is known. The collection has been described in detail by Waley.[2] It contains eighteen dated works, the earliest 864, and the latest 938. Tun Huang was a remote provincial city on the North-west Frontier of China famous for its cave-temples and Buddhist sculptures, some of which date back to the fourth century. In the days before sea traffic it was an

[1] It is interesting to note that the *Ku Kung Shu Hua Chi* (Reproductions of Paintings from the Palace Collections) is confined to Buddhist paintings of the Sung, Yüan and Ming. Presumably there are no T'ang Buddhist paintings to reproduce.

In the first 30 numbers the following Buddhist paintings are reproduced:—

Vol. iv, No. 4, "Wên Shu (Manjusri)," by a Sung artist (anonymous); No. 11, "Bodhisattva (? Kuanyin) in a Bamboo Forest," by Hsia Ch'ang, Ming dynasty.

Vol. vi, No. 6, "Lohan," by Liu Kuan Tao, Yüan dynasty.

Vol. vii, No. 2, "Bodhisattva," by Ku Shih, Sung.

Vol. viii, No. 14, "Kuanyin," by Hsing Tz'ü Ching, Ming.

Vol. xxiii, No. 6, "Proclaiming scriptures amid a rain of flowers," by a Yüan artist (anonymous).

Vol. xxiv, No. 4, "Lohan," by Li Sung, Sung.

Vol. xxvi, No. 16, " Goddess from over the Sea," by Chên Shu, Ch'ing.

Vol. xxvii, No. 20, "Lohan," by Ting Yün-P'êng, Ming.

[2] Waley, A. *Catalogue of Paintings recovered from Tun Huang by Sir Aurel Stein.*

The cave has been described by Pelliot in *Les Grottes de Youen Houang*; in the *Ruins of Desert Cathay*; and in *Serindia* by Stein himself.

XII. BODHISATTVA (PUSA) WITH
TRANSPARENT BOWL
T'ang dynasty (618–906). Brought by
Sir Aurel Stein from Tun Huang.
The British Museum. (2′ 11″ × 1′ 0½″)

important caravan station on the road across Chinese
Turkestan to India. It was along this route that the great
bulk of pilgrims passed to and fro, and it is not surprising to
find that an immense cache of Buddhist paintings, such as
would have been sold to pilgrims, should have been preserved there. The place was occupied by the Tibetans
from the middle of the eighth to the middle of the ninth
century when it was to a great extent cut off from the
world. In this way it escaped the rigorous persecutions of
845. The pictures which Stein discovered were provincial
and archaic survivals of the T'ang period. Most of them
are anonymous and must have been painted by artisans
entirely out of touch with the living tradition of their own
day. But they are copies of copies of originals that must go
back to the seventh century. Waley remarks that despite
the provincial incompetence of the monks who painted
them, a curiously impressive abstract quality has been
preserved.

The Yüan dynasty, which succeeded the Sung, brought
a race of simple Mongolian horsemen from the Steppes.
Fighting and hunting were the salt of their existence. They
had little use for the contemplation, the peace, the care of
animals that Buddhism enjoined. The refinements of Taoism
were unsympathetic to this primitive people; the ethics of
Confucius carried no message. It was the crude and blood-
thirsty practices of Tibet, so closely akin to the howling
and dervish dances of their own Shaman, that appealed to
them. From then onwards it was only the Tantric (magical)
form of Buddhism which flourished in Tibet which had
any serious influence. In 1283, when Kublai Khan lost his
heir, it was forty thousand Lama monks who were engaged
to chant his soul to paradise.[1] Lamaism supplied a vitality
and a missionary zeal which the Buddhists of China could

[1] Grantham, A. E. *Hills of Blue*, p. 411.

71

not provide. Its influence extended all over inner and outer Mongolia and into Manchuria. On political grounds alone it had to be placated. By the Ming period Tibetan prelates came to take precedence over the Chinese. Yung Lo sent to Tibet for his chaplains. The Ch'ing dynasty was also from the Steppes. It was openly hostile to Buddhism which had by now sunk into complete decay, but it maintained an outward respect for all Tibetan forms. The Lamaism of Tibet is a Tantric (magic) form of Mahayana Buddhism, overlaid with the mystical practices of Northern India, and diluted by the devil worship native to the country. Pictures of Yama, the God of Hell, standing astride a bull, which symbolizes desire, or trampling upon blood-stained human forms, take the place of the benevolent pity of Kuanyin.

Buddhism reached Tibet in 632 (640?) [1] when Sron San Gampo was converted by his two wives, one a Chinese princess, and the other a daughter of the King of Nepal; both were later incarnated as consorts of Avalokitesvara in the shape of white and green Taras. By the eighth century it had been contaminated by the addition of ingredients from the native Bon pantheon. The Bon religion must have resembled the Shamanist practices of Mongolia. It was a gruesome worship of nature in which blood-smearing and human sacrifice played a part. The mongrel child of these forbidding elements was Lamaism, but it was not until the eleventh century that it assumed the name.[2] In 1038 (1040?), under the direction of the Indian priest Artisa, a reformation was carried out; the dogma of the living Buddha was introduced and the sect of the Yellow Caps. By the end of the

[1] Waddell, L. A. *Lamaism*, p. 9.
[2] Waddell describes it as (p. 30) : "a mixture of Sivaite mysticism, magic and Indo-Tibetan demonolatry overlaid with a thin varnish of Mahāyāna Buddhism."

fifteenth century the title of Grand Lama, an incarnation of Avalokitesvara, had been invented, and in 1640, the title of Dalai Lama. Soon after, he was recognized as king of Tibet by the Chinese. Lamaism was dominated by the fear of punishment in the next world, and the expiation of sin was its chief anxiety. A fear of evil penetrates all the ritual of the Lama church. To this end every family dedicated a son or daughter to the church to pray for their sins. Lhasa became a hive of monks. Monasteries of ten thousand or more are not uncommon, and Tibet is probably the most superstitious and priest-ridden country in the world. Charms are carried on the person or in the shoes; incantations are swallowed when they are not memorized; an endless stream of liturgies ascends to the heavens; even the wind and water are set to contribute their share. The priests worship the gods with howlings, and masks, and devil-dances with the aid of conch, and drum, and trumpet, and tambourines made of human skulls cemented to a wooden disc, which they shake to mark time between their incantations. The trumpets are often made of human bones, "the bones of a criminal or of those who have died a violent death being preferred." [1] The skulls used for libations of blood are elaborately mounted in brass and copper and studded with coral and turquoise. Offerings of this nature are so popular that a regular system of craniology has been adopted for making a suitable selection.

"There are indications from which a good skull can be told in a live person; if he has soft and smooth hair of lustrous black; if his forehead is broad and his eyebrows thick; if on his forehead there is a mark; if he has most teeth in the upper jaw; if the tip of his tongue can touch his nose (this is a peculiarity possessed in even greater degree by all Buddhas); if his voice is high-pitched and

[1] Laufer, B. *Use of Human Skulls and Bones in Tibet*, p. 2.

73

complexion fresh; if in walking he throws his left hand and left foot first." [1]

The banner paintings which decorate the Lama temples invariably depict the Lamaist divinities (Tibetan landscape painting does not exist). They are painted on coarse cloth in pigments mixed with glue, and their oily appearance is due to the lamps fed with butter which have burnt before them in Lamaist temples. They very seldom date back to earlier than the Ming. The pigments with which they are painted possess a delicate pastel opaqueness. Some of the colours used in the Ming paintings are very beautiful, but they are applied in a thick dead manner, and heavily out-lined. Few of them rank as works of art. The scowling faces of the black and green-skinned gods of the Tibetans are not easily forgotten; round their necks hang necklaces of skulls, and on their heads grows flaming red hair. They are often clad in human skin and they brandish thunderbolts in a thousand arms with which they subjugate devils or they crush underfoot the bleeding corpses of the damned and clasp their çakti (consorts) to them in the act of coition. When we reflect that Buddha forbade the taking of life, and that his priests were dedicated to a life of peace and contemplation, one is astonished that his religion could be so twisted to serve completely different ends.

In the second half of the thirteenth century Kublai Khan adopted Lamaism as the State religion. It became the political buttress of China's northern frontiers. The great Lamaseries of Peking and Jehol were built to secure the allegiance of the nomads living in their shadow.[2] The *Pai Ta Sŭ* temple in Peking, built in the Ch'ing dynasty to house the relics of Buddha, was turned into a Lama temple

---

[1] Laufer, B. *Use of Human Skulls and Bones in Tibet*, pp. 7, 8.

[2] Stuart Lillico. *China Journal*, July 1934: "Ruined Temples of Jehol," pp. 14–18.

XIII. TIBETAN BANNER PAINTING OF AVALOKITESVARA
Ch'ing dynasty (1644–1912).

By permission of Messrs. Luzac. $(2'\ 7\frac{3}{4}'' \times 1'\ 10\frac{1}{2}'')$

by Kublai Khan and the *Yung Ho Kung,* which in the early part of the eighteenth century had been the residence of the Emperor Yung Chêng, became the seat of the Yellow sect of Lamaism. China realized that to keep Tibet and Mongolia she must keep the Tashai and Dalai Lamas. But the power of the Tibetan priesthood in China has had little influence outside Peking. Its message was entirely unsympathetic to Chinese traditions. Tibetan art bears a superficial resemblance to the art of China, but the spirit and iconography are more akin to that of Northern India.

The great rival of Buddhism was the native Taoism which it tended to supplant in the popular imagination. Taoism is associated with the name of Lao Tzǔ, a hypothetical personality whose life and death are shrouded in mystery: but this has not in the least deterred Taoists from producing elaborate descriptions of his personal appearance. We are told that "his complexion was white and yellow. His ears were of extraordinary size and were each pierced with two passages. He had handsome eyebrows, large eyes, ragged teeth, a double-ridged nose and a square mouth; on each foot he had ten toes, and each hand was ornamented with ten lines." His name, Lao Tzǔ (the 'Old Child') was derived from his appearance, for he combined the white hairs of old age with the complexion of a youth. He is supposed to have foreseen the fall of the Chou dynasty under which he held office, and to have ridden away on a black ox into the West. At the *Han Ku* pass he was encountered by the Governor Yen Hsi who besought him to leave some teachings for the use of mankind, upon which he produced the *Tao Tê Ching* and then disappeared for ever. There is also a highly improbable account of his meeting Confucius. As Waley points out, there is no proof that such a man ever existed. Ssǔ-Ma Ch'ien, who attempted to write his life as

early as the first century B.C., was unable to gather sufficiently convincing information and had to abandon it.
Probably we shall never know who wrote the *Tao Tê
Ching* which has been attributed to him.[1] It is impossible to
explain the strange paradoxes of this fascinating book,
which has been more often translated but less understood
than any other Chinese classic. The text is full of obscurity,
and we have little knowledge of the conditions under
which it was written and to the perplexing circumstances
to which it refers. The whole subject is discussed most
lucidly and informatively by Waley in his introduction to his
own translation. The *Tao Tê Ching* teaches that the road to a
high existence is the Way (*tao*). This Way is the right path
of conduct. Those who practise it cease to strive; they live
in harmony with themselves and their surroundings. But
it is a strangely elusive *tao* that they must pursue.

"You can look at it, and you cannot see it. You listen to
it and you cannot hear it. You use it and you cannot exhaust
it. It is not to be expressed in words. It is still and erect; it
stands alone and changes not; it circulates everywhere and
is not endangered. It is ever active but it leaves everything
undone. From it phenomena appear, through it they dis-
appear. Formless it is the cause of form. Nameless it is the
origin of heaven and earth, without a name it is mother of
all things." [2]

The ideal society of the Taoist is a state of simplicity and
innocence. "Fill your stomach and empty your mind," Lao
Tzŭ is supposed to have said. Language, literature, civilization were nothing. To live in harmony with the powers of
nature was the ambition of the Taoist. But the philosophy
of the *Tao Tê Ching* was too subtle and too difficult to be

[1] Waley, A. *The Way and its Power*, p. 106.
[2] See also Zen, S. H. C. *Symposium of Chinese Culture*: "Religion and
Philosophy," by Hu Shih.

XIV. LAO TZŪ
By Mu-Ch'i, thirteenth century.

popular. Lao Tzŭ spoke for the individual mystic; he left no creed and founded no priesthood, and his philosophy has become the basis of a religion which would have amused him. His original and cryptic message has been obliterated by later acquisitions of folk-lore, necromancy and alchemy. The pursuits of the Taoist sage have degenerated from the search for harmony to the hope of changing snow into silver and cinnabar into gold. The search for the elixir of immortality has obscured "the Way." A mass of magical incantations and the grossest superstitions became associated with Taoist rites and assisted in their decline. The pursuit of a life beyond death became their only objective.

Taoism resented the arrival of Buddhism which threatened to supplant it in the popular estimation, and in order to preserve its own popularity it borrowed wholesale from her rival. It built monasteries in imitation of Buddhist monasteries. It adopted liturgies, chants, legends and a whole pantheon of gods, none of which had existed before the arrival of its opponent. It founded a priesthood (but it was not celibate); in fact it took over the whole Buddhist organization. Buddhism returned the compliment; in order to adapt itself to the Chinese temperament it reshaped itself along Taoist legend. The Shadowland of the Taoist was developed into the Buddhist hell. The Taoist worship of nature, and particularly of mountains, was extended to include the four sacred Hills of Buddhism. Each strove to outdo the other in the popular estimation. The worst Buddhist persecutions were due to Taoist instigation, for there was a bitter feeling between the two. It is said that Chang Sêng-Yu painted a picture entitled "A drunken Buddhist priest," which caused much annoyance and embarrassment to the pious, and was a source of malicious glee to the Taoists. Eventually a

77

subscription was raised to induce Yen Li-Pên to paint a reply entitled "The drunken Taoist priest." [1] There is a picture in the Boston Museum to-day attributed to Li Kung Lin entitled "Buddhist Patriarchs triumphing over Taoist Heretics." Taoism, when it could rely upon imperial favour, took the first opportunity to compass the destruction of Confucianism as well as Buddhism. The holocaust of books and scholars in the reign of Shih Huang Ti was directly due to Taoist instigation. Taoist influence was particularly strong during his reign (246–209 B.C.). This monarch passed his later days building palaces and in the search of the fungus of immortality. In 219 he dispatched Su Shih with "several thousands of boys and girls" in search of the Three Fairy Islands of the Immortals. A mania for building palaces is typical of all Chinese monarchs who have been under the influence of Taoism. Shih Huang Ti had plans drawn up of the palaces of every ruler he defeated, and built replicas of them up to the number of two hundred and seventy on the banks of the Wei.[2] It is to this man that we owe the great wall of China. The Han Emperor Wu Ti (140–87 B.C.), under the influence of Taoists, perpetuated Shih Huang Ti's search for immortality and his love of building. In 133 he sent magicians in search of the islands of the genii. In 106 he built on the banks of the River Wen a "Ming T'ang" (hall) in the form of a Greek cross supposed to be in the tradition of the building of the mythical Yellow Emperor, and in the palace grounds of Ch'ang-an he erected a copper statue holding a bronze bowl to catch the dew, which when mixed with crushed jade, and drunk out of golden bowls, was supposed to induce everlasting life. The palace of Chien Chang which he built had a tower 500 feet high and a terrace of the gods decorated with

[1] Giles, H. A. *Chinese Pictorial Art*, p. 41.
[2] Grantham, A. E. *Hills of Blue*, p. 149.

78

representations of the earth and sky and spirits of the wind and water.[1] He seems to have been a prey to all dabblers in the supernatural. A magician called Chao Wang, who produced an apparition in the form of a dead concubine, was rewarded with the title of "Marshal of Learned Perfection," but in 119 when he gave a silk book to a cow to swallow in order to deceive the emperor, his handwriting was unfortunately recognized and he was executed.[2] His successor when failing to produce the immortals, was cut in two in the market place. It was the heyday of soothsayers, witches, and spiritualists. One had seen supernatural beings many feet high and had heard unearthly voices. Another had observed "divine footprints on the ramparts of the city and a pheasant-like creature hovering about them." Towards the end of his reign Wu Ti became the subject of illusions, until he believed his own son was trying to bewitch him. He embarked on a civil war which involved the death of his two sons, their wives and families. But before his death he was forced to admit the sad failure of his dreams. "I have afflicted the people with my follies and cruelties. I repent of the past but cannot amend it. In the future I will avoid everything that oppresses my subjects. . . . I have acted madly. I was the toy of dishonest magicians. They deceived me. There are no immortals. . . ." [3] The influence of the buildings laid out by Shih Huang Ti and Han Wu Ti has promoted a Chinese architectural tradition in which the influence of Taoism can be traced. Since the days of Han Wu Ti there has been a semi-artificial lake within the palace precincts in the style of the T'ai I Lake which he built. The San Hai or the three seas of Peking is a survival of this tradition.

[1] Grantham, A. E. *Hills of Blue,* p. 124.
[2] Faber. *Chronological Handbook of the History of China,* p. 43.
[3] Grantham, A. E. *op. cit.,* p. 130.

The Taoist believed in a class of beings that had achieved immortality and lived in paradise. They were the *Hsien* (immortals). There were thousands of them, but eight of them were particularly famous. Those who had become *Hsien* had abandoned the struggle for the wealth and honours of the world, to cultivate a life of harmony with nature among the hills and forests, where they practised a spiritual and mental discipline in order to achieve immortality. They shunned the earthiness of cooked food and lived on nuts and dew. Pine cones were one of their delicacies, for the everlasting greenness and the hoary old age of the pine was symbolical of immortality. The immortals are pictured in the company of the crane and tortoise among the peach blossoms and jade mountains of the Three Paradises (there are several others); of the three, P'êng Lai Shan is the most famous ; the immortals who walk its terraces or ride through its clouds on their crane and tortoise steeds, live on sesamum and coriander seeds. The waters that surround its promontories lack buoyancy and are unapproachable. The second paradise, Ying Chou, is situated in the Eastern Sea opposite Kiangsu and seventy thousand miles distant from the mainland. This is the island which Shih Huang Ti and Han Wu Ti sought in vain to discover, and which the Japanese have identified with their own country. Upon its shores grows the *Chih*, the famous fungus of the immortals, the food of the gods, and a rock of jade stone from which flows a spring whose waters confer eternal life.[1] Another paradise is in the K'un Lun Mountains at the source of the Yellow River. At the foot of the mountains grows the famous peach tree whose fruit confers immortality. Every six thousand years the peaches ripen and then Hsi Wang Mu gives a banquet. This lady is the fabulous Queen of the Immortals (the Jesuits of the eighteenth century identified

[1] Mayers. *Chinese Reader's Manual*, p. 278.

XV. THE EARTHLY PARADISE
Painter unknown. Ming dynasty (1368–1643).

(7' 8" × 3' 10")

The British Museum.

her with the Queen of Sheba). The Shan Hai Ching says, "Her appearance is that of a human being. She has a panther's tail and dog's teeth and can howl loudly. Her hair hangs down and she wears a coronet. She presides over the calamities and punishments sent by God." [1] Yet in Chinese paintings she is not represented with a panther's tail or dog's teeth but as a beautiful woman, who rides through the skies on a phœnix steed, followed by a host of other immortals on dragons, tigers, lions and winged horses. In the K'un Lun Mountains by the Jasper Lake is her palace. Artists have vied with one another to portray the splendour of its surroundings which are indescribable; its walls piled high with ninefold gradations; its trees laden with precious gems. Here Hsi Wang Mu attended by her phœnixes and fairy handmaidens received Mu Wang of the Chou dynasty, and from here she sent seven precious peaches on a platter of jade to Wu Ti of the Han, from the tree which blossoms and fruits once in six thousand years. The emperor preserved and planted the stones with great care, but they did not take kindly to the air of this world. [2]

The *Hsien* are frequently subjects of Chinese paintings. They are generally shown in a setting of wild natural landscape clad in skins or strange cloaks of leaves and accompanied by the animals with which they are associated, but there are also groups luxuriously clad. Sometimes an individual *Hsien* is represented as a hermit living in seclusion among mountain streams, at others a group appear together. The most ordinary group of *hsien* numbers eight. Each has his or her appropriate emblems and can be easily distinguished. Why and when these eight immortals came to be associated and to be separated from the rest it is difficult to say. Mayer does not think that the tradition

[1] Giles, H. A. *Adversaria Sinica*: "Hsi Wang Mu," p. 5.
[2] See Strehlneek. *Chinese Pictorial Art,* p. 284.

was established earlier than the Yüan period. Yetts points out that one of them, Ts'ao Kuo-Chiu, is said to have lived as late as the Sung, while Lü Tung-Pin may have existed as early as the T'ang. But most of the paintings of the eight *hsien* can be attributed safely to the Ming.[1]

Taoism was at its height before Buddhism came to charm away its followers, and Confucianism was not fledged. In its struggle with Buddhism, Taoism borrowed so widely and exhaustively that it lost its own identity. The two have blended and intermingled until it is not always easy to distinguish the *Lohan* from the *Hsien*, and to-day they live in harmony side by side.

The Taoist worship of mountains and rivers goes back to the most remote antiquity. The five Taoist peaks have been held sacred for a much greater time than those of their four Buddhist counterparts. They are T'ai Shan in southern Shantung, Hêng Shan in Hunan, Hua Shan in southern Shênsi, Sung Shan in north-west Honan, Hing Shan in north-east Shansi. The worship of T'ai Shan is mentioned in the Books of History, Rites, Odes and the Analects.[2] A popular story identifies the spirit of these mountains with the jade lady dressed in feathers and crowned with clouds who was seen in 2650 B.C. and in 65 A.D. Li Po mentions several versions of her in his poems. This worship was extended to rivers. In the *Peking Gazette*, No. 13 of 1891, we read that it was necessary to erect a shrine at the capital of Shantung to guide the spirit of the Yellow River. After this, the *Gazette* retails, the autumn freshets passed without incident, and the emperor placed a tablet there in recognition.

[1] It would take too long to describe all eight in detail. (Professor Yetts in a valuable pamphlet entitled "The Eight Immortals," reprinted from the *Journal of the Royal Asiatic Society*, Oct. 1916, has discussed each in detail.)

[2] Moule, A. C. *T'ai Shan*, p. 5.

The Taoist monk was contemptuous of official life. He was devoid of duty or personal ambition. The famous Taoist sage Chuang Tzŭ, when approached with the offer of official emoluments, was found dangling his legs in a mountain stream. After pondering a few moments he asked the leader of the embassy whether he would prefer to be the dead shell of a sacred tortoise, wrapped in brocade and kept in a temple, or a live tortoise in a muddy pool. "Begone," he said, "I, too, will wag my tail in the mud." In the same way the Emperor Wu Ti (502–506) made repeated efforts to secure the services of the painter T'ao Hung-Ching, who sent him back as an answer a picture of two oxen, one wandering free amid brooks and trees and the other in a gilded head-stall led by a herdsman with a goad.[1] Hsi K'ang wrote to Shan T'o who had recommended him as his successor to the position of secretary to the Local Service Board, comparing himself to a bird or a deer: "if they are domesticated when young they submit meekly to all sorts of chastisement and restraint; but when restraint commences after they are grown up, they look about in a frenzy, tug wildly at their fastenings, and rush unhesitatingly into boiling water and flames to free themselves. Even though you should adorn them with ornaments of gold and feed them with the most tempting morsels of food, you would only succeed in quickening their thoughts of deep woods and their desire for its rich pastures."[2] At the head of the Taoist church is the Taoist pope, supposed to have been descended from one of the immortals, Chang Liang, a counsellor of the first emperor of the Han. Under the empire he was the chief exorcist of the Government and was reputed to have the power to travel to and from

[1] Giles, H. A. *Chinese Pictorial Art*, p. 32.
[2] Agnes E. Meyer. *Chinese Painting as reflected in the Thoughts in Art of Li Lung-Mien*, p. 77.

the capital unseen. On his death he is reincarnated in an infant of the same family.

But the gods of the people were not the shadowy figures of the immortals in a distant paradise, but a thousand small friendly idols of paper, stone, wood and clay.[1] Each trade had as its patron saint, the figure of one who had been particularly famous in his profession, and who after his death because of his reputation, had been enshrined as the divine protector of his fellow craftsmen. The majority of these deities were men who had been raised to the rank of gods. They suffered from the same disabilities and displayed the same qualities. They ate, married, quarrelled and slept. To those who prayed to them they bequeathed skill and help in time of trouble. The people kept them in their homes, but the larger effigies were carried round the streets in procession by their guilds on their appropriate festivals. Sometimes they were of entirely local significance. If they were suspected of losing their efficacy they were destroyed and replaced. There is Shen Nung, the God of Medicine, who possessed a transparent body from tasting many herbs; Lu Pan, the God of the Carpenters, whose dexterity brought a drought into the land of Wen; Lao Lang, the God of the Actors, who was once Chuang Tsang of the later T'ang dynasty; Mei and Ko, the Gods of the Dyers; Huangi-Ti, the inventor of boats and wheeled vehicles. Kuan Ti, the God of War, as a boy was a seller of bean curd; in his youth he committed murder, but during the war of the Three Kingdoms he distinguished himself so prominently that he was canonized by imperial rescript in 1594 A.D. But the three most frequently represented are Tsao Wang Yeh the Kitchen God, Ts'ai Shen the God of Wealth, and Ch'ung Kuei the demon dispeller. The first is perhaps the

[1] Plopper, C. H. *Chinese Religion seen through the Proverb*, p. 164 et seq.

XVI. TSAO WANG YEH, THE KITCHEN GOD

By permission of Dr. Otto Samson.   (Approx. 1′ 6″ × 1′ 0″)

most popular of all the domestic gods. He can still be found in the Chinese homes of the poor. The last two are the subjects of innumerable humble drawings exchanged at the Chinese new year by the people to secure wealth and happiness. The Kitchen God is the god of the hearth. He is supposed to preside over the family and to return to heaven every Chinese New Year to report on the behaviour of individual members of the family. Before he ascends, the household are careful to smear his mouth with a kind of treacle, so that he shall speak sweet words of them if the stickiness does not prevent him from speaking at all.[1] Chung K'uei, the God of the Demons, was an unsuccessful scholar, Chung Chang-Shih, who committed suicide because he could not pass his examinations. He owes his existence partly to a dream of the Emperor Ming Huang and partly to the brush of Wu Tao-Tzŭ. Ming Huang was tormented by a demon in his dreams, until the shade of the scholar caught and ate his tormentor. He revealed his history to the emperor who canonized him as Chung K'uei and commanded Wu Tao-Tzŭ to make a representation of the dream. If this is true, the figure of Chung K'uei, as conceived by Wu Tao-Tzŭ, is the original of all later portraits. His name is often painted on doors to frighten away the demons, as is that of Chiang T'ai-Kung, who was once a fortune-teller, and who is now the Controller of the Offices of the Gods. "Chiang T'ai-Kung is present, a hundred evils are warded off," is seen to-day as a charm over street doors. The pictures of the poor are paper charms. They cannot afford paintings. These charms are painted on red paper and stuck on to the lintels of the door on Chinese New Year. *Wu fu li men* (May the Five Happinesses approach the door) is one of the commonest in the south. The Five Happinesses are generally interpreted

[1] Plopper, C. H. *Chinese Religion seen through the Proverb*, p. 183.

85

as longevity, riches, peace, virtue and children. They are frequently pictured in the form of five bats. Another red paper charm runs "May voices be heard in front of the house singing of a hundred blessings, good luck and long life for those within."

The struggle of the three religions runs through all Chinese history. The one which enjoyed imperial patronage persecuted the other two. At first Taoism was in favour, at intervals it continued to regain its ascendancy. Buddhism arrived on the scene in the first century of the Christian era and proved a dangerous rival. But both went down during the Ming before the onslaught of Confucianism, which remained in power up to the Revolution of 1912. K'ang Hsi, in a famous edict (reprinted in the second year of his son Yung Chêng, 1724) launched against heterodox doctrines, dismissed all doctrines that are not contained in the Five Canons and Four Books as twaddle. As I feel that Young China would echo his sentiments, I cannot resist quoting some passages. ". . . all these renowned bonzes living retired upon distant mountains, and in pagodas, ex-plaining their sacred books, keeping the abstinence from flesh-meats, and mortifying themselves, beating drum and bells, they have not reached beyond the word 'heart'. And those old Taoist priests who live in caverns, trying hard to become immortal spirits; they do nothing but refine cinna-bar to nourish their vital fluids, eat the petals of flowers and drink the dew, in the hope of living on without old age overtaking them. They thus reject the great rules of human life, about which they never say anything.[1] These men withdraw themselves into lone forests; there they burn incense, recite prayers, give themselves to alchemy and magic, and nevertheless fail to become either Buddhas or

---

[1] This lack of public spirit the Confucians found particularly exas-perating.

spirits. If what they pretend is possible, how is it that no-body has ever seen them going to the Western Paradise; who ever saw them in broad daylight flying through the air? All their talk is nonsense. . . . But there are gangs of good-for-nothings, who, idling away all their time, fail to provide themselves with food or clothing; and so they go in search of a quiet life in some pagoda, cut off their queue and say they have renounced the world. . . . They make people believe that to give them alms is a means of acquiring titles to felicity; that the more they give them, the richer will they become. Then fearing that they should not be believed, they threaten people, saying that those who injure the bonzes, refuse to believe in Buddha or in the spirits, do not pray to Amida, or who passing a pagoda fail to prostrate themselves, or omit to give bountiful alms when necessary, will surely go to hell, or be struck by lightning, or suffer from lootings and fire and will endure all sorts of evils. They stop at no threat so long as they can make the people believe them and support them. . . . All these nonsensical tales about fasts, invoking Buddha, meet-ings, the erection of pagodas and casting of statues, the painting of images, all this is the work of those idle vaga-bonds, who, after having forsaken their family, become bonzes, or Taoist priests, to get hold of your money. Yet you obstinately persist in believing in them. Not only do you go yourselves to worship and burn incense in the pagodas and make the prostrations, but you also suffer your wives and daughters to frequent the pagodas. With their hair oiled, their faces painted, dressed in scarlet clothes trimmed with green, they enter the temples under pretext of making offerings, or fulfilling a vow, and associate with these old bachelor bonzes and Taoist priests; a practice of which I do not see the utility. . . . But nobody is more mistaken than those who seek in this life to assure their happiness in the next. Hence the hopes of the bonzes or the Taoists to become Buddhas or genii in the next world are but vain and idle dreams; and thus all is said." [1]

[1] Wieger, L. *Moral Tenets and Customs in China*, p. 115 et seq.

3

The Relation to Calligraphy

ONE of the first impressions of a visit to China must
be the beauty and decorative qualities of Chinese
writing, in which strokes and splashes and blobs are
woven together in sweeping lines to form the happiest
patterns. Writing is everywhere in evidence. The streets are
hung with shop-signs and banners, painted or embroidered
in large characters with the name of their owners and their
wares. All restaurants, most places of business, and many
private houses, are hung with quotations from the poets or
the classics extolling the beauties of nature or offering the
most impeccable moral sentiments: some businesses confine themselves to such practical maxims as "chattering and
gossiping interfere with business," or "No credit given here
—we have grown wise by experience." [1] It is not long
before the foreigner realizes the Chinese affection for the
written word. The Chinese language is monosyllabic and
pictographic. The most primitive characters are conventionalized pictures of objects as a primitive people must
have represented them on stone or wood. The earliest extant
writings that we know of are records scratched upon bone
and tortoiseshell that go back to the Shang Yin dynasty
(1766–1122 B.C.), but writing was already fully developed
by that date. Each ideogram throws upon the mind an
isolated picture: there is no grammar, nothing equivalent
to our parts of speech, and no punctuation. The language

[1] Dukes, E. J. *Everyday Life in China.*

reached maturity at such an early date that it has been simplified to a degree that has made it clumsy in the hands of a European. It can be described as a telegraphic language, for the old "pidgin" English of the Treaty Ports was a literal translation. Instead of saying "There are many ships but few men to man them," the Chinese would say literally "Ships many, men few." Without a practical knowledge of the Chinese mind every sentence presents an indefinite series of meanings, but acquaintance in time breeds familiarity with the turn of the phrase. Because the number of monosyllables are limited the Chinese rely upon "tones"; without the use of these they would be unable to find sufficient breadth of expression. By use of tones one syllable may take on several meanings according to the inflexion of the voice. Pekingese is said to have five tones, but Cantonese is generally supposed to have nine. It is possible to know the meaning of every individual character in a Chinese sentence and yet be quite unable to understand the general trend of thought, for each character has a tremendous width of meaning which varies with its combinations; it is only in this way that one can discover the tone in which it should be pronounced.

There is another factor to be taken into account. The literary and colloquial languages have diverged; and while the literary language has stood still, the colloquial has continuously changed. By the Yüan period the novel and the drama had produced a written colloquial language which was completely ignored by the official world, which up to the rise of the Republic continued to conduct the affairs of State in a language which was so full of literary allusion as to be incomprehensible to any but scholars. To-day all the papers are printed in colloquial and the literary language is falling out of use. "The literary language has been an artificial thing for a thousand years and more, and for all

THE RELATION TO CALLIGRAPHY

its variations it has been essentially the same throughout the ages. Once a Chinese has succeeded in mastering it, it is the same to him, from the point of view of the language whether a poem he is reading was written at the time of Christ, a thousand years later, or yesterday; it is just as comprehensible and enjoyable in either case. In other countries, where the written language follows the execution of the spoken, a practically new literary language has been evolved in the course of a few hundred years. An ordinary Englishman of to-day can hardly go further back than a few centuries in his own literature; the earliest he can only appreciate after special philological study. To the Chinese the literature of millenniums is open; his unrivalled love for and knowledge of the ancient culture of the country is largely due to the peculiar nature of his literary language." [1] There is a tremendous divergence of dialects throughout the country, but the written language has produced a common bond which has held China together as a cultural unit; this is the chief objection to any form of romanization.

To-day the Chinese write with a brush dipped in ink in the same way as their ancestors did during the Han period. There are combinations of pictures that naturally form ideas.

Bright: 明, a combination of sun and moon.

Good: 好, a combination of mother and child (the relationship between mother and child could not be anything else).

Family: 家, a roof with a pig under it (pork is the staple meat of the Chinese).

Peace: 安, a roof with one woman under it (a heartfelt comment on the disadvantages of polygamy).

To the Chinese writing is very much more than a vehicle of expression; it has the pictorial brevity associated with

[1] Karlgren, B. *Sound and Symbol in Chinese,* p. 37.

painting, and the same appeal to the imagination, and so there has come about in China the closest relationship between painting and writing. The same materials, ink (Chinese pictures were almost invariably outlined in ink), paper and silk were used for both. Calligraphy is mounted and exhibited in the same way.

Every Chinese had to learn to write well before he could paint. The linear qualities of Chinese paintings are the direct result of this calligraphic training. With the exception of the Literary school that rebelled against the technique of the brush stroke and the "boneless style" of painting flowers originated by Hsü Ch'ung-Ssü and perpetuated by Yün Nan-T'ien (in which colours are applied direct without an ink outline), the whole of Chinese painting is calligraphic in feeling. In the running hand you can trace the feeling that inspired the pictorial design, and the sense of spatial relationship in painting is directly due to the influence of the written word. Painting and calligraphy are dealt with as one subject in Chinese books. Calligraphy is frequently used as a complement to pictures, for the Chinese are very fond of hanging antithetical phrases on each side of their paintings or inscribing the pictures themselves with quotations and descriptions. A "literary man" has been the Chinese ideal. It was not the military heroes of the period of the Three Kingdoms that the small Chinese boy was brought up to respect, but Chiang Pi who studied his books by moonlight, Chi Yu who gathered fireflies in a sack for the same purpose, and Sun K'ang who read by the reflected light of the snow. In this way a reverence for the written word has arisen that can only be compared to the English respect for the Bible. The San Chieh Ming says that the ancients thought that to save a single character leads to respectability. It became a work of merit to rescue fragments of the written word, to wash, dry and burn them

92

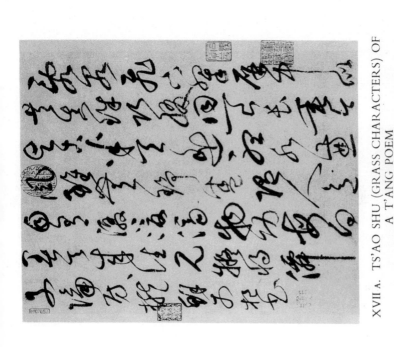

XVII B. STANZA IN A SEVEN
WORD 'STOP SHORT'
By Tung Ch'i-Ch'ang
(b. 1555, d. 1636)
(3' 2" × 1' 4")
The National Collection, Peiping.

XVII A. TS'AO SHU (GRASS CHARACTERS) OF
A T'ANG POEM
By Hsien Yu-Shu, Yüan dynasty (1206–1358).
(5' 3" × 1' 8")
The National Collection, Peiping.

and scatter the ashes. In public places small altar furnaces provided for this purpose by literati can still be seen in provincial towns. In 1875 an official proclamation in Foochow called attention to the prevailing disrespect exhibited towards the written character: "Shopkeepers who, in shameless disregard of propriety and ancient usage, have the audacity to paint words upon the papers and wrappers used in the ordinary course of business, the characters they often tore or soiled with dirt in a way that excites one's strong indignation." [1] Merchants were urged to use trade marks and shop signs of birds, flowers and insects in the interests of public morality.

Calligraphy is the structure on which Chinese painting is built. As Professor Chytel has put it, the Chinese painter "writes his pictures." When a Chinese critic says a picture "has strength" he refers to the calligraphic vigour of the brush stroke. The painters of the North have been more calligraphic than the South as the Literary school was a revolt against this technique. There is little good calligraphy practised in China to-day. The fountain pen is ousting the native brush. It is probable that Chinese painting will become increasingly less and less calligraphic in feeling. It is impossible for us to appreciate the niceties of Chinese calligraphy without many years of study. We can without difficulty distinguish individual handwriting, and perhaps we may be able to recognize style, but there are many factors to be taken into consideration: the disposal of space, the pressure of the brush, the size of the writing, the manner of connection, the speed and direction, the materials and the historical determination of the signature.

Chinese critics of calligraphy are never tired of dwelling on its relation to natural phenomena. To the Chinese calligraphy calls up visions of flying birds, dancing dragons, rising

[1] Dukes, E. J. *Everyday Life in China*, p. 200.

93

clouds and dripping dew. It was said that the secrets of ts'ao shu (the grass style) could only be mastered while listening to the ripple of flowing water or watching snakes in combat. San Kuo-T'iang (a T'ang calligraphist) says, in the Shu P'i, "in writing one sees the hanging needle, the dropping dew, crashing thunder, falling rock, flying bird, startled beast: (it is) heavy as breaking clouds, light as a cicada's wings, graceful as the new moon and dependent stars—it equals the exquisiteness of nature. . . ." [1] Ts'ai Yung (A.D. 133–52) compared good calligraphy "to worms eating leaves, sharp swords and spears, strong bow and hard arrow, water and cloud, sun and moon all freely shown." [2] It was said of Yen Chen-Ch'ing's writing, "his dots are like balls of stone, his strokes like summer cloud, his hooks like bent gold, and his curves like bent bows. The movement of his strokes are instinct with a sense of form and their goings up and comings down have a style of their own." [3] The calligraphy of Wang Hsi-Chih (321–379), who was the most admired of all calligraphists, was "bright as floating clouds but vigorous as a startled dragon."

The picture that the Chinese ideogram raises in the Chinese imagination is beyond us, because the written character does not convey its full meaning. The Chinese say that calligraphy is a portrait of the mind. European opponents of graphology say it depends upon the muscular construction of the hand, the materials, the school teaching, and the mood of the writer rather than his character. [4] Kuo Jo-Hsü wrote: "Speaking of the ink tones of one's autograph, some say that they are Hsin-yin or the 'Seal of the Mind.' In other words, ink tones are but the external

[1] Lucy Driscoll and Kenji Toda. *Chinese Calligraphy*, p. 15.

[2] *Ibid.*, p. 13.

[3] Zen, S. H. C. *Symposium of Chinese Culture*, p. 76: "Painting and Calligraphy," by T'sai Yuan-P'ei.

[4] But see Robert Sandek. *The Psychology of Handwriting*.

94

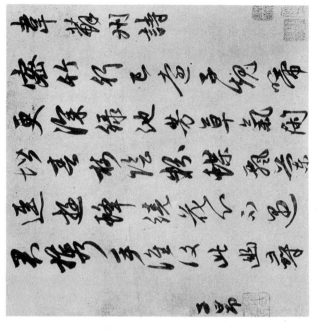

XVIII b. CALLIGRAPHY OF CHAO MÊNG-FU
The National Collection, Peiping.

(4′ 0¾″ × 1′ 9¾″)

XVIII a. HORSES
Attributed to Chao Mêng-Fu (*b.* 1254, *d.* 1322)

(1′ 10½″ × 1′ 6½″)

The British Museum.

manifestations of the mind, and there must be a coinci-
dence between the mind and its external manifestations. This
relation is something like that which exists between the seal
and its impression. . . . Paintings and writings are seals, for
the sentiments and feelings of their authors can be traced in
them. It is nothing surprising that in painting and calligraphy
Ch'i-yün [1] should become high or low according to the
personalities of the authors. Painting is fundamentally the
same as calligraphy. To quote the saying of Yang, 'Language
is the voice of the mind; calligraphy the painting of the mind.
And both speak out unerringly as to whether the speaker
or the painter is a high-minded soul or a man of a low
character.' " [2] Chao Mêng-Fu's (Tzǔ-ang) writing was supposed to have been lacking in nobility but artistic in execution. Chang Ch'ou wrote: "Tzǔ-ang's style of writing was
very gentle, elegant and harmonious. He was a follower of
the real Wang Hsi-Chih school. It was indeed too gentle
and seductive because it lacked the spirit of men who cannot be forced to desert their principles. As for instance
Wen T'ien-Hsiang, whose style was clear, penetrating,
straight and inspiriting." No Chinese ever forgets that
Chao Mêng-Fu accepted service under the Mongols; he was
cabinet minister, confidential adviser to several Yüan
emperors, and his loyalty and efficiency enabled the Mongols
to bridge the gap between the Chinese people and their
barbarian conquerors.

Good writing is often compared to good riding. To
ride a good horse was a metaphor for a good hand. It was
said of Mi Fei that his writing was like a "good horse which
will trot or gallop as the rider chooses." [3] This eccentric

[1] See page 42 for explanation of this term.
[2] *Kokka*, No. 244, p. 69.
[3] Zen, S. H. C. *Symposium on Chinese Culture*, p. 83: "Painting and
Calligraphy," by Tsai Yuan-Pei.

95

figure dressed in the style of the T'ang period (he lived in the Sung), learnt a hundred poems a day, painted beautiful landscapes in ink and was most unscrupulous in his ways of adding to his collections. It is recorded that he borrowed a picture of a cow that he particularly fancied, copied it and returned the copy. On a boating expedition when he was shown the calligraphy of Wang Hsi-Chih he became so excited that he threatened to jump overboard unless it was given him. There is a delightful description of a meeting between him and Su Tung-P'o quoted by Sirén from the *Shih Lu Pi shu lu*: "Once he invited Su Tung-P'o to dinner. Two long tables were placed facing each other and on them were piled fine brushes, exquisite silk and three hundred sheets of paper, with some food and drink at the side. When Tung-P'o saw this arrangement he laughed heartily. Between each drink they would flatten the paper and write. Two page boys were kept busy grinding the ink but they could hardly keep on making enough of it. Towards evening the wine was giving out and so was the paper. Then each of them took the other's papers and said good-bye. Afterwards they found that they had never done better writing." [1] Su Tung-P'o was particularly fond of painting bamboos in ink. Mi Fei said of him, "The strangest things were coiled up in his chest" and speaks of a picture of his containing "an old tree with trunk and branches bent like dragons and masses of sharp and cracked stones." [2] He mentions another picture which Su Tung P'o painted of two bamboos and a dead tree when he was drunk at Hangchow, "but the picture was borrowed by Chieh Chou and never returned."

The history of the Chinese ideogram is one of continual simplification. Tradition ascribes its origin to the mythical

[1] Sirén, O. *History of Early Chinese Painting*, vol. ii, p. 28.
[2] *Ibid.*, p. 36.

七澤山圓碧
水三湘雲重
蒼天何必重
尋姓氏直稱
海岳家傳
乾隆丙子御題

XIX. MOUNTAINS UNDER SNOW
In the style of Mi Fei (*b.* 1051, *d.* 1107), by an anonymous painter of
the Yüan dynasty (1206–1358)
The National Collection, Peiping.   (3′ 6″ × 1′ 2″)

Fu Hsi, who deduced methods of keeping records from the
pa kua (eight trigrams) which were brought to him by the
heavenly horses of the River Lo; and to a system of
knotted cords invented by Shên Nung.[1] Ts'ang Hsieh, a
minister of the Yellow Emperor (another mythical figure),
is credited with the development of the script by observing
the marks on the shell of the tortoise and the footprints of
birds on the sand. In October, 1928, Dr. Li Chi of the
National Research Institution of History and Philology of
the Academica Sinica, excavated at Anyang in Honan
quantities of fragments of bone and tortoiseshell engraved
with characters scratched on them from the Shang Yin
period (1766–1122 B.C.). These are the earliest forms of
Chinese writing at present known to us. At this early period
the script was fully developed, and it must go back to an
even earlier day. Professor Yetts considers the calligraphic
quality of some of the inscriptions on old bronzes may take
the use of the brush back to very much earlier times than
Mêng T'ien (third century B.C.) to whom the invention of
the brush is credited by the Chinese.[2] The earliest writing
in ink with a brush that has survived is probably from the
Han period. By the first century the invention of printing
had placed books in the hands of the masses. The Chinese
characters have become increasingly simplified as they pro-
gressed.[3] There are a large number of archaic styles which
have survived, and although these are not in general use
they are often inscribed on antiquities to endow them with
a hypothetical age. The earliest form of script in use before
the invention of paper and the brush was the *Chuan Shu*.
We find it engraved on early bronzes, stone or bones and
written in lacquer on wood. It was a complicated script;

[1] Yetts, W. P. *Eumorfopoulos Collection*, vol. i.
[2] Yetts, W. P. *Recent Finds Near Anyang*, p. 470.
[3] *Kokka*, No. 197, p. 471: Sei-ichi Taki.

H

and it was never standardized until about 800 B.C., so that
there are endless varieties of characters surviving which
make it difficult to read. Of the 3000-odd characters that
the Anyang finds brought to light only some 600 have
been read. The earliest forms of the Chuan are the "great
seal," in which the famous stone drums of Shensi in the
Confucian Temple in Peking are said to be inscribed. The
"big seal", was laborious to write and it gave way to the
"small seal" invented in 220 B.C. by Li Ssŭ at the command
of the Ch'in Shih Huang Ti, who burnt the books in 213
and built the great wall; but the two forms are still far
from distinguishable. In A.D. 121 the son of a retired official
Hsü Shên, published his father's *Shuo wên chieh tzŭ*, an
"explanation of ancient figures and an analysis of com-
pound characters," in which the history of writing is out-
lined.[1] The *Li shu* that followed the *Chuan Shu* is attributed
to one Ch'eng Miao. The next simplification is the *K'ai
Shu* which is credited to the famous calligrapher Wang Hsi
Chih (A.D. 321–379) who also wrote in the *Ts' ao Shu* or
running style. The *Chuan Shu* is still used for seals and to
invest antiques with a factitious age. The *K'ai Shu* is
still in use for printing, and the *Ts'ao Shu*, and a simplified
form of it, the *H'sing Shu*, are in general use to-day. These
are the four most important forms but there are several
others.[2] There are, so far as I am aware, no collections of
Chinese calligraphy in this country, and as it is not easy
to know where to look for reproductions I submit a list of
calligraphy from various dynasties (for those who care to
pursue the subject) taken from the first thirty odd numbers
of the *Ku Kung Shu Hua Chi*.

[1] See Yetts. *Eumorfopoulos Collection,* vol. i.
[2] *Kokka,* No. 197, p. 471, No. 320, p. 157: "Chinese and Japanese
Calligraphy," by Sei-ichi Taki.

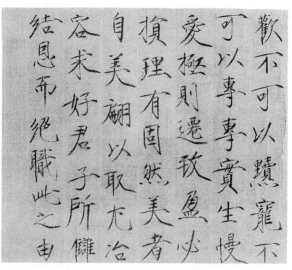

XX A. CALLIGRAPHY ATTRIBUTED TO THE
EMPEROR HUI TSUNG
(b. 1082, d. 1135).
From the Ku K'ai-Chih scroll, the British Museum.

$(10\frac{1}{2}'' \times 9\frac{3}{4}'')$

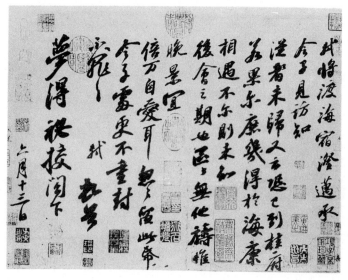

XX B. CALLIGRAPHY OF SU SHIH (SU TUNG-P'O),
(b. 1036, d. 1101).
The National Collection, Peiping.

$(4' 5\frac{1}{4}'' \times 1' 8'')$

APPENDIX

CALLIGRAPHY

Vol. 2, No. 11. Sung K'o. Ming.

Vol. 2, No. 18. "Poem on eating crabs." Ho. Ch'ao. Ch'ing.

Vol. 3, No. 3. Letter from Su Shih. Sung. (Su Tung-P'o.)

Vol. 4, No. 8. Chang Yu. Yüan.

Vol. 4, No. 14. Wang Ch'ung. Ming.

Vol. 5, No. 2. Wu Chu. Sung.

Vol. 5, No. 19. Chang Chao. Ch'ing.

Vol. 6, No. 9. Shên Tu. Ming.

Vol. 6, No. 10. Shên Ts'an. Ming.

Vol. 7, No. 9. Shên Ts'an.

Vol. 8, No. 9. Poem. Ch'en Pï. Ming.

Vol. 10, No. 13. Mei Han-Wên. Ch'ing.

Vol. 12, No. 14. Lou Chien. Ming.

Vol. 14, No. 11. Tung Ch'i-Ch'ang. Ming.

Vol. 15, No. 17. Chang Ying. Ch'ing.

Vol. 16, No. 19. Liu Yung. Ch'ing.

Vol. 17, No. 9. Poem by Hsuan Tsung. Ming.

Vol. 20, No. 13. Tung Ch'i-Ch'ang. Ming.

Vol. 21, No. 16. Couplet. Chang Chao. Ch'ing.

Vol. 22, No. 9. Seven word stanzas. Wang Fêng-Yüan. Ming.

Vol. 23, No. 12. Calligraphy and painting, by Ch'ên Chi-Ju. Ming.

Vol. 24, No. 8. Calligraphy, by Chang Yu. Yüan.

Vol. 24, No. 9. "The story of the drunken old man of the tea house." Wên Chêng Ming. Ming.

Vol. 25. No. 2. Verses by Wan Chu. Sung.

Vol. 25, No. 13. Calligraphy by Yen Chên, Ch'ing, in the style of Tung Ch'i-Chang.

Vol. 26, No. 8. Sung Ts'ao. Ming.

Vol. 29, No. 5. Hsien Yu of the Yüan.

Vol. 29, No. 16. Shên Chuan. Ch'ing.

Vol. 30, No. 2. Su Mai. Sung.

Vol. 30, No. 6. Yang Wei-Chan. Yüan.

Vol. 30, No. 20. Poetry. Ka'i Shu, by Wang Tan-Lin.

Vol. 31, No. 6. Calligraphy of Chao Mêng-Fu. Yüan.

Vol. 31, No. 7. Calligraphy of Yu Chi. Yüan.

Vol. 31, No. 14. Tung Ch'i-Ch'ang. Ming.

Vol. 32, No. 2. Mi Fei. Sung.

Vol. 32, No. 6. Hseh Ming-P'ên. Yüan.

Vol. 32, No. 7. Ni Tsan. Yüan.

4

The Patronage of the Throne

IT is not at all easy to capture the essence of Chinese painting. Time has dealt kindly with the silks and papers upon which the Chinese painted, and the rich golden brown, soft grey backgrounds which supply a charming setting to bright pigments, but there is something above and beyond that indefinable quality which is the work of time; there is a mellowness of spirit. Filial piety has taught the Chinese to pay great respect to old age. China has often been compared to an old man among the nations. As the oldest extant civilization she is too wise to be deceived by the confusing passions and enthusiasms of a young people. A whimsical humour mingled with a mild benevolence colours the sentiments of her artists. A wistful scepticism has crept into her poetry and her painting. It is not of love but of the frailty of human pleasure which her poets sing. It is not the glory of the battle-field but the beauties of friendship and the sadness of farewell that her painters would choose to portray. Dead artists occupy different places in the estimation of each generation according to how they reflected its own aspirations. Each generation reacts against the ideals of its predecessor. The romantic succeeds the classical and in turn gives way to a new tradition. It has been said that an age of scepticism gives way to an age of faith. The ink landscapes of the Sung and Yüan were succeeded by the colour and glitter of the early Ming, which in turn gave way to the severity of the Literary school. The simple joyful world of the T'ang's gave way to the doubts and difficulties of the Sung period; just as the security and confidence of the Victorian world has given way to our own uncertainty. The seventeenth century in Europe saw a collapse of the social fabric, for the Reformation undermined the whole organization of society. That generation saw the passing of the papal domination of the divine right of kings. Both China and Europe are passing through just such an age of transition to-day.

To understand the influences that have led to the formation of a Chinese tradition of painting in the past, a bird's-eye view of Chinese society, as it existed before the impact of Western influences, is necessary; without it the relation of the painter to that society cannot be clearly visualized. China was, and is still, apart from its great coastal cities, an agricultural as opposed to an industrial country. At a very early age she abandoned feudalism for government by village clans under the loose control of monarchy. In the north, Tartar, Mongol and Manchu were granted landed estates, and in the neighbourhood of great cities rich merchants have bought land, but the vast interior of the country is controlled by the semi-isolated and self-supporting clan villages. Communications were so bad that these villages were cut off from their neighbours. They remained self-supporting and self-reliant. Each village had its own militia, and apart from paying certain taxes to the central government was left largely to follow its own devices. The land that belonged to the village was let on behalf of the community by the elders. The revenue was put to the cost of village administration, the repair of the walls and streets, the upkeep of the militia, the decoration of the village temples, and perhaps once a year a public theatrical display. Provincial governors, as represented by the local viceroy, visited the villages at intervals to settle cases which the village elders had been unable to arrange themselves, and to collect taxes. The viceroys from time to time memorialized the throne as to affairs of the province. Chinese society was a perfect example of communism functioning within a hierarchy. Within the village, traditional handicrafts were carried from father to son for generations. There was no competition, no fluctuation of wages. Each trade was governed by its own guild, and the same standard articles in traditional taste were on sale everywhere at a standard price. As there was no competition the shops of each trade were grouped together. It was an ordered and static society such as you find in Europe before the Renaissance. There was a low standard of living for the workmen, long hours, poor food and poor pay, but also no great profits for the employer. There was security of tenure and an easy-going relationship between master and man. Each business was small; there was none of that impersonal relationship and insecurity of employment which the existence of huge combines, vast profits and high standards of efficiency has tended to produce and which has made for all the bitterness and class hatred in the great industries of the modern world. This was the background of Chinese life until the Western individualism and industrialism began to undermine the power of the family and the guild. The process of disintegration and reconstruction still continues. The discoveries, the conquests and the scientific achievements of the white races that began in the fifteenth century came to a climax in the nineteenth. Their impact upon China has shaken the fabric of her culture.[1] The history of China is an almost continuous cycle of the conquest by absorption of foreign dynasties. Invasion after invasion swept over the great wall from the north, was digested, and disappeared. The strength of China lay not in her soldiers but in her culture. She might be conquered by the nomad,

[1] See Lothrop Stoddard. *Clashing Tides of Colour.*

103

but he invariably became her slave. She emasculated him by the luxury of her great courts. She fascinated him with all the wiles of an old and superior civilization. But in the early nineteenth century the Chinese came up against European races. The old civilization failed to absorb the red-haired "foreign devils." It is the old Chinese traditions that have broken down, and the ethics of Confucius and the family have collapsed before the scientifically equipped armies and rapacious American business methods of the West.

Chinese painting particularly reveals all the advantages and disadvantages of a strong national tradition. Tradition classified the styles that would be used, and governed the composition, the brush stroke, and the use of pigments. It is impossible to say that certain pleasant qualities did not accrue to artists working under these rigid conditions. The association of each traditional theme became common property. The fact that previous generations had tried their hand at them did not prevent the living artists from discovering fresh angles of interpretation, and the subject matter of Chinese painting became invested with an imaginative significance and a depth of philosophical and religious meaning from continuous handling. Tradition has kept Chinese painting simple and unambitious in design, and pure in colour. The humblest sketches reflect something of the great designs of the old masters even though copied at tenth hand. The Chinese thought that the art of painting, like the art of living, must conform to certain standards and conventions. To live without a pattern was to live without dignity and style. The elaborate etiquette that Confucius constructed enabled the Chinese to live graciously and harmoniously. China in both life and painting strove for perfection of form within narrow channels. As a result she achieved distinction in certain directions which was entirely beyond the art of the West.

The absolute power of the throne in China provided monarchs with facilities for expressing their fancies. It is difficult for us to imagine the refinement of the Chinese courts of T'ang, Sung, Ming and Ch'ing at the height of their power. As has been said before, every luxury that the mind could devise and the ingenuity of the hand evolve was provided to enable the emperor to pass a life of extravagance and irresponsible leisure. Nor do the Chinese people seem to have given unwillingly to support the whims of the Son of Heaven. Mencius says: "What a sovereign loves, his subjects will love with even greater ardour." But even in those spacious days the life of an emperor was ordered by the most rigid etiquette; shut up in the walls of the Forbidden City, surrounded by hordes of eunuchs and beauties, he must have found the hours hang heavy on his hands. Chinese court painters have left us pictures of past emperors at audience or surrounded by their harems at music or theatricals: we see them in the banquet hall, partaking of the Eight Precious Dishes (bear's paw, deer's tail, lark's tongue, torpedo roe, camel's hump, monkey's lip, carp's tail, and beef marrow). Very often the emperors took a lively interest in painting. We hear of imperial collectors as early as the first century A.D. Ming Ti of the Han, Yüan Ti of the Liang dynasty, Wen Ti and Yang Ti of the Sui dynasty, T'ai Tsung of the T'ang, were all great collectors, but no satisfactory records of their collections remain. A number of both emperors and empresses were talented painters.[1]

But by far the most important imperial painter and connoisseur was the Sung Emperor Hui Tsung who reigned

[1] See *Catalogue of Writings and Paintings by Chinese Emperors, Empresses and Princes, dating from the T'ang Dynasty to the End of the Ch'ing Dynasty* (A.D. 618–1912). Collected and Compiled by Reikichi Kurosawa, pp. 8 *et seq.*

from 1101–1126. The catalogue of his vast collection has survived. His paintings are described in the *Hsüan-ho-hua-chi-pu* (a description of the paintings in the Hsüan-ho Palace). He was not only a great connoisseur but also a painter of some merit. He specialized in fur and feathers. A picture entitled "A She Monkey with her Baby, a Tuft of Dandelion and Two Beetles" is among other paintings in the National Peiping Collections attributed to him. He was especially fond of painting birds and flowers. In the Fine Arts Museum, Boston, is a picture attributed to his brush, entitled "Five-Coloured Parrakeet." On the picture is inscribed a poem supposed to have been composed by the emperor himself.[1]

But he was most famous for his pictures of white eagles, copies of which have been continuously painted since his day. The British Museum possesses several pictures attributed to him in this vein, but the earliest is probably a copy not earlier than the Ming. He painted them sometimes after a banquet in the presence of his guests. The eyes of his birds, we are told, were rendered in exquisite and elaborate detail by repeated coatings of lacquer so that the eyeballs stood out, which was an invention of his own. His long nervous handwriting (or is it that of his great-nephew?) has come down

---

[1] "The five-coloured parrakeet came from Lingpiao. Reared in the imperial enclosure, he has become docile and is lovable. He flits and sings as he pleases, moving to and fro in the garden. Now in mid-spring the apricots are in full bloom and over them he is flying. He is noble and placid, and possesses a dignity peculiarly his own. As I gaze upon him he seems to present a sight superior to a picture. Therefore I compose this verse: Heaven produced the parrakeet, this strange bird. From far away he came to the imperial precinct. His body is complete with five colours and his nature rare. Blessed is he uttering many a speech, its tone most beautiful. When flying high, to be envied is he, his feathers elegant. When walking about, contented is he, fed with choice grain. His yellow breast and purple feet are truly perfect. Thus I compose a new verse and sing as I stroll."

XXI. BIRD ON A BOUGH
Artist unknown. Sung dynasty (960–1279).
The British Museum (Eumorfopoulos Collection). (10″ × 8¾″)

to us on the scroll of the Ku K'ai-Chih.[1] The paintings in his catalogue in twenty volumes numbered 6,396. Two hundred and thirty artists are represented. They include most of the famous names. The country must have been ransacked to produce his treasures, and we are led to conclude that the pictures were requisitioned in a shameful manner and often without his knowledge by the officials, Ts'ai Ching and Chu Mien, who were anxious that he should be so absorbed in sifting, cataloguing and admiring his collection as to have no time for State affairs, which were left entirely in their hands.[2] The introduction to the catalogue is dated 1120; it is arranged according to the ten classifications of subject.[3]

(1) *Tao shih* (Taoist and Buddhist scenes). Vols. 1–5. Religious painting. Forty-nine artists represented; 1,179 paintings.

(2) *Jên wu* (human affairs). Vols. 5–7. Illustrations of manners, morals and legend. Thirty-three artists represented; 505 paintings.

(3) *Kung shih* (palaces and houses). Vol. 8. Architecture (which includes ships and vehicles). Four artists represented; 71 paintings.

(4) *Fan tsu* (foreign tribes). Vol. 8. Five artists represented; 117 paintings.

(5) *Lǎng yü* (dragons and fish). Vol. 9. (This included crabs and shrimps.) Eight artists represented; 117 paintings.

(6) *Shan shui* (mountains and water). Vols. 10–12. Landscape. The oldest landscape painter represented was Li Ssǔ-Hsün (651–716). Forty-one artists represented; 1,108 paintings.

(7) *Ch'u shou* (domestic animals and wild beasts). Vols. 13–14. (Li An-Chih contributed a delightful picture entitled "Drunken cats.") Twenty-seven artists represented; 342 paintings.

(8) *Hua niao* (flowers and birds). Vols. 15–19. This included butterflies and bees. There was no pre-T'ang picture in this group. Forty-six artists represented; 2,786 paintings.

[1] The genuineness of this calligraphy (see plate facing page 26) has been questioned by Prof. Yashiro who believes it may be by the hand of his great-grandson.

[2] Grantham, A. E. *Hills of Blue*, p. 354.

[3] Hirth, F. *Native Sources for the History of Chinese Pictorial Art*, pp. 16–22; and *Kokka*, No. 308, p. 160: "Art Encouragement under the Sung Dynasty."

(9) *Mo chu* (ink bamboos). Vol. 20. Twelve artists represented; 148 paintings.

(10) *Su kuo* (vegetables and fruit). Vol. 20. Six artists represented; 25 paintings.

There were in addition twelve hundred pieces of calligraphy. These categories were further sub-divided. Buildings were divided into *Lou-t'ai* (houses and terraces of several storeys), *Ts'un t'ien* (villages and fields) and *Kung-yüan* (palaces and parks); and landscape and religious paintings were sub-classified in the same manner.

All these pictures were said to have been stamped with the seal "Hsüan Ho," indicating that they belonged to the Imperial Collection and were housed in the Hsüan Ho Palace. At his capital Pien Liang (K'ai-Fêng Fu), Hui Tsung set up the Hua Yüan academy.

The custom of appointing special artists to the imperial household goes back to as early as the Six Dynasties,[1] but little information of the activities of the court academy under the Six Dynasties and the T'ang remains. Early in the Sung period court artists were allowed a scarlet-purple dress, and during the reign of Hui Tsung the academy were permitted to wear the *p'ei-yü* or fish-shaped jewel made of gold or jade over the garment, until then only worn by persons of rank. Members of the Hua-yuan (the Academy) were always in attendance night and day in the imperial departments.[2] The life of a court artist had its cares. Yen Li-Pên [3] when he was sick was commanded to attend the Emperor Kao Tsung to paint a strange bird seen in his garden. On his return he is supposed to have advised his son, "Be either an artist or an official, but not both at the same time." The menageries in the imperial gardens were a constant source of pleasure to the throne and embarrass-

---

[1] See *Kokka,* No. 274: "Origin and Growth of the Academy in China," p. 205.

[2] *Ibid.*

[3] Died 673.

ment to the court painters. Ku K'ai-Chih, Lu T'an-Wei, Ku Ching-Hsiu, were all at different times requested to paint peacock, parrots and waterfowl for the imperial pleasure. It was probably during the T'ang dynasty that the painters began to specialize in national history. The catalogue of Hui Tsung's Collection contained no pre-T'ang examples of the subject. The name of Pien Luan (who excelled in birds and cut flowers) and Tiao Kuan Yin have come down to us. We do not know in what style these men painted but we suspect that they subscribed to the sentiment expressed in the biography of one court painter of the same period, "To study painting one needs no masters. To copy objects from life and to strive to imitate nature is sufficient."[1]

By the Five Dynasties (907-960) bird and flower painting is divided into two different schools; those of Huang Ch'üan and his son Huang Chü-Ts'ai and that of Hsü Hsi, which consisted in painting direct in colour without an ink out-line. The latter was revived by Yun Nan-T'ien, of the Ch'ing dynasty, who was famous for his peonies. It was the style of Huang Ch'üan that established itself at the Sung court. As Hui Tsung was himself so fond of painting birds and flowers from nature, members of the academy painted pictures of those subjects; from this time onwards bird and flower painting is almost entirely associated with the academic style. From the beginning, the academy must have carried with it a flavour of court sycophancy, and under the Ming dynasty the court painters became a byword for flattery and vulgarity. Mi Fei refers to them in disparaging terms as mere brush-holders whose daubs were only fit for the walls of the wine shop.[2] Kuo Jo-Hsü says : "It is popularly believed that Huang was rich and aristocratic and Hsü simple and unaffected. This difference is well revealed

[1] *Kokka,* No. 299, p. 243.
[2] Sirén, O. *A History of Early Chinese Painting,* vol. ii, p. 32.

in their painting. Huang first served under the court of Shu, and when it was overthrown went over with his son to that of Sung and there painted the rare birds, animals and flowers within the precincts of the imperial gardens; hence the style of his painting is rich and gorgeous. Hsü Hsi was a man of good family in the south. He loved to wander through beautiful landscapes and to paint from life the animals and plants he came across. His colouring is light but striking. Each of these two schools had its merits, so that we hesitate to assign the superiority to either." [1] Hsia Wên-Yen of the Yüan dynasty says that most of the Sung painters were interested in colour, but Hsü Hsi alone attached more importance to the life and spirit of the brush stroke. There seems to be a rough approximation to the Northern and Southern schools of landscape painting.

The *Hua Yuan* of Hui Tsung had many famous members and provided a great impetus to the art of the day. The emperor himself presided at the competitions. He was anxious that artists should combine ancient models with original sentiments. One of the subjects he set was a line from a poem, " the hoof of his steed comes back heavily charged with the scent of the trampled flowers,"[2] was won by the candidate who depicted butterflies fluttering at a horse's hoof. Artists had to submit rough sketches for imperial approval. "Once a plant in front of the palace bore some fruit. As the emperor was admiring it, a peacock came along and jumping upon a mound, began to peck at the fruit. The emperor immediately summoned a number of his Hua Yuan painters and ordered them to paint the scene. They all vied with one another in producing elaborate paintings. But the emperor was not pleased with any of them and they all wondered why. He then assembled them

[1] *Kokka*, No. 299, p. 241.
[2] Giles. *Chinese Pictorial Art*, p. 137.

XXII. PEONIES
Attributed to Yün Shou-P'ing (*b.* 1633, *d.* 1690).
(4′ 3″ × 1′ 7¾″)

together and said that the peacock, when he jumps upon an elevation, always puts his left foot forward, but that in all their peacocks the right foot was leading. From this incident it is clear to what minute details his observation extended and how much he interfered with their work." [1] From this and other references one can only infer that he did not approve of paintings, however novel, which were not faithful representations of nature.

A picture by Chang Tse-Tuan painted of Pien Ling at the orders of Hui Tsung, 1126, the year before the sack by the Tartars, and entitled "Going up the River for the Spring Festival," has brought down to us an idea of the wealth, beauty and the happy jostling crowds of his capital. "As we look" (writes a Ming critic) "at the crowded hamlets and houses, at the magnificence of the courtiers and boats, at the abundance of merchandise, surfeiting desire and exceeding superfluity, we cannot refrain from regretting that we did not ourselves live in those times, and see these things with our own eyes. But the thought that no state can reach its zenith without subsequent decline is one that chills a wise man's heart." [2] Hui Tsung's reign was a glorious failure. His academy did not shield him from the raids of the Nuchens. At first they were bought off with gold, silver and silk, but so pressing did the danger become that in 1126 Hui Tsung abdicated in favour of his son; in 1127 Pien Liang was besieged for forty days, was captured, and then pillaged. Hui Tsung and his son were taken prisoners and in 1135 he died a captive on the banks of the Sungari.

The Ming emperors were no such patrons of art as Hui Tsung. Hsüan Tsung (1426–35) and Hsiao Tsung

---

[1] *Kokka,* No. 308, p. 167. "Art Encouragement under the Sung dynasty."

[2] Waley, A. *Burlington Magazine,* vol. xxx, No. clxvi, Jan. 1917, p. 4 : "A Chinese Picture."

(1486–1505) were amateur painters but of indifferent merit. The academy suffered a corresponding decline. Academic painters of the Ming, such as Tai Chin, Pien Wien, Lu Chih, Lü Chi, Ch'iu Ying, still maintained a certain standard. The Emperors Shun Chih and K'ang Hsi of the Ch'ing dynasty were supporters of the academy. Ch'ien Lung (1736–95) was both a painter and a poet of indifferent quality, but he was genuinely interested in the arts. He was very fond of superscribing porcelain and paintings that met with his approval with the lofty sentiments of his own poems in the imperial hand-writing. The Ku K'ai-Chih carries a sketch of an epidendrum by his hand and an inscription dated 1746, part of which runs: "At an odd moment in the summer I came across a Ku Kai-Chih picture, 'The Admonitions of the Instructress,' and under its influence I sketched an ink spray of epidendrum as an expression of sympathy with its profound and mysterious import. . . . It has not lost its freshness, an achievement not to be compared to the after born. Of the painter's four works it is the best. It has always been preserved in the quiet retirement of the palace." [1] In 1743 he began a revision of the paintings and calligraphy in the imperial palace in Peking. In 1744 a catalogue of his Buddhist and Taoist paintings in four volumes was completed under the title of the *Pi-tien-chu-lin*. In 1745 the rest of the paintings were catalogued in the *Shi-ch'u-pao-chi*. There seems to have been a revision in 1791—93 and another in the reign of Chia Ch'ing in 1815–17.[2] In the reign of Ch'ien Lung and his son, Tao Kuang, collecting became very fashionable in court circles. Ch'ien Lung's minister, Ho Shen,[3] amassed an

---

[1] Waley's translation.

[2] Mr. Tanaka (*Kokka*, No. 351) gives a full account of these catalogues and their contents in Japanese.

[3] Who was impeached and allowed to commit suicide.

XXIII. PAIR OF GEESE ON A SNOWY SHORE
By Lü Chi (*c.* 1500).

The National Collection, Peiping. (6' 6" × 3' 6")

enormous pile of treasures. We hear of his hundred and forty gold and enamel watches, his nine thousand sceptres of old gold, his four hundred and forty-four couches of lacquer inlaid with gems, his two thousand three hundred and ninety snuff-bottles of topaz, carnelian, amber and jade.[1]

The collection that Ch'ien Lung brought together is not intact to-day. In October 1860 the Yüan Ming Yüan, which he had built with the aid of his Jesuits, was looted and burnt by the forces of France and Britain. During the Boxer trouble of 1900 Peking was occupied by the combined forces of Britain, France, Japan, America, Russia and Germany. On both these occasions parts of the collection must have been looted or burnt; and on the fall of the dynasty in 1912 other pieces made their way out of the palace. The old-fashioned Chinese official who was so often a collector of jade, porcelain and paintings, has given way to young men educated in the West, who are rarely interested in such things. To many of the young, old China is anathema. Its customs, folklore, art, architecture must be swept away. It stands for a period of degradation and humiliation; a period of unequal treaties and decay. Nathaniel Pfeffer, in a passage from "The Death of Chinese Civilization," [2] reproduces a conversation with a Chinese student on the shores of a lake which I take to be Hangchow. "Here emperors came to take their ease in pavilions of red beams and green and golden tiled roofs built for their pleasure. On the hills which gently rise above, the monasteries lie in cool, serene retreat half hidden in groves of bamboo. About us lay the deposits of the greatness and glory of China's ancient days. He was telling us of his plans for the 'development' of the lake shore—he used just that

[1] Grantham. *A Manchu Monarch,* p. 56.
[2] Published in *Harper's Magazine,* 1930, and quoted by Lothrop Stoddard, " Clashing Tides of Colour."

word. There would be a public library with classes for the illiterate; there would be a building for commercial exhibits and so forth. 'What kind of buildings would they be,' I asked. ' Would they follow the architectural lines of those around us, with dipping roofs and broad courtyards, and winding shaded paths of old gardens? 'They would not,' he answered; 'decidedly not.' 'Would they be adaptations from the Western style to make them more comfortable and economical of space?' ' No, that was cheap, serving neither one thing or the other.' They would be Western, pure Western—as complete a break with the past as possible. Yes, those that were here now were beautiful. They would never be surpassed. And they embodied the traditions of the race. That was just it—they tied the race to her past. Above all else those ties had to be broken. Then he spoke with a passionate intensity. 'If I thought it were necessary in order to make that break sure,' he said, 'I would tear all these down and put up new factory buildings in their place.' "
It is only to be expected that in a period of transition, civil warfare and foreign agression there is little time to devote to the arts. Young China is too busy in her struggle to discover national ideals and Western standards of living to establish a new tradition of painting. Since the Republic economic conditions have thrown the collections of old Manchu houses on the market. China has been forced to sell her treasures abroad, but she has of recent years quite rightly increased the control over the flow of objects of national importance.

There is a strange parallel in all this to the opening of Japan in 1868. For some thirty years afterwards the indigenous culture was out of fashion. Japan set herself to assimilate Western methods. During this period her art was sold extensively abroad. The West for the most part failed to take advantage of the opportunities. The bright and over-decorated wares of Satsuma and Kioto were bought instead of tea ceremony pottery, and colour prints instead of ink paintings, because the finer periods of Japanese art were not appreciated. Since the turn of the century, all that was good has gone, or is going, back to Japan because the Japanese are prepared to offer higher prices than Europeans in the European markets. Is the same story likely to be repeated all over again? There are magnificent collections of Chinese porcelain in this country, but we have few paintings. The opportunity of buying them in such a favourable market is not likely to last. It is perfectly understandable that as the flow of treasures grows less, China should prevent important pieces from leaving the country. China is afraid lest the foreign explorers take anything of scientific or æsthetic interest out of the country. In the field of archæology she has not the capital to finance expeditions on an extensive scale, but she is not always prepared to avail herself of the opportunities that foreign capital offers, because she is determined that her material shall not be exploited by foreigners. She would naturally prefer to await conditions under which she could carry out her work on her own, but unfortunately, while the world waits much valuable material is passing away. The deserted cities of the Gobi desert are perishing before our eyes, and as Sowerby has said, while *bona fide* travellers are hampered and hindered or kept waiting on the doorstep, native antique dealers dig up, mutilate and steal or destroy material in a most haphazard manner without tabulating scientific data, material which the foreign archæologist would hand over after a careful excavation to some Chinese cultural institution. Never before has there been such a lively interest in the culture of China or so many European students backed by wealthy institutions eager to work there. It will reflect sadly on both sides if it is not possible to come to some amicable arrangement.

The painting of China has been concerned with expression of ideas that were representative of fact; that is why it has been misunderstood by us in the past. "To our eyes they (Chinese paintings) appear either hideous or ludicrous. Even the most sedate specimens of Chinese art seem to have been intended as high burlesque. By some oriental process which the European is unable to follow the Chinaman sees what it is intended to be taught by the picture which offends most outrageously against all laws of proportion, perspective, and correctness of colour. . . . They are really very curious specimens of ingenuity." [1] Chinese academic painting was at its best during the Five Dynasties and the Sung, when it possessed a spiritual quality which raised it above mere representation, but from the Ming onwards its highest aim was copies of nature true to life. Sketches of birds and flowers, chariots, headdresses and implements, scenes from the life of foreign races, beautiful women and architecture were all patronized in turn. Even the most academic paintings are arranged to suggest symbolic meanings and literary allusions, which we do not understand. Yet it is a mistake to say that there were not Chinese painters at any period whose real aim was to reproduce faithful representations from life, although in practice they seldom sank to the photographic levels of European art of the nineteenth century. An imaginative significance, an impish humour, and a delicious sense of the fantastic, interfere to prevent it. But when all is said, the vast majority of Chinese paintings which find their way to our shores belongs to the poorer productions of the academic school; they are usually decorative and they often possess delightful designs in charming colours, but they are not great art.

[1] Dukes, E. J. *Everyday Life in China*, p. 29, written towards the end of the last century.

5

The Choice of Materials and Technique

ALL painting must be conditioned by the choice of materials which are employed. The interest in Chinese painting lies in the wealth of suggestion supplied by slender means. It is no use to ask of it qualities that it cannot possess; it would be as foolish as to complain that the volume of a flute is unequal to that of an organ; but the pitch and tone may be as or more true; moreover, the flute possesses a lyrical charm which is entirely its own. The Chinese paint in water colours on silk or paper. Chinese paintings are seldom framed or hung, but are kept rolled up and only exhibited on special occasions; sometimes they are bound up in albums. The scrolls, which are unrolled vertically and suspended, from a piece of twine attached to the top, are called *chou* (Japanese, Kakemono); they are weighted at the bottom by a wooden roller. Another variety which unwinds horizontally off a roller from right to left, cannot be suspended, but must be unrolled on a table a few feet at a time; this is called *chüan* (Japanese, Makimono). Both are mounted with borders of paper or silk. Whereas the Chinese generally use paper, the Japanese prefer heavy brocades.[1] Each painting carries its title and origin on a label stuck to the mount of the roll so that it can be consulted before it is unrolled. Chinese paintings

---

[1] Two narrow strips of brocade hang down from the top of some kakemono, but this feature is peculiar to those mounted in Japan. It is difficult to discover their purpose, but it has been seriously suggested that their duty is to frighten small birds who might perch on top.

may be either single or in pairs; sets of four with subjects of the four seasons of the year are not uncommon. A series of scenes with progressive actions or one long rambling landscape is typical of the *chüan*. The rolls upon which they are wound are often finished with knobs of jade, ivory or lacquer or other expensive materials. Some of them possess rich brocade covers. According to Mi Fei, the scrolls of the Emperor T'ang Ti of the Sui dynasty were finished with "covers of brocade, embroidered labels, gold fasteners, scroll-ends of precious stones." Hirth tells us the rolls belonging to the collection of the Emperor Hüan-Tsung were made of white sandal wood with end-pieces of red.[1] The strips of brocade with which the outside of the rolled scroll was mounted were chosen with great care by the connoisseurs of the Sung period. Too much attention to these details called forth delightful ironies from Mi Fei, who wrote that "Amateurs and students form two different classes of people. To the latter may be counted those who are earnest in their love of painting, who have studied extensively and recorded their observations. They have taken it unto their hearts and they have learned how to paint themselves. What they collect is consequently of a high order. But these present-day people who possess wealth without a great love of painting and whose ambition is to pose as connoisseurs in the eyes or ears of other people may be called amateurs. They place their pictures in silk bags and provide them with jade rollers, as if they were most wonderful treasures, but when they open them, one may break down with laughter." [2]

The earliest paintings were in body colour on bricks, plaster walls and wooden panels, but few of them have survived. The Chinese do not seem to have experimented with

[1] Hirth, F. *Native Sources for the Study of Chinese Pictorial Art*, p. 5.
[2] Sirén, O. *A History of Early Chinese Painting*, vol. ii, p. 31.

oils until a comparatively late date. Professor Liu Hai-Su tells me that the earliest oil he knows of is a Buddhist painting on a wooden panel that dates from the Sung, in the possession of Dr. Hu Shih. Mr. Sei-ichi Taki does not think oils were unknown in China before the arrival of the Jesuits in the latter half of the sixteenth century.[1] But they were a medium of expression in Japan as early as the eighth century;[2] the crusade against Western influences caused it to fall into disuse and it must have been reintroduced later by the Dutch traders at Nagasaki.[3] In China oil paintings from the seventeenth century onwards by the hands of the Jesuits and their Chinese followers are by no means uncommon.[4] The use of coloured frescoes, which are the descendants of the original wall-paintings, has never died out. Colour washes made of water and powder, mixed after the manner of gouache, are applied thick with a large brush either on a wet or a dry plaster surface, and sometimes covered with a varnish. Frescoes of this kind in red and green in a style attributed to the fourteenth century were presented to the British Museum by Mr. Eumorfopoulos and can be seen hanging on the staircase below the Print Room. The use of tempera has also not been neglected. Most of these fresco paintings, even when they are as late as the Ming, are done in T'ang style; this period must have been the heyday of that particular medium.

[1] *Kokka*, No. 265.

[2] Binyon. *Flight of the Dragon*, p. 58.

[3] Petrucci, R. *Les caractéristiques de la peinture Japonaise* (Extrait de la *Revue de l'Université de Bruxelles*, Jan.–Feb. 1917).

[4] The Irish painter Chinnery, who died in Macao in 1852 (1847?), had a number of followers in Canton. There is an anonymous three-quarter length portrait of a Chinese gentleman in oils reproduced on p. 15 in the June number of the *China Journal*, 1934, which might well be by the hand of a painter of this school. There is a portrait of a Cantonese merchant, How Kua, by Chinnery, in the National Gallery of Ireland.

Sirén states that there is no mention of paintings on silk until the reign of Ming Ti (A.D. 59–75) or on paper until the reign of Ho Ti (A.D. 89–106). There is a popular idea in the West that Chinese paintings on silk are better than those on paper. But the Chinese themselves prefer paper as it is less likely to crack and flake. The invention of paper is accredited to Ts'ai Lun (or Lin), an officer of the Imperial Guard, who, according to the records of the Han dynasty, made it from tree bark, hemp rags and fish nets in A.D. 105. He was deified as the God of the Paper Makers.[1] Sung paintings on paper are rare, for paper was never in general use before the Yüan. Paper is more sympathetic than canvas and the Chinese are particularly fortunate in their dirty grey and yellow papers which are not artificially tinted. The blotchy outline of the ink strokes derives a delightful quality from the blotting-paper-like texture of the grain. On the other hand, silk treated with glue and rubbed with chalk or mica produced a beautifully smooth surface. Some names of famous papers and silks have come down to us, but we cannot identify them to-day. There were the "mind clarifying paper" of the Southern T'ang, the Shê paper, "smooth glossy white and very lovable," and the "wild goose white" and "Kuanyin (Goddess of Mercy) watermark paper" of the Sung.[2] The older Chinese papers were made from the paper mulberry and fir bamboo, but some of the Ch'ing papers from cotton and flax plants. "In the province of

[1] Clapperton quotes from a Chinese source. "During the 5th year of the reign of Yong Yuan, Ts'ai Lun was minister of public works; . . . In ancient times writing was generally done on a piece of bamboo, or on a piece of silk. . . . But silk being costly and the bamboo heavy, the two materials were not convenient. T'sai-Lun thought of making paper from the bark of trees, waste linen, old rags and fishing nets."— *Paper-Making by Hand: an Historical Account*, p. 1. See also Florence Ayscough. *A Chinese Calligraphy and Painting*, p. 44.

[2] Mayer. *Chinese Painting as reflected in the Art and Life of Li Lung Mien*, p. 237.

Szechuan they made paper from hemp, in Fou Kien from young shoots of bamboo, in the north of China from bark of the mulberry tree and from osiers. Dwellers near the sea made papers from moss, and in other provinces corn stalks and rice stalks were used, also cocoons." [1] There are Chinese who profess to be able to deduce the date and authenticity of a painting from the fibre of the paper or web of the silk; but, as Waley points out, even if it were possible to say that a particular type of silk or paper was manufactured at a certain period it would not mean that the painter could not have painted at a much later date. In a spur of the Great Wall Sir Aurel Stein discovered in 1911 the earliest written Chinese paper document known. It has been dated c. A.D. 151. The earliest dated papers at present known were discovered at Lou Lan by Sven Hedin, and the three earliest dated MSS. are of A.D. 252, 266 and 310. Mr. Clapperton believes that the evidence goes to support the attribution of the invention of paper to the time of T'sai Lun as a very reasonable one. It would appear from his book that paper was in use in China some six centuries before it was anywhere else. Mr. Clapperton has made a very interesting analysis supported by microphotographs of the paper brought back from Tun Huang by Stein. He says the earliest papers were white, thin, transparent and exceptionally well made. Some papers in the fifth century were a dull buff and in the sixth a golden yellow. In the seventh the papers were brittle, and in the eighth a rapid deterioration set in, probably due to the rebellion of An Lu-Shan. He gives a detailed account of some sixty pieces, taken from the Stein Collection. The papers examined dated from the fourth century A.D. varying greatly in texture and quality. "The most striking feature about them is that from the fifth century to the tenth they deteriorate in quality and texture, and from beautiful

[1] Clapperton, R. H. *Paper-Making by Hand: an Historical Account*, p. 4.

thin, well-made papers taking ink well and showing excellent resistance to hard wear, they become thick, flaky and soft like blotting-paper or coarse wrapping-paper.[1]

All Chinese painters have preferred to use the old materials when they could get them. It is the same with pigments and with inks; Chinese connoisseurs have hoarded them and passed them from hand to hand. Our dating of these materials is likely to be very untrustworthy for some time to come. We know that, generally speaking, the T'ang silks are thick and coarse, and that the woof of the Sung silks is uneven, and in many the surface was sprinkled with chalk or mica after it had been sized with glue. The Yüan silks were coarser than the Sung, and the Ming have often a cross woof that can be distinguished; this period had a predilection for painting on gilt paper for fans while the Ch'ing preferred yellow. But there must have been a very extensive and varied output of silks and papers, and it is impossible to be definite without a much more exact knowledge than we possess. If generalizations could be substantiated and coordinated on some scientific principle it might one day be possible to date pictures along these lines.[2]

The Chinese have discovered that the use of ink outline gives full play to the rhythm of line. The ink stroke provides "the bones" of the Chinese painting to which the colour is added afterwards. Nearly all Chinese paintings are sketched in this ink, but there are also other schools of painting (such as flower painting by Yün Shou-P'ing) in which the colour was applied direct. Many Chinese artists

[1] He shows microphotographs of some of the papers in Plates xiv and xv: Clapperton, R. H. *Paper-Making by Hand: an Historical Account*, p. 22.

[2] For a Chinese description of silk and paper, see Petrucci, R. *Encyclopédie de la peinture Chinoise*, p. 88. A translation of the *Chieh tzu yuan shu chuan*.

have confined themselves to the use of ink alone. The ink of China, miscalled in England "Indian ink," is made from fine wood charcoal, lamp-black combined with a little sesamum oil, and the glue from ox or donkey hides, to which camphor and various perfumes are added. Ink-cakes and ink-sticks are made from wooden moulds in many fantastic shapes, tastefully gilded with landscape designs and calligraphy. They are sought after for themselves by the Chinese. Every Chinese writing-table boasts of one ink-slab on which the cake or sticks are ground before water is added for use. A great variety of inks has been made, and famous names, as in the case of silks and papers, have been preserved. The invention of ink has been attributed among others to Tien Chên of the time of the Yellow Emperor, and to Hsing I the originator of the seal characters. The Chinese are never at a loss for an origin. The first ink-cakes are reputed to have been manufactured by Li Ch'ao, a native of Chihli, in T'ang times. One Chang Yu of the Sung made a famous ink from a mixture of oil and soot which he stamped with a goldfish and christened "Combination of dragon's essence." [1] Ink painting is favoured by Japanese and Chinese connoisseurs who prefer a strong command of the brush to a highly elegant finish in colours. Part of the fascination of the ink sketch is that it permits no correction. It provides a perfect medium for the inspiration dashed off in the heat of the moment. The pen and wash drawings of Rembrandt and Dürer are the European equivalent. Perhaps J. R. Cozens, who reinforced his outline with washes of India ink and pale colours, comes nearer than any other English artist to the feeling of Chinese landscape. In China the power of the brush and the quality of the ink-tone are the two factors that command attention. One of the

---

[1] For Chinese inks see Petrucci, R. *Encyclopédie de la peinture Chinoise*, pp. 39-42.

commonest remarks of a Chinese critic before a good painting is that "it has strength." He refers to the strength of the brush strokes. Ch'ên Chieh-Chou of the Ch'ing dynasty wrote: "Ink applied meaninglessly to silk in a monotonous manner is called dead ink, that appearing distinctly in proper chiaroscuro is called living ink. The former has nothing of the attractive lustre of the latter. This is the first point to be laid to heart by painters. . . . Colouring in a true pictorial sense does not mean a mere application of variegated pigments. The natural aspect of an object can be beautifully conveyed in ink colours only, if one knows how to produce the required shades. . . . In ink sketches the brush and the ink stand in relation of a general and a lieutenant, but in coloured paintings colours and the brush are like master and servant; in other words, ink complements but colours supplement the work of the brush." [1] The greatest painters use this medium more powerfully than any range of colours. They modulate the tones of their sketches by the addition of more or less water as they work, so that their brush strokes range from the deepest black to the palest shades of grey. The first ink paintings are ascribed to the fourth century A.D. Before the downfall of the T'ang ink paintings were popular. In the Sung period romantic ink paintings came to dominate the popular taste in the hands of the Ma family and Hsia Kuei. During the Yüan dynasty Huang Kung-Wang, Kao K'o-Kung and Fang Fang-Hu continued the tradition which was upheld in the Ming dynasty by Tung Ch'i-Ch'ang; whereas the Sung and Yüan painters concentrated on the calligraphic qualities of line, the Ming and Ch'ing ink painters (the so-called "Literary school") concentrated on ink-tones. The ink-tone which was so assiduously studied by the "literary painters"

[1] *Kokka,* No. 203, p. 647: "On Oriental Ink Painting," by Sei-ichi Taki.

corresponds to our chiaroscuro (light-dark). In the Chinese painting the study of half-revealed tone takes the place of light and shade. Suggestion has particularly appealed to the Literary school. A list of Chinese painters in ink would be an extensive one. Besides the Sung and Yüan painters of the Calligraphic school and the ink-tone painters of the Literary school there were others like Mu Ch'i who fall into no category. He was not appreciated in China, but his works have found great favour in Japan. The *Hua shih hui yao* remarks, "he painted in a coarse and repellent fashion, not in accordance with ancient rules and really not for refined enjoyment." [1]

The earliest conceptions of colour were based upon symbolic use.[2] This influence still lingers in the colours of the masks in the Chinese theatre which denote the character of the wearer. In the days of the Chou Li blue or green (for the character used does not distinguish between the two) was associated with spring, the genesis of things, and the eastern hemisphere, red with the south, and summer and the influence of yang (the male element in nature). Red is the colour of rejoicing and good fortune.[3] White is the colour of Chinese mourning, for it typifies autumn, death and the western hemisphere. Black is the symbol of the north, symbolical of wickedness and winter [4]; Buddhism favours black as the colour of oblivion and blue as the colour of the gods. The curls of Buddha are represented as blue. But the favourite colour of the Chinese is yellow,

[1] Sirén, O. *A History of Early Chinese Painting*, vol. ii, p. 93.

[2] *Kokka*, No. 214, p. 253.

[3] On festive occasions the small children are dressed in red silk. Eggs dyed in red pigment are eaten at the Spring Festival or at the celebration of the birth of a son. Felicitous inscriptions on red paper are painted over the lintels of the door in the Chinese New Year.

[4] Black masks are worn by characters to denote treachery and cruelty in the Chinese theatre.

symbolical of the earth and life.¹ The power of colour to influence emotion is recognized by modern psychology. The juxtaposition of colours absorbed the Chinese; they were not interested in the play of light and shadow. Unfortunately Chinese pigments are impure and many of them have not lasted. The fugitive qualities of some pigments must be attributed to the fact that they were selected from unsuitable materials and ground and prepared by the hands of the artist themselves.² The Chinese never fail to apply them fresh and direct; all muddy colours are particularly disliked. The stippling and sponging and rubbings which were the secrets of Turner's effects could not be permitted by Chinese materials.

Popular tradition attributes the origin of the brush to Mêng T'ien, a general of Shih Huang Ti (246–210 B.C.), but this cannot be taken too literally. The earliest writings were scratched on bone or tortoiseshell; later characters and rough drawings were inscribed with a stylus in lacquer on wooden tablets. Sirén believes that the earliest existing specimens of writing with a brush are not earlier than the Western Han.³ Yetts believes that the originals go back to a very early date.⁴ Sei-ichi Taki says that writing on paper with a brush did not set in till after the Han.⁵ The state of our knowledge does not at present permit an accurate estimate.

One account tells us that Mêng T'ien used hairs from the back of a deer and another account from hare's

¹ Yellow sand was scattered in the streets of Peking when the emperor went abroad to worship at the Temple of Heaven, and yellow played a greater part than any other colour in the robes that he wore and the porcelain dishes from which he ate. It has been used to glaze the tiles of the great yellow roofs of the Forbidden City.

² See Petrucci for a description of Chinese pigments from a Chinese source: *Encyclopédie de la peinture Chinoise*, pp. 48–62, 411–424.

³ Sirén, O. *A History of Early Chinese Painting*, vol. i, p. 2.

⁴ Yetts. *Eumorfopoulos Catalogue*, vol. i, p. 30.

⁵ *Kokka*, No. 203, p. 645.

fur; [1] yet another account speaks of camel hair. The calligraphist Wang Hsi-Chih is reputed to have used rats' whiskers for softness. Most of the brushes in use to-day are made from goat or sheep's hair. The size of the brush varies. Wu Tao-Tzŭ is said in late life to have painted with one the size of a cabbage. But the Chinese artists did not limit themselves to brushwork. Tradition tells us that Chang Hen-Han specialized in water-demons sketched with his toe. Lu I (who is reputed to have lived about 200 B.C.) is said to have been able to fill his mouth with coloured water and spit out demons.[2] Kao Feng-Han of the Ch'ing,[3] whose right hand was paralysed, painted with his finger-tips. Another finger painter was Kao Ch'i-P'ei. Mi Fei sketched with anything that came to hand. Paper and silks, sugar canes, calices of lotus were all tried in turn. It is to the brush, however, that we owe the calligraphic qualities which make Chinese painting unique. That the Chinese are first of all calligraphists cannot be too often emphasized. They teach drawing by the same methods that we teach writing. All written characters can be divided up into their component parts. The various strokes that go to make up the complete character have been carefully arranged by tradition. Each character has been assembled from a number of strokes brought together in a pre-arranged order, and it can be reconstructed stroke by stroke. The grouping of elements in painting has been

[1] Petrucci, p. 36, *Encyclopedie de la peinture Chinoise,* speaks of several brushes with strange names including the "hsiao tchao" (crab claw brush) made out of weasels' fur combined with goats' hair or sheep's wool.

[2] How sad, as Mr. Lee remarks, that our gum and tobacco chewers have not adopted this technique. "How many a small saloon in Texas or Tennessee might have become a place of artistic pilgrimage."—*China Journal,* vol. iii, 1925, p. 59.

[3] He retired from Government service in 1727.

arranged in exactly the same way. Figures, trees, birds, animals and houses are each classified under certain styles, and analysed and explained in the more elementary manuals. Nothing is left to the individual initiative. There is a wrong and a right way of making each stroke, and tradition has classified the various styles which may be used. You may paint, so to speak, an ash tree in the style of Gainsborough, or Constable, or Morland, but you must confine yourself to the choice of one style and not a mixture of any two. Only the greatest painters were strong enough to break away and originate a style of their own. They were severely frowned upon during their lifetime. From this tradition has sprung the Chinese command of the brush. "The hand rushes over the paper rapidly like a storm and the effect reaches out where the brush has not touched." [1] Chang Ts'ao of the T'ang "would grasp two brushes and bring them down simultaneously, with one painting a live and the other a dead bough. Then from his brushes vertically and horizontally with jagged edges or in scaly masses as the fancy smote him would burst forth mist, vapour and glowing skies and the terrors of frosts, wind and rain. The living branch would be fresh with the sap of spring and the dead branch withered under autumn blight." Chinese calligraphers often use wrist-rests when writing; and the old-fashioned Mandarin used to toy with two walnuts in his spare time in order to encourage the play of muscles of the hand and forearm, and in order to keep his fingers subtle; when he wrote he kept the forearm stiff and held the brush perpendicular to the paper; as a result he was able to draw lines of great delicacy or coarseness. This calligraphic quality (by which I mean linear rhythm) is natural to all Chinese painting except the Literary school of the Ming and Ch'ing.

[1] Liu Hai-Su. *China Review*, April–June, 1935, p. 31: "The Spirit of Chinese Painting."

This technique lends itself to suggestive drawing in a few strokes. Chinese painting is remarkable for the intervals of spacing and the balance of masses. The training in calligraphy must have developed this ability; in writing, each character, whatever the number of its strokes, must take up the same space as its neighbour on the written page.

The Chinese have never wished to represent solid form. They did not attempt to model in relief. Rhythm of line is the foundation of nearly all Chinese painting. During the Sung and Yüan dynasties, when the landscape painting of China was at its height, artists worked entirely in ink monochrome and relied upon line to obtain their effects. Fry speaks of it as the "graph of a dance executed by hand." "Botticelli," he remarks, "is one of the few European artists who possesses the same melodious ease." We do not in the West associate calligraphic qualities with great painting. Chinese painting should appeal particularly to the English, because both nations have found in the water-colour the proper expression of the national genius, and because the whole tradition of English painting is linear and not plastic. The English love of line has continually asserted itself, despite the imposition of plastic standards from the Continent. If we go far enough back in the history of English painting we come to the Landisfarne Gospels which were an entirely national expression of Celtic England. The linear quality of their entwining ornament and the soft pastel colours are entirely oriental in sympathy. The book might have well been painted in Persia. In the cultivation of what Cotman called the "Art of leaving out" the Chinese are unsurpassed. The Chinese use it as effectively in their paintings as in the lay-out of their architecture. The great intervals of empty space between high walls of the Temple of Heaven are more effective than anything the most elaborate architecture could supply. They carry a sense of the vast space and the silences of the plains in which they were conceived. This suggestive quality is always present in Chinese painting. Binyon describes it as "an invitation to the imagination to leap in and supply the unexpressed." Understatement as the Chinese use it, is more effective than any *tour de force*. The very economy of means may suggest force which the finished drawing is at a loss to represent.

It is a commonplace to remark that the Chinese have no knowledge either of tone or perspective. It is true that their drawings are without a correct vanishing point, and they possess no exact laws of foreshortening figures. But perspective is nothing more than a convention by which artists endeavour to represent three-dimensional objects.[1] The Chinese are content to work in two dimensions. Distance is represented by height. The more distant the figure the higher it is placed on the paper. The Chinese also allow for displacement of the view-point. Nearly all Chinese landscapes are seen as from a height. Again there is no projection or recession of masses by the use of high lights or shadow. But the Chinese have studied the relation of light and dark just as carefully in chiaroscuro instead. It cannot be argued that their painting lacks both tone and perspective; rather that they achieve the convention in a different way. As M. Vignier once expressed it "similarly, we would say of a man wearing a turban that either he does not possess a hat or that he is wrong to be thus attired." The Chinese artists draw with a brush in washes of colour. The medium lends itself to the swift interpretation of passing impressions. It demands decision and concentration, for it

[1] Some may consider perspective a great deal more than a mechanical aid to representation. European art shows immense superiority over the Chinese in this direction.

leaves little time for consideration and mistakes cannot be
rectified. Water-colours suit the Chinese and British
temperament equally well. Our water-colours are more
translucent than theirs because the pigments that we use
are much purer, and the white non-absorbent paper upon
which we paint provides a transparent background. Nearly
the whole of the Chinese palette is semi-opaque (that is to
say the pigments are mixed with white), and the grey paper
and brown silk that they use provide a delightful foil for the
soft pastel effects of these colours. Their painting approxi-
mates to our painting in body colours on tinted paper, such
as was executed by Sandby and the early water-colour
school. But they draw rather than paint in water-colours
and they never attempt to cover the whole surface with a
wash, but sketch their design in strokes and blobs and allow
the natural tint of the silk or paper background to contribute the rest. The sixteenth, seventeenth and eighteenth
centuries saw a revolt against the calligraphic technique in
China. At the worst the academic school laboured after
detail without imagination. Han Fei-Tzu speaks of a painter
who spent three years to paint a bean with birds, beasts and
chariots for a prince of Chou. It is to be hoped that the
Chinese will not completely abandon their ancient calligraphic training. The work of many modern Chinese
painters is becoming less and less calligraphic in style, for the
fountain pen is fast supplanting the native brush and there
is a danger that the connection between calligraphy and
painting may be entirely broken.

The training of Chinese artists was confined to copying
old masters. Hsieh Ho places copying as one of the six
principles of painting. It is the spirit, not the lines, of a painting the copyist must attempt to capture. The Japanese
Tanyu of the Tokugawa era made a copy of every fine
painting he came across until in his old age he could count

them by the thousand. We know that Li Lung-Mien and Chao Mêng-Fu were copied extensively in their own life-time. To copy the styles laid down by tradition was the duty of every young artist. The sixteen methods of painting hills in landscape are described and illustrated in the *Kokka*.[1] Trees, birds and figures were classified in the same way. Of course the system had its critics. Su Tung-P'o expressed the opinion that "to copy the masterpieces of antiquity is only to grovel among the dust and husks." In their choice of subjects the Chinese are unpretentious and even common-place. There is no search for novel or lofty themes. The traditional themes are continually repeated. The peach remains for ever emblematic of the fruitfulness of nature, and its blossom a fragrant symbol of the beauty of maiden-hood; while the tough pliancy of the bamboo, whose green leaves defy frost and snow, are emblems of the urbanity, strength and constancy of the Chinese scholar. The beauties of the seasons have a never-failing appeal; their fleeting beauty is indirectly contrasted with the swift passage of human life. Spring and autumn are their favourite moods. The titles of Chinese landscape paintings are careful to tell us the season of the year. There is no attempt to portray social evils or to caricature fashionable society. Love scenes and political propaganda are equally absent. The themes chosen are the eternal pleasures and tragedies of all time, the balm of spring and the glory of autumn, the frailty of human pleasure, the sadness of farewell, and the in-evitability of decay. The landscape paintings of China do not picture the peasants' life of toil and hardship, but a life of ease and pleasure under shaded trees. We are carried away in the disinterested search for beauty to an imaginary world, where horsemen ride up through dark forests to ruined monasteries on solitary hills, or where sages sit

[1] No. 196, p. 415, *Chinese Landscape Painting*, III, by Sei-ichi Taki.

XXIV. LANDSCAPE
By Hsia Kuei, c. 1180–1230.

teaching wisdom by the shores of a lake beneath weeping willows stirred by the summer breeze. Perhaps it is the influence of Buddhism which has encouraged these introspective qualities. It is to the world of dreams that they turn for inspiration.

The Chinese never painted landscape direct from nature. Their pictures were the fruit of contemplation and meditation. Wu Tao-Tzŭ returned from a visit to the Yangtze gorges without a picture, but he had them all in his heart. Chinese artists have sought inspiration in different ways. Some went through a system of purification and shut themselves in secluded places, while others excited their imaginations by music or debauch. Kuo Hsi, of the Sung dynasty, wrote: "In painting any view, whether it be large or small, whether it contain many details or few, the artist must concentrate his powers in order to unify the work. Otherwise it will not bear the peculiar imprint of his soul. His whole soul must attend the completion of the task, otherwise his energies will be dulled. He must have deep seriousness wherewith to dignify his work, else it will lack depth of conception. He must use reverent toil to perfect it, else it will be incomplete. If a painter forces himself to work when he feels lazy his productions will be weak and spiritless, without decision. This is because he cannot concentrate. If, when he is feeling distracted and bothered, he decides to muddle through, his forms will be fogged and frightened; they will have no freshness. This is because his soul has not attended at the completion of the task. If the work is dashed off light-heartedly, the forms will be evasive and incomplete. This defect comes from lack of seriousness. If it is hurried on feverishly the composition will be rough and arbitrary; it will lack consistency. This defect comes from lack of reverent toil. Now indecision leads to loss of lucidity; lack of freshness destroys charm; incompleteness

133

mars composition; lack of consistency leads to sudden transitions. These are the main defects of painters. But they can only be discussed with those who understand the subject." [1]

His son provides a footnote to the effect that his father would put aside work if he felt disinclined, and that "on days when he was going to paint, he would seat himself at a clean table, by a bright window, burning incense to right and left. He would choose the finest brushes, the most exquisite ink; wash his hands, and clean the ink-stone, as though he were expecting a visitor of rank. He waited till his mind was calm and undisturbed, and then began. Is not this what he meant by saying that one should not dash off one's work light-heartedly? What he had completed, he would sift again. What he had enlarged, he would amplify. When once might have seemed enough, he would not even be content with *twice,* but would improve upon it. He would recommence each picture many times, as though at war with a pitiless adversary, till at last he was content. Is not this what he meant when he said that the work of art must not be hurried on?" [2] This is far from the extravagant self-advertisement of Ku Shêng who, we are told, "began by spreading out his silk upon the ground and mixing his colours, meanwhile he caused a number of men to blow horns, beat drums and make a general hubbub; in the midst of which he would put on an embroidered robe and with an embroidered turban round his head would drink himself half tipsy. He would then sketch the outline to his picture and lay on the colours with a large brush, mountain peaks and island shapes starting into existence in a wonderful manner." [3] Wang Fu preferred to work

[1] Waley, A. *Burlington Magazine,* vol. xxxviii, No. ccxviii: "Chinese Philosophy of Art—IV," p. 247.
[2] *Ibid.*
[3] Giles, H. A. *Chinese Pictorial Art,* p. 77.

XXV. OLD CYPRESS
By Kuo Hsi (c. 1020–1090).

to the strains of a flute by moonlight, while tradition has it that Ku Chiu-Chih [1] would retire to a tower from which he pulled up the ladder to prevent intrusion by his family. He would only paint on clear, bright days. Wu Tao-Tzŭ drew one of his best paintings in the T'ien Kuan Temple in Loyang, inspired by a sword dance of General P'ei Mu from which all the other spectators fled in terror. It is a sad descent from these two lofty characters to Wu Wei, who was so fond of wine and women that if you wished for a specimen of his painting you had to supply these accessories. On one occasion when he was summoned to the Imperial presence tipsy, he upset the ink slab but produced a fine fir tree in spring out of the blot on the floor. Or to Wang Mêng, who admitted openly, "I love eating, drinking and painting, and if people offer me good food, good wine and good silk why should I refuse?" [2] Wine seems to have been a never-failing source of inspiration for both painting and poetry. The painter Ts'ai Ying (133–182) was known as the "drunken dragon," and the Japanese painter Kiosai signed himself "Kiosai, sober," or " Kiosai, drunk."

But while painters like Wang Mêng were only too ready to sell their services to any patron for silk, food or wine, others had an intense dislike of patronage of officials and the world of wealth and fashion. Ni Tsan received a messenger from a prominent man with gifts of silk and money with the remark, "I have never during my whole life painted for high fliers," [3] upon which he tore up the silk and returned the money. He was a strange character who distributed his wealth among his friends and spent his

[1] *Kokka,* No. 244, p. 68.
[2] Giles, H. A. *Op. cit.,* p. 17.
[3] Sirén, O. *A History of Early Chinese Painting,* vol. ii, p. 142.

life in travelling by boat on the lakes and rivers of Kiangsu, stopping at Buddhist temples when he felt inclined. Like other Chinese artists he would give away his sketches freely at a drinking bout to those who appreciated them, or shower them on some humble peasant, but it pleased him to keep the fashionable world waiting years for an order, which he might never complete. Kuo Yü, we are told, "when persons of rank tried to get pictures out of him, would stare at the roof and count the beams without making any reply. If they persisted he would jump up excitedly and finally rush out of the room with a howl." [1] Lu Chih, when he had retired from official life to the hills, would entertain visitors who pleased him in the garden with honey served in a bamboo joint, but an unprepossessing stranger would find the door shut in his face and a stone against it. Some artists would never sell their work unless poverty compelled. If any one wished to obtain a landscape from the painter Liu Wei he had to climb the bell tower of the temple close by where the artist lived, and if he could detect no smoke rising from the chimney of the kitchen he knew that Liu had no money and might soon be ready to part with some of his treasures.[2] His style was characterized by dots like nail-heads and he was so eccentric that he was called by his neighbours Liu Ch'ih (Liu the fool).

All art criticism in China is based on six principles laid down by Hsieh Ho who lived A.D. 479–501. He left a description of twenty-six painters who had preceded him, dividing them into six categories according as they achieved his own standards of excellence. He seems to have been the first Chinese to formulate any system of art criticism. Waley describes him as a realistic portrait painter, whose doctrines

---

[1] Giles, H. A. *Chinese Pictorial Art*, p. 182.
[2] *Kokka*, No. 318, p. 115.

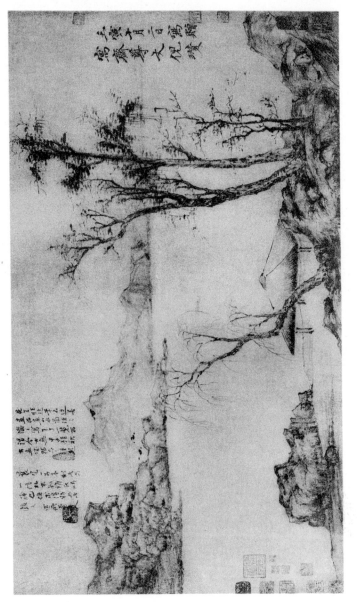

XXVI. LANDSCAPE
By Ni Tsan (*b.* 1301, *d.* 1374).

were not very different from those of our own nineteenth-century academicians. He did not originate, but gathered, arranged and edited the thoughts of earlier Confucian and Taoist philosophers. His six principles of good painting have been much written upon and variously translated. I give the translations of Waley [1] and Sei-ichi Taki [2] and Hirth [3] in that order.

1. *Ch'i-yün-shêng-tung.*

    (1) Spiritual harmony—life and motion.

    (2) Spiritual tone and life movement.

    (3) Spiritual expression and life movement.

This is the most important principle of the six. Giles translated it "rhythmic vitality" and Okakura "the life movement of the spirit through the rhythm of things." Taki and Waley associate it with the Confucian spirit of heaven and earth found in the *Book of Changes,* and Petrucci with the "Tao" of the Taoists. Binyon devotes some interesting pages to it in the *Flight of the Dragon.*[4] It is not easy to improve upon these translations. The conception is a philosophical one and the meaning is difficult to capture in words. Hsieh Ho refers to the spirit that moves the mind of the artist to paint. He is attempting, as I see it, to describe the source of artistic inspiration which is outside the mere ability to interpret thought and emotion. He speaks of it as the spark that sets alight the sensibility of the artist. Most Chinese critics say this quality cannot be cultivated. Great artists are born and not made. But Tung Ch'i-Ch'ang believed that "by reading ten thousand books and travelling ten

[1] *Burlington Magazine,* vol. xxxvii, No. ccxiii, p. 309.

[2] *Kokka,* No. 244, p. 67.

[3] Hirth, F. *Native Sources for the History of Chinese Pictorial Art,* p. 8.

[4] P. 12 *et sequitur.*

thousand miles one can cultivate something approaching spiritual rhythm." [1]

2. *Ku-fa-yung-pi.*
   (1) Bone means—use brush.
   (2) Manner of brushwork in drawing lines.
   (3) Structure and style.

Here he refers to the importance of the brush stroke of which I have already spoken. The vigour, turn and duration of the brush stroke is one of the first criteria of any Chinese painting, but this must not be confused with the flourishes of mere dexterity.

3. *Ying-wu-hsiang-hsing.*
   (1) According to the subject depict shape.
   (2) Form in its relation to objects.
   (3) Representation of form according to object.

Which is summed up in accurate reproduction of form.

4. *Sui-lei-fu-ts'ai.*
   (1) According to species apply colours.
   (2) Choice of colour appropriate to the object.
   (3) Spreading colour according to the nature (of the object).

This is nothing more than a reference to accurate use of colours.

5. *Ching-ying-wei-chih.*
   (1) Planning and disposing degrees and places.
   (2) Composition and grouping.
   (3) Organizing and constructing picture according to space.

This is composition.

[1] *Studio*, May 1935: Professor Liu Hai Su.

6. *Ch'uan-mu-i-hsieh*.

  (1) By handing on and copying, to transmit designs.
  (2) Copying of classic masterpieces.
  (3) Tracing and copying.

This can either be interpreted that to copy masterpieces is the highest form of art training or that the observance of traditional design is one to which all pictures should concede. Copying has received a much higher position in the East than we should permit, but it is the spirit, not the design, that the Chinese would copy. There are traditional subjects, comparable to the theme of the "Last Supper" in Italian religious painting, which occur continually in all branches of Chinese painting, particularly in landscape. Hsieh Ho would seem to support the use of these motives against subjects chosen by the artist himself. Hsieh Ho's claim to fame lies not so much in the six principles themselves, but in the influence they have had upon Chinese art. The six principles may not strike us as very conclusive, but the Chinese have woven round them a wealth of philosophical subtleties. Records do not lead us to believe that Hsieh Ho's own work was very inspiring, and it is doubtful whether his judgment was reliable. He places Ku Kai-Ch'ih in the third class of painters. The critic Chang Yen-Yüan of the T'ang was very sceptical of the six canons and Hsieh Ho does not seem to have fared much better at the hands of Sung critics. But as Waley says, "each age and class has made its attempt to define artistic beauty, has produced its convenient phrase and grown tired of it. Who shall say Hsieh Ho's formula is any more nebulous than the rest?"

In the *Chieh tzu yuan shu chuan* (the Book transmitted in the Mustard Seed Garden) there is a description of the six methods (the six principles according to Hsieh Ho), the six necessities, the six superiorities, the three qualities and the three vices. This book was compiled with an introduction by Li Li-Wêng towards the end of the seventeenth century. It has often been reprinted since in China and Japan. The original notes were by Li Chang-Hêng (Li Liu-Fan) 1575–1629. These notes were given to Li Yu by Shen Hsu-P'u his son-in-law, who owned the Mustard Seed Garden, the scene of the conversation that led to the gift. They had already been revised and completed by one Wang An Chieh before Yu saw them. The book was first published in 1679, but the fourth part was never printed until 1818 when it was published under the care of a painter Ting Kao, to whose publication an introduction was added by Ch'ao Hsun in 1888. The whole book has been translated into French by Raphael Petrucci in 1918 under the title *Encyclopèdie de la peinture Chinoise.*[1]

APPENDIX

Extract from " Chieh Tzu Yuan Shu Chuan "

Lu Ch'ai said : "Some who study painting esteem intricacy, others simplicity. Neither intricacy or simplicity is sufficient in itself. Again some prefer facility and others laboriousness. Both facility and laboriousness can be bad. Some value method; others lack of method. To be without method is bad but to rely entirely on method is even worse. Now you must first vigorously observe the rules and afterwards modify them according to your intelligence. To use method to the right purpose is to appear as if you were eschewing it. . . . First Han Kan prayed, then he painted and inspiration visited him. So you can

---

[1] A translation from a small part of the Chinese text may be found in the Appendix. From it I hope it may be possible to obtain an inkling of the philosophical approach of the Chinese to painting.

paint with or without method. But first you must bury (your-self under?) a complete pile of brushes and grind the iron (ink slab) to mud.

"You must take eleven days to draw a river and five days a boulder. The landscape of Chia Ling took Li Ssu-Hsün several months to complete. Wu Tao finished it in one evening with a few strokes of the hand. So it can be said facility is good and laboriousness is good.

"You must store up in your breast the five peaks, and not concentrate on the whole cow.

"You must study ten thousand volumes and travel ten thousands roads. You must gallop up to and jump over the barriers set by Tung and Chu.

"You must straightway penetrate into the inner sanctum of Ku and Cheng. Mountains loom up and springs spurt forth, as you make limpid waters and lonely forests, and like Kuo Shu-Hsien release a paper kite on a thread.

"One stroke of his brush represents many tens of feet. He drew (with equal facility) the storied buildings, the pelts of oxen and the threads of silkworms. So intricacy is permissible and simplicity also permissible. For if you wish to draw without method you must first master method. If you wish to obtain facility you must first acquire laboriousness. If you wish with practised brush to depict austere simplicity you must first have at your finger tips a mastery of complexity and of luxuriant detail.

"The six methods, the six necessities, the six superiorities, the three qualities, the three vices, the twelve things to shun, how can you neglect them?"

(The six methods are the six principles of Hsieh Ho which I omit.)

The six necessities.

Liu Tao-Chun of the Sung dynasty said:

"(1) The transformation of the spirit must be united with strength.

"(2) You must paint according to tradition.

"(3) Changes and differences ought to conform to reason.

"(4) The colour must have richness.

"(5) Method must be spontaneous.

"(6) In imitating and learning relinquish the deficient."

The six superiorities.
"(1) In coarseness and rudeness search for a strong brush.
"(2) In rustic roughness search for talent.
"(3) Through delicacy find strength.
"(4) Through madness and strangeness find reason.
"(5) Without ink find depths.
"(6) In flat painting find space."

The three qualities.
Hsia Wen-Yen said: "The movement of the spirit produces animation. This quality comes from heaven in its perfection. Mankind cannot gauge its subtlety. It is called *Shên* (the spiritual quality). When brush and ink are at their height, when in painting you arrive at the absolutely suitable. When you have ideas in abundance. This is called *Miao* (the marvellous quality). When you get hold of form and yet do not lose the compass and the square this is called *Nêng* (the quality of ability)."
Mr. Lu Ch'ai said: "This contains everything in a nutshell, but Chu Ching-Chên of the T'ang dynasty added over and above the three qualities, the quality *I* (extravagant or luxurious). Wang Hsiu-Fu placed the quality *I* first and afterwards *Shen* and *Miao*. His ideas are derived from Chang Yen-Yüan. Yen-Yüan says: '(If a painting) fails to be natural then it will be spiritual; if it fails in spirituality then it will be marvellous; if it escapes the marvellous then it will be careful and meticulous.' This discussion is truly strange. When a painting has achieved the spiritual it has then attained its objective. How can it not be natural? The quality *I* ought of course to be placed outside the three qualities. How can we discuss its inferiority or superiority to *Miao* and *Shen*. If one loses oneself in the fine and delicate one may put yourself beyond criticism, for the world likes to be flattered with pleasant gratification in the guise of painting, and the man of the world by the slave and concubine. I will not follow the matter further."

The three vices.
Kuo Jo-Hsü of the Sung dynasty said: "The three vices all lie in the use of the brush. The first one is *Pan*. *Pan* is weak wrist and faulty brush. Entirely deficient in taking and giving, which makes things flat and level and is not able to make them round and complete.

"The second vice is *K'o*. *K'o* is when the movements of the brush are uncertain in the middle (of the stroke). The heart and the hand are uncoordinated at the moment of painting and wrongly produce the angles of the Kuei.

"The third vice is called *Chieh*. *Chieh* is to wish to advance but to fail in that objective. To be in a position to progress but not to progress. As if something holds up and obstructs (the brush) so that it will not flow freely."

The twelve things to shun.

Tao Tzu Jan of the Yüan dynasty said: "The first thing to shun is to arrange the composition without spacing. The second to make no distinction between distance and foreground. The third to make mountains with no breathing passages (geomantic term). The fourth to depict water without a flowing spring. The fifth scenery without hill and dale. The sixth, roads without entries or departures. The seventh, stones with only a single surface. The eighth, trees with less than four branches. The ninth, figures of human beings, humped backed. The tenth, towns and pavilions placed higgledy piggledy. The eleventh inappropriate smudges and blurs. The twelfth to spread colour with no method."

6

The Treatment of Landscape and the Human Figure

IT is often assumed that the portrait has played a small part in Chinese painting. It would be more truthful to say that figure painting developed at a very early date, and that so little has survived that it is easy to forget its existence. We know that pictures of sages, generals and ancient emperors were painted to adorn the Han palaces, so that the reigning emperor might be constantly reminded of his predecessors.[1] A representation of thirteen famous emperors, beginning with the Han and going down to the last emperor of the Sui, A.D. 618, which is attributed to Yen Li-Pĕn, is in the Museum of Fine Arts, Boston.[2] By 100 B.C. mentions of portraits are frequent in Chinese literature. In 51 B.C. the Emperor Hsüan Ti had the portraits of victorious generals painted for Ch'i Lin tower, the Chi-lu-ko temple.[3] Chang Yen-Yüan mentions six portrait painters between the years 43 and 33 B.C., and by the time of the Emperor Yuan, if the tragic story of Chao Chün can be trusted, Court beauties were regularly painted.[4] The art of the Han was particularly concerned with figure painting, but only engraved stone has survived. The works of Chavannes show us that Han

[1] Sirén, O. *History of Early Chinese Painting,* vol. i, p. 5.
[2] *Burlington Magazine,* vol. xxxv, 1919.
[3] Zen, S. C. *Symposium on Chinese Culture,* p. 67: "Painting and Calligraphy," by Ts'ai Yuan-Pei.
[4] Hirth, F. *Native Sources for the History of Chinese Pictorial Art,* p. 1.

XXVII. SECTION OF A RUBBING FROM STONE BAS-RELIEFS AT THE CEMETRY OF THE WU
FAMILY CHIA-HSIANG-HSIEN, SHANTUNG

Han dynasty (206 B.C.–A.D. 264).

(2′ 5″ × 10″)

artists loved to depict chariots and horses, feasts and fights and the chase.[1] Most of the Chinese portraits that are met with to-day are portraits of ancestors. These are seldom works of art; reference to them is generally omitted from Chinese books on painting. They are the work of anonymous artisans who, instead of dealing in funereal statuary, painted pictures to house the spirits of the departed.

At funeral ceremonies the portrait hung directly over the coffin, and in the procession it was carried near the corpse. When the funeral was over it was stored in the ancestral hall; from there it emerged together with all the other ancestral portraits on the first six days of the Chinese New Year. They were hung, and worshipped with incense and prostrations, after which they were returned to store until the same ceremony the next year. In some of the pictures the faces are carefully painted. The portraits were often painted in the lifetime of the subject at the order of his or her children. The position and clothes of the subjects were strictly conventional. Both men and women are depicted full-face in a sitting position on a chair with a tiger mat at the feet. They wear the finest official raiment to which they are entitled, and their pictures are painted in the brightest colours and touched up with gilt. No attempt is made to portray movement or gesture. It is possible to see in Canton rows of partly finished paintings lacking heads, which will be added at the time of the order from a glimpse of the corpse or a sitting in a studio at the back part of the shop.

The lack of plastic qualities in Chinese painting has always put it at a loss to reproduce solid form. Water-colour is not really a suitable medium for figure painting, it is better

[1] See also Petrucci. "La Peinture des figures en Chine," *Gazette des Beaux Arts,* tome xi.

adapted for rendering atmospheric effects. To the Chinese, interest in human form seldom displaced the intellectual idea. The head of the male Chinese figure is generally drawn at a certain angle to the body to depict the stoop of the scholar, which is the national ideal. Figures are often treated as part of the pattern of a design.[1] There is a tendency to draw the ruler bigger than the subject, the sage larger than his disciples. In the Buddhist paintings from Tun Huang secondary figure subjects on a smaller scale are shown in the margin. When an individual official is painted, the aim is to seize upon significant accessories; his robes display his official distinction; a background of hills, his love of nature; a display of pen, paper and ink slabs, his literary taste. His expression should be austere, serene or thoughtful as befits a scholar.[2] The Chinese are far happier in their paintings of the legendary lives of heroes. They were also particularly fond of painting pictures of the birds, beasts and people of foreign lands which fired their imagination and gave full range to their fancy. Taoist and Buddhist subjects were invested with something of the same attraction. They delighted to depict tribute bearers from strange countries in fantastic clothes. There is a design after a picture by Li Lung-Mien which has been extensively copied in which foreign envoys are painted bringing an ibex, elephants' tusks, petrified wood, peacocks and a bird in a cage. Li Ssŭ-Hsün said of Yen Li-Pĕn, "he painted envoys of many countries arriving at Court with tributes of jade and other precious things from the T'u mountain; he painted the procession of barbarian people with their high hair ornaments, their hu tablets and their strange and startling manners such as drinking through the nose and making the

[1] *Kokka*, No. 244, p. 72: Sei-ichi Taki.
[2] The secret of *ch'uan shen* (portrait painting), wrote Ku K'ai C'hih, "lies in the proper rendering of the pupil of the eye."

XXVIII. PORTRAIT OF A GENTLEMAN
Painter unknown, late Ming dynasty (1368–1643).
The British Museum. $(2' 2\frac{1}{2}'' \times 1' 6\frac{1}{2}'')$

head fly, and he did it all with the greatest accuracy down to the smallest details." [1]

There is nothing in China comparable to the figure painting of the Ukiyoé school of the seventeenth and eighteenth centuries in Japan. But it must be remembered that the colour print was till very recently beneath the notice of the Japanese connoisseur. Painting in both China and Japan was considered to be the hobby of the scholar and the aristocrat. Japan, during the seventeenth and eighteenth centuries, created popular art in the colour prints. Chinese coloured woodcuts are seldom more than vehicles of reproduction, while in Japanese hands they became an original force. The woodcut illustrations to the *Dream of the Red Chamber*, *The Three Kingdoms* and other popular Chinese novels cannot compare with the prints of Utamaro or Harunobu; but some of the early Chinese woodcuts of flowers, fruit and birds are exceedingly fine. It is not extraordinary in these circumstances that caricature and satire are completely absent except in the humblest forms of Chinese painting, which have for the most part perished. As early as the twelfth century in Japan we have the monk Tobo Sojo caricaturing in pictures of frogs, mice and monkeys the lazy priest and the arrogant daimyo. It was a brave man who ventured along these paths; for a mild caricature of Hideyoshi (who had been dead a century), Utamaro, Toyokuni and two others were kept in prison for two months with their hands tied behind their backs. The Shogunate kept a very strict censorship on painters and writers. In the same way Chinese poets seldom dared to criticize the throne except through its ministers and then only in elaborate symbolical language. It has been said with truth that a Hogarth in China or Japan would have been immediately executed or exiled.

[1] Sirén, O. *A History of Early Chinese Painting*, vol. i, p. 55.

Nature provided the safest and most illusive vehicle of criticism. It has been suggested that Korin, when he painted fields of blue iris amid pointed flags, was portraying at once the beauties of nature and the splendid arrogance of the daimyos amid the spears of their numerous retinues.

In China "small views" of the middle-class family are not uncommon. The whole family is pictured in the Zoffany manner, the wife at her embroidery, the husband at his books, and their children at play: often the background is the garden. Another subject is one of the four elegant occupations, *i.e.* tea, music, calligraphy, or checkers. The life of the retired official surrounded by his family, entertaining his guests to music at his country seat, taking the air in his garden, driving over the fields in a canopied cart, or riding on the back of an ox or mule led by a boy attendant, is also represented. Other subjects are young exquisites assembled in groups beneath trees from which they have suspended birds in cages, while they match their quails, gamble, or listen to the rival melodies of the "yellow eyebrow" (a whistling thrush) or larks from the plains of Tsien tung. The Chinese are particularly fond of painting sages and old men. Shou Hsing, the god of longevity, a swollenheaded person holding a peach and a staff; Lu Hsing, the god of rank, in official costume with a winged hat; and Fu Hsing, the god of happiness, holding a child, are all common motives. Besides the Eight Immortals and the Eighteen Lohan who have been referred to elsewhere, there are the Seven Sages of the Bamboo Grove, an association of convivial men of letters,[1] who were accustomed to meet for discussion and relaxation in a bamboo garden.[2] The Chinese are fond of portraying bands of worthies who gathered

[1] C. A.D. 275.
[2] Mayers. *Chinese Reader's Manual*, p. 27.

XXIX. LADY ASLEEP ON A LEAF
By T'ang Yin (b. 1466, d. 1524).

(Length approx. 2′ 0″)

By permission of A. W. Bahr, Esq.

together in secluded gardens to discuss over a cup of wine philosophy and the beauties of nature.[1]

Portraits of beautiful women have always been in demand in court circles. The *Hsi ching tsu chi* tells how the Emperor Yüan Ti (48–32 B.C.) employed court painters to portray his harem which had grown to such proportions that he had no longer the time to receive all his ladies in audience. The beauty, Wang Chiang (Chao Chün), did not pay the huge sum demanded by the court artists for a flattering portrait and was neglected. When it became necessary to provide a bride for Hsiung Nu she was chosen. At her parting audience the emperor was so astonished at her beauty that he tried in vain to repurchase her for a camel-load of gold. He was so enraged by the duplicity of his painters that he ordered six of them to be executed. One of these was the court painter Mao Yen Shou.[2] Chao Chün died a few years later outside the Wall. Poetry tells us that the grass on the mound over her grave was always green despite the barrenness of the surrounding country. Female beauty is invariably associated with natural beauty. The analogy of flowers appeals to the Chinese mind. Whereas the Greek personified nature in a thousand legends, the Chinese naturalized woman. The commonest female names are those of flowers. A Chinese artist when asked to paint a young girl would sooner sketch a sprig of blossom than the girl herself. It is the symbol of her maidenhood which interests, not her personality. There is a practice of painting a woman surrounded by butterflies. It was said of Ch'in Lien, a beauty of the T'ang period, that whenever she

[1] One club was that of the Four Recluse Grey Heads (Tung Yüan Kung, Hsiu Huang-Kung, Ch'i Li-Chi, Chio Li Hsiu-Sheng) who during the reign of Shih Huang Ti retired from the disorders of official life to the mountain of Shang, from which they emerged in the Han to enter official service. (Mayers. *Chinese Reader's Manual*, p. 305.)

[2] Giles, H. A. *Chinese Pictorial Art*, p. 6.

stepped from her house butterflies would hover round this human flower. The "hundred beautiful women" is a not uncommon subject. There is Lo Fu, a beautiful and chaste woman of the Han. One day, when she was out picking mulberries, the Prince of Chao, in whose service her husband was, began to make advances to her. "She at once seized her lute and broke into song in order to express her feelings." [1] Of Li Küan, a beauty of the harem of Wu Ti of the Han, we hear that "the exquisite delicacy of her complexion at the age of fourteen was such that her imperial lover dreaded, it is said, lest the mere touch of a silken fringe should cause her injury. The emperor playfully expressed the fear, moreover, that the zephyrs, however gently blowing, might carry her away from earth." [2] Chinese history is full of the infatuation of emperors for court beauties whose reckless extravagance cost them their thrones. [3] The definition of a beautiful woman is a "kingdom breaker." Mei Hsi, who overthrew the Hsia dynasty, conducted drunken revels on a lake of wine from which two thousand people drank like cattle at the beating of a gong, and dwelt in an underground palace; Ta Chi, who caused the downfall of the Yin dynasty, for whose vanity Chou Hsin built the "Deer Tower," the highest structure known, was called the "hen that heralds the dawn of day." The smile of Pao Ssü (773 B.C.) of the Chou dynasty cost Yu Wang his life and his crown. Tradition says that she was so hard to please that to make her smile her lover had all the beacons lit; at the disgust of his nobles, who arrived in hot haste for the defence of his land, she was very much amused. Later, when the Dog barbarians invaded the land, the emperor lit his bonfires in

[1] *Catalogue of Chinese Paintings, Ancient and Modern, the property of Liu Sung Fu,* compiled by Florence Ayscough, p. 90.

[2] Mayers. *Chinese Reader's Manual,* p. 116.

[3] See *Outlines of Chinese History,* Li Ung Bing.

XXX. COURT BEAUTY

Painter unknown. Ch'ing dynasty (1644–1912).

$(2' \, 0'' \times 10\frac{1}{2}'')$

vain. But the most famous and the most often illustrated of all beauties was the lady Yang Kuei Fei, a favourite of Ming Huang of the T'ang dynasty. Her beauty and her extravagance ruined the country and fomented the rebellion of the Tartar general An Lu-Shan, who, it has been suggested, was her lover. On the flight from the capital before An Lu-Shan's advance the imperial troops threatened to mutiny unless she was strangled. The emperor gave in. An Lu-Shan was defeated and the emperor was reinstated in the capital, but he never recovered from the loss. Her story is told in a poem by Po Chü-I under the title of the "Never Ending Grief."

Chinese artists give as much attention to the clothes as to the human face. It was said by Kuo Jo-Hsü, "Ts'ao t'a's (Ts'ao Chung-Ta) figures were clad in garments that clung to the body; they looked as if they had been drenched in water whereas the mantles on Wu's (Wu Tao-Tzǔ) figures were dressed in billowy folds and looked as if they had been caught by the wind." [1] Ts'ao Pieh-Hsing of Wu of the Three Kingdoms (according to T'ang Hou, an art critic of the Yüan) painted the creases in the clothes of human figures so faithfully that there arose a saying "Ts'ao's clothes look as if they have just come from the wash." [2] The coiffure, the headdress, or the make-up of a picture of a court beauty may indicate her date. The ladies of the Han period are represented as wearing jade plugs in the ears. The T'ang artists powdered the nose, the lips and brows of their subjects.[3] The *Tieh shih* (butterfly coiffure) of T'ang heads is famous. Probably the painting of women reached its height in this period. Chou Wen Chu painted the "golden beauties" of the Southern T'ang, and the opulent charms of the beauties of Chou Fang (780–810) were famous.

[1] Sirén, O. *A History of Early Chinese Painting,* vol. i, p. 39.
[2] Giles, H. A. *Chinese Pictorial Art,* p. 15.
[3] The triple white method.

This painter is supposed to have originated "spring pictures" (erotic paintings). His masterpiece, entitled "The Secret Frolics of a Spring Night," [1] does not seem to have survived. The T'ang ideal of female beauty was full cheeks, round small mouth and full red lips. There was much painting of female beauty during the Ming; Ch'iu Ying, who flourished early in the first half of the sixteenth century, was one of the most popular painters of court beauties, and no one could approach him in delicacy of colour. The tradition was continued in the eighteenth century by Yu Tsi (1743–1823) who held a sinecure as Imperial Supervisorate of Instruction,[2] and K'ai Ki (1795–1832), a Mongolian. A contemporary critic said that if the latter would discard the habit of painting rouge on the cheeks of the ladies, his ladies would be still better.[3] Hirth mentions a well-dressed sing-song girl (without rouge) painted in 1795. But it would not be untrue to say that the painting of women was confined to court artists, and was an insignificant part of the main body of Chinese painting.

The Chinese word for landscape is *shan shui* (hills and water). Every Chinese landscape contains mountains, waterfalls, rocky water-courses, broad lakes and winding rivers heaped together in one composition. Scenery is most usually treated in panoramic view. The wild confusion of these landscapes is incomprehensible to the European mind. Mountains rise sheer from plains in the foreground, trees tangled with creepers hang over precipices, monasteries are perched high above rivers that surge through the gorges below. It is difficult for us to imagine that such scenery can exist outside the imagination. These scenes are not typical

[1] Waley, A. *Burlington Magazine*, No. clxxi, vol. xxx, p. 214, Jan. 1907.
[2] Hirth, F. *Chinese Painters*, p. 42.
[3] Hirth, F. *Op. cit.* p. 42.

XXXI. THE PEACH AND PLUM GARDEN
By Chiu Ying (c. 1522-1560).
Chi-on-in Temple, Kyoto.   (6′ 8″ × 3′ 9″)

of China, but are confined to certain regions in Shansi, northern Chekiang and southern Anhwei, but it is the scenery that the Chinese most admire, and as they never paint landscape from nature, their imagination finds fullest range in the impenetrable mountains and forests of their distant provinces. "To gaze upon the clouds in autumn, a soaring exaltation in the soul; to feel the spring breeze stirring wild exultant thoughts—what is there in the possession of gold and jewels to compare with delights like these? And then to unroll the portfolio, spread the silk, and transfer to it the glories of flood and fell, the green forest, the blowing winds, the white water of the rushing cascade . . . these are the joys of painting." [1] There is a wide divergence between English and Chinese landscape. We seek to interpret a fruitful nature, tamed to the grazier and broken to the plough. The nature the Chinese know is hostile and capricious, whether it be the great deserts, or barren mountain ranges of the north, or the tropical rice-fields and the malarial swamps of the south. It is not strange that an entirely different conception of nature should have arisen, which has tended to a fatalism in their relationship with it.

It has been the fashion for Chinese priests, poets, artists and disappointed politicians to retire to the mountains to end their days. Both Taoism and Buddhism have taught that this is the shortest road to spiritual enlightenment. Both built monasteries in remote places in which their devotees might find a refuge. Nature worship is the oldest of all the Chinese religions. As far back as they can remember they have built altars to the earth, the moon, the sun and the heavens. Buddhism and Taoism have between them carried down the tradition unbroken to the present day.

[1] Giles, H. A. *Chinese Pictorial Art,* p. 25: quotations from Wang Wei (A.D. 420–479).

"From what motives springs the love of high-minded men for landscapes? In his very nature man loves to be in a garden with hills and streams whose water makes cheerful music as it glides among the stones. What a delight does one derive from such sights as that of a fisherman engaging in his leisurely occupation in a sequestered nook, or of a woodman felling a tree in a secluded spot, or of mountain scenery with sporting monkeys and cranes? Nothing is so distasteful as the bustle and turmoil of a city, and one naturally envies the lot of sages and hermits who always abide amidst the beauty of nature. But in this day of peace when the emperor and people are in perfect accord, each striving to promote the weal of the empire, it would be contrary to justice, if a man should egoistically leave society and retire to a mountain. This is no time for us to abandon the busy worldly life for one of seclusion in the mountains, as was honourably done by Hsia Huang, Kung Chi, and Chi Ying in their days. The ancient poems on Pai Chu and on Tzu Chio were undoubtedly productions of high-principled persons who, unable to forsake the earthly life, consoled themselves by leaving to posterity verses expressing their ideals. Though impatient to enjoy a life amidst the luxuries of nature, most people are debarred from indulging in such pleasures. To meet this want artists have endeavoured to represent landscapes so that people may be able to behold the grandeur of nature without stepping out of their houses. In this light, painting affords pleasures of a nobler sort, by removing from one the impatient desire of actually observing nature." [1] The Chinese love of nature amounts to a mystical experience. Binyon has written that they have taken for their subject all that is august or elemental in nature, "Peace and storm

[1] *Kokka,* vol. xvi, No. 182-193, p. 332, *et sequitur*: "On Chinese Landscape Painting," Part II, by Sei-ichi Taki.

154

范中立別
號寬陝西
崋原人
上以玆畫特
賜內閣大學
士商丘
宋公玄平先
生畫之傳玄
奇與气骨玄
迴用荊關童
巨運之一機而
靈韻雄邁兀
為古今第一
佗如薄淺草
隘小奇致璧
营邦小國本非
坫壇盟長
公以第一流人
錫天下第一畫
懸昭道德勳
業對揚大亦
休命其博大亦
可知己

XXXII. BUDDHIST TEMPLE IN SNOWY HILLS
By Fan K'uan (c. 990–1030).
The National Collection, Peiping.   (3′ 6¾″ × 1′ 10″)

upon the mountain top, wild geese flying through the autumn sky, the willow bending its soft streamers to the wind of spring." He goes on to quote a Chinese poem: "It is midnight—all is quiet. The water clock stopped, but I am unable to sleep because of the beauty of the trembling shapes of spring flowers thrown on the blind by the moon outside." [1] The painter Fan Kuan is said to have sat up all night under the moon admiring the snow.[2]

The Chinese landscape painters were adept at rendering a panorama in a few square feet. Trees and streams are seen in a plain in the foreground; buildings and waterfalls occupy the foothills in the middle distance; high mountains stretch away to infinity beyond. "When sequestered from the world, in the quiet enjoyment of wine and the music of the harp, I face my paintings and contemplate them in the serenity of peace, I see the whole universe before my eyes. Nature reveals herself in all her reality, and I feel as if I were walking through a beautiful land alone, with no one to disturb me. Yonder towers a mountain peak, there a forest is dimly visible through the mist. In the midst of this sublime scenery methinks I see the spirits of the ancient saints and sages. All Nature seems to be in harmony with the Divine. The soul can wish for nothing more." [3] Waley remarks that the sentiment of association often intervened between the painter and his subject. Kuo Hsi's essay on landscape painting begins: "Wherein lies the reason that good men so much love landscape? It is because amid

[1] Binyon, L. *Painting in the Far East.*

[2] He is described as "a stern and old-fashioned man, careless of his behaviour, fond of music, with no command of the ways of the world." Critics complained he used too much ink. (Sirén, O. *A History of Early Chinese Painting,* vol. i, p. 135.)

[3] *Kokka,* vol. xxv, July 1914–June 1915, No. 297: "Landscape painting under the Six Dynasties," Part I, p. 185 ("Introductory Notes on Landscape Painting," written by Tsung Ping).

orchards and hills a man has ever room to cultivate his natural bent; because streams and rocks never fail to charm the 'rambler who goes whistling on his way.' It is because fishing and wood-gathering are the natural vocations of the hermit or recluse, hard by where the flying birds and chattering apes have made their home. Noise and dust, bridles and chains—these are what man's nature is ever weary of. Haze and mists, saints and fairies—for these man's nature pines eternally, and pines in vain. Now comes a painter, and by his skill all these things are suddenly brought to us. Still in our home, stretched on the divan, we hear the cries of gibbons by many streams, the song of birds down many valleys; while our eyes are flooded by the gleam of hills, the hues of falling streams. Does not this illustrate the saying 'Charmed by another's purpose, I attain my own desire'?" [1]

Landscape painting appears at a remarkably early period in China. The roll of the " Admonitions to the Instructress" attributed to Ku K'ai-Chih, but thought to be a T'ang copy, contains a landscape scene, but as in European countries landscape is a later development. The great landscape painters were the artists of the Sung and Yüan, and the landscape came to exclude all others in the hands of the literary painters of the Ming and Ch'ing. As it was a comparatively late manifestation, a greater number of good landscape paintings has survived, and there has been, perhaps in consequence, a tendency to over-emphasize its importance. Tradition has divided all Chinese landscape painting into the Northern and Southern schools. It is no easy matter to decide when this division occurred. Some critics write that it existed in the T'ang, others that it did not occur till the Ming. The Northern school is indebted to the genius of

[1] Waley, A. *Burlington Magazine,* vol. xxxviii, No. ccxviii, May 1921, p. 244: "Chinese Philosophy of Art."

XXXIII. SECTION OF A LANDSCAPE ROLL
By Ma Yüan (c. 1190–1224).

$(2' 8'' \times 1' 4\frac{1}{2}'')$

The Freer Gallery, Washington.

Li Ssŭ-Hsun and his son Li Chao-Tao, the Southern school to Wang Wei. The vast plains and mountain ranges of the north gave rise to a bold, hard, angular style, while the hills and streams of the south promoted gentler technique.[1] The northern style could be simple and romantic in the hands of Ma Yüan and Hsia Kuei or delicate and sentimental in those of Li Ssŭ-Hsün and his son; these two drew landscapes with infinite patience and in exquisite detail, in coral and gold, malachite green and azure blue. The painting of the south was soft and suggestive. It lent itself to rapid painting. Wu Tao-Tzŭ who is accredited to the south painted ten thousand miles of landscape in a day. Wang Wei did not adhere closely to nature. A picture of his entitled "Bamboo in Snow" was a source of unceasing criticism to his more academic brethren. The northern style became flat and harsh or dead and ornate in academic hands during the Ming, and the southern style also declined to blots and blurs that aped noble sentiments under the Ch'ing. The strength and simplicity (at its best) of the north were contrasted with the subtlety and grace of the south. In practice there was no dividing line, as many painters painted alternately in both styles or in a judicious mixture of the two. But the northern style was more often in favour at court.

There are sets of landscape that appear over and over again, such as the proverbial eight views of the Hsiao and the Hsiang. The subjects are as follows:[2]

(1) Geese flying towards a sandy beach.
(2) Homeward bound.

[1] See *Kokka*, No. 196, p. 423, where a long list of painters of the two schools is given by Sei-ichi Taki.

[2] We are told that the River Hsiao begins at the boundary of Tao Chou in Kuangtung and the Hsiang in Chuan Chou in the province of Lei Hsing. The two unite and flow together into the Tung t'ing Lake. (*Kokka*, No. 216, p. 273.)

(3) A mountain inn at twilight.

(4) The snowy lake side.

(5) Moonlight night in autumn on Lake Tung t'ing.

(6) Evening rain on rivers Hsiao and Hsiang.

(7) Evening bell of a distant temple.

(8) Fishing village at sunset.

These eight views are supposed to have been originated by Sung Ti of the Sung dynasty, but were reproduced by Mu Ch'i, Ma Yüan, Mi Yu-Jên, and Hui Tsung.[1] Later they found great favour in Japan. Shubun, Sesshu, Masanobu Kano and Sesson all painted them, and Soami seems to have been particularly familiar with these subjects. We learn of another famous set of views which came from the West Lake at Hangchow.

(1) Broken-off bridge of late snow.

(2) Pavilion of the peaceful lake and harvest moon.

(3) The three pools and the printed moon.

(4) Su's dancing spring road.

(5) The lagoon of fish and flowers.

(6) The windy hill of fragrant breeze.

(7) The southern mountains evening bell.

(8) The evening illumination of the thunder peak.

(9) The willow bay where the eagles are heard.

(10) The two clouds pierced by peaks.

Each of the views had some historical association or was famous for its particular scenic beauty. The first was a famous vantage point from which snows could be seen against the waters of the lake. The second was connected by sentiment with an old pavilion built in T'ang times and demolished but rebuilt during the Ming, from which one could see the reflection of the moon in the surface of the

---

[1] *Kokka*, No. 343. Five of the seven are reproduced by the hand of Chang Lung-Chang, a Ming artist.

随意沙趣不必在人
有此乱雲西丹邱真
向毫端出入
白雲溪史壽平

XXXIV. LANDSCAPE
Attributed to Yün Shou-P'ing (*b.* 1633, *d.* 1690).
$(2' \, 0\frac{1}{2}'' \times 1' \, 1\frac{3}{4}'')$

lake. Here are a few further titles of landscapes from the *Ku Kung Shu Hua Chi*:

"A hill path under whispering pines," by T'ang Yin.[1]

"Gazing at distant mountains wreathed in mist," by Wang Chiu.[2]

"In silent idleness under dark trees," by Tung Pang-Ta. Ch'ing dynasty.[3]

"In the shade of the bamboos winding up the summer," by Ch'iu Ying. Ming dynasty.[4]

"Clear sky after snow in the Min Mountains," by a Sung artist.[5]

"Penetrating the mysteries of a pine-covered ravine," by Yang Jung. Ch'ing dynasty.[6]

"Light on the stream and shadow from the clouds," by Tung Ch'i-Ch'ang. Ming dynasty.[7]

The titles alone reflect a beauty which is outside our experience. This world the West has seldom entered because she has not the key.

[1] Vol. i, No. 13.
[2] Vol. i, No. 16.
[3] Vol. iii, No. 16.
[4] Vol. vii, No. 10.
[5] Vol. xi, No. 3.
[6] Vol. xxv, No. 19.
[7] Vol. xii, No. 12.

7

The Use of Bird, Flower and Animal Motives

THE Chinese possess a peculiar intimacy with nature. It has been said of them that they manage to combine the love and understanding of nature which belong to all primitive peoples, with the sophistication of an old civilization. The nature-worship of the race has never died. Taoism insisted that the only road to perfection lay in a life in harmony with nature. Buddhism by its doctrine of reincarnation knit together the personality of man with those of the birds and flowers and plants around him. Both perpetuate the idea that human life was only part of the universal life of nature.[1] In their paintings of birds and flowers in particular the Chinese have never been surpassed. A certain plant, bird or animal, or a combination of these, raises a series of images in the Chinese mind. These motives serve as indirect forms of stating a wish or implying a greeting. The reason for many of these traditional combinations has been lost. Some seem to be as incomprehensible to the Chinese as to ourselves. Hirth remarks that once a model had been established it seems to have been faithfully copied for centuries. To find the reasons for these heterogeneous combinations of bird, flower and beast we must search the pages of history, folklore and religion. Sometimes the origin may come from some literary allusion in the *Shih Ching* (The Book of Poetry) or the *Pên tsao*

[1] Binyon, L. *The Flight of the Dragon*, p. 31.

XXXV. FISHING IN AN OBSCURE RETREAT ON A RIVER
IN AUTUMN
By Ma Yüan (c. 1190-1224).
The National Collection, Peiping.   (1′ 4″ × 10½″)

kang mu (the famous *Materia Medica*). We know why the Chinese painters have selected the crane as the natural companion of the pine, as they both symbolize longevity, and why the cock is usually represented with peonies, as they are both emblems of the *yang* principle, and lovers of the sun. But why should the swallow be combined with the willow or the apricot, the sparrow with the bamboo or the quail with the millet? In some cases the subject matter has been invested with certain qualities that are admired in mankind. The winter plum, fir and bamboo (the "three friends") have become an emblem of endurance and constancy, because even in the winter the fir and bamboo are evergreen, and the winter plum blossoms defy the last frosts. The "hawthorn pattern" is found on the blue-and-white porcelain ginger jars, which are particularly associated with the reign of K'ang Hsi; these were New Year's gifts (Chinese New Year falls in our February) and they carried the wishes of the season. The veined underglaze blue background against which the flowers are so often painted depicts the cracking of the ice of winter; the plum blossoms the first breath of spring. There is a Chinese proverb "If it was not for the time of cold penetrating the stems, how could the plum blossoms obtain the fragrance they give forth." "My life," wrote a Buddhist poet Ching an, "is a fleeting thing like the plum blossom that appears amid the last snows of winter." Since the days of Mêng Hao-Jan (689–740 A.D.) "To go over the snow in search of plum blossom" has become a synonym for seeking poetic inspiration. Mêng was a scholar-poet of the T'ang dynasty who was accustomed to seek inspiration by riding over the snow on a donkey in search of plum blossom, and he is not infrequently depicted in this rôle.

The plum may also be used to symbolize female beauty. "Plum flower" is a common name for a Chinese girl. In

M

the *Shi Ching,* Pt. 1, it is used as a figure of speech to illustrate the anxiety of an unmarried girl. "Dropping are the
fruits from the plum tree; there are (but) seven (tenths) of
them left. For the gentleman who seeks one this is a fortunate time." There is a Chinese proverb "The peach and
the plum are silent yet a path is trod beneath them." Here
the flower is used to symbolize persons whose natural
qualities attract without effort.[1]

The Chinese are fond of using homonyms; that is to say,
the name of a bird, flower or animal is used to suggest
another word of the same sound with a different meaning,
and often of a different tone. Their language, because of
the number of monosyllabic words of the same sound
differing only in the inflexion of pronunciation, lends itself
very happily to this sport. Thus a picture of a deer (鹿), *lu,*
can be used to suggest another form of *lu* (祿), income from
official position. The picture of a bat (蝠) *fu,* can in the
same way suggest another *fu* (福), which means happiness.
The rebus, which is an enigmatic representation of a
word by pictures suggesting its syllables, is continually

[1] For plum blossom, see *Ku Kung Shu Hua Chi*:

Vol. 1, No. 6. By I Kuei. Ch'ing.

Vol. 7, No. 14. "Narcissus and plum," by Sun Chih. Ming.

Vol. 11, No. 1. "Tier upon tier of wild plum," by Ma Lin. Sung.

Vol. 18, No. 4. By Ch'ên Li-Shan. Yüan.

Vol. 19, No. 12. "In search of plum blossom," by Chu Tuan. Ming.

Vol. 21, No. 3. "Gazing at plum blossom," by a Sung artist.

Vol. 22, No. 18. By Ching Chao. Ch'ing.

Vol. 24, No. 17. By Ching Jo-Ai. Ch'ing. Combined with camellia
and narcissus.

Vol. 25, No. 7. By Ko Chiu-Ssu. Yüan.

Vol. 25, No. 8. By Chên Li-Shan. Yüan.

Vol. 26, No. 14. By Ch'ên Hung-Shou. Ch'ing.

Vol. 26, No. 15. By Yung Chin. Ch'ing. Combined with bamboo,
orchids and rocks.

Vol. 29, No. 13. "Plum and narcissus," by Wang Ku-Hsiang. Ming.

Vol. 29, No. 20. By Fei Erh-Ch'i. Ch'ing.

Vol. 30, No. 19. By Huang Wei. Ch'ing.

utilized in painting. Strehlneek, in his *Chinese Pictorial Art*,[1] represents a picture by Li Yüeh or Yün Ko consisting of a sprig of prunus, a twig of pine, a cluster of narcissus, an ancient stone, a jar of melon seeds, two walnuts and two squirrels and suggested that it composes a rebus reading "May you have three kinds of abundance (good fortune, years and male offspring) in combination with peace and harmony." The plum we have already dealt with, but I know of no context in which it symbolizes prosperity. According to Strehlneek the presence of a narcissus represents good fortune. He gives no examples and I should like to know his reason. The narcissus ,"water hsien flower," is found at New Year in every Chinese home growing in dishes amid stones set in water. Sometimes its bulbs are slit and stuffed with cotton wool to dwarf the blossoms. Its fragrant flowers and graceful growth have rendered it a popular subject among painters of every school. The *Pên ts'ao* tells us that the bulbs are used in a poultice for swellings, and the flowers for preparation of cosmetics. It is probably not a Chinese plant but an introduction by the Portuguese. It may be used to personify beauty, fragrance, but scarcely good fortune. The fir, Strehlneek goes on to say, represents longevity. The gnarled roots and twisted stems of old pines have impressed the Chinese with their age. Pine cones and pine needles form part of the diet of the Taoist hermit seeking immortality. The red seeds of the *Nandina Domestica*, the "Heavenly Bamboo," the melon seeds and the squirrels all represent sons, for the Chinese character *tzŭ* (子) represents both son and seed, while the squirrel represents *tzu* among the twelve animals of the duodenary circle. Strehlneek suggests that the vase (*p'ing*) (瓶) and the walnut (*ho t'ao*) (核桃) are partial homonyms for peace (*p'ing an*) (平安) and harmony (*ho ho*) (和合). Hence the rebus of the

[1] Page 186.

picture is composed partly of symbols and partly of homonyms.

"May you live as long as the tortoise and the crane" is a not uncommon Chinese felicitation. P'an Ku when he made the world had a tortoise attendant; thus the tortoise is supposed by the Chinese to have been the first created and the basis of living things. Hence the tortoise stelæ that support stone monuments all over Northern China and Korea. Sowerby notes the custom of every carter on passing such monuments beside the road to take out the brush from its bottle slung under the shafts and to dab oil on the nose of the tortoise for luck.[1] The tortoise is one of four sacred animals of the Taoists. The long-haired specimens which accompany the hsien are supposed to be unable to grow their hairy tails until they have lived 10,000 years.[2] The tortoise in one of the four quarters of the universe represents the north—the earth, the winter and darkness; it is usually combined with an entwined snake. Chinese folklore has it that the male tortoise is unable to copulate and so the female consorts with a snake instead.[3] From at least Shang-Yin times the tortoiseshell has been used in divination. Lionel Hopkins,[4] in an article entitled "Working the Oracle," gives us eight different topics for which the tortoiseshell was consulted. They

[1] Sowerby, A. de. *China Journal,* Jan. 1934. p. 30.

[2] In actual fact the origin of their "green hair" is a vegetable growth which sometimes attaches itself to the shell; a similar growth (*achlya prolifera*) attaches itself to the gills of fish and the bodies of frogs. (Bushell. *Notes and Queries on China and Japan,* vol. iii, No. 10, p. 158.)

[3] In Canton the expression "tortoise egg" is a term for bastard and to wear the green hat (the head of the male tortoise is supposed to be green) a description of a cuckold. Yet the tortoise was used as an emblem in battles. Tortoise and falcon banners are mentioned in the *Shi Ching.* (*Shi Ching.* Bk. i, Ode viii, p. 263, Pt. ii; decade of Luh Ming, Legge's translation.)

[4] *New China Review,* vol. i, p. 111.

include hunting, military expeditions and the harvest. He tells us that only the plastron and not the carapace of the tortoise was used; the latter was too thick and uneven. A hollow was gouged in the back of the plastron, and the application of heat resulted in fine vertical and lateral fissures on the surface of the shell, which bifurcated on a second application, and it is from these lines that the diviners interpreted the wishes of the heavens. At least a tenth of the Shang-Yin oracle bones that have come to light are fragments of tortoiseshell. In the *Shi Ching* (Book V, Ode I, Pt. II, p. 331, Decade of Min) we read a lamentation on the recklessness and incapacity of the councillors of Yen.

"Our tortoises are wearied out
   and will not tell us about the plans.
The councillors are very uneasy
But on that account nothing is accomplished."

A much more elementary system is still in use among humble folk in the south of China. Even to-day an elderly woman with an open umbrella may be seen going round the streets of Canton crying *Sün Meng* (算 命), "calculate destinies"; her apparatus is a hollow tortoiseshell in which she places pieces of wood, and she shakes them on the pavement and from the way in which they fall she will supply a happy day for a family festival or the felicitous name for a child.

The word for fish, *yü* (魚), is a homonym for the word *yü* (餘), superfluity. As fish are extremely plentiful in Chinese waters, they have come to represent the reproductive powers of nature. A pair of fish interlocked in the form of a pottery jar or a jade ornament is a common gift at a wedding to the bride. Fish were included among the auspicious signs on the footprints of Buddha. As in the

water a fish moves easily in every direction, so in the
Buddha state the fully emancipated knows no obstructions.[1]
Fish are never supposed to sleep. The Buddhist monk must
copy their vigilance. The wooden gong which their priests
beat at intervals through the night is shaped in the form of
a fish. Fish-ponds are a characteristic of all Buddhist monasteries; their inhabitants are fed by the pilgrims as a reminder
of the Buddhist commandment to refrain from the slaughter
of living things. Angling is a common subject in Chinese
paintings and as a sport that lent itself to meditation particularly congenial to the scholar and the recluse.[2] Even the
Buddhist monk fished, but without bait or hook. Fishing is
also continuously compared to the art of ruling, for just as
the unskilled angler catches no fish, the foolish ruler fails to
win over his people. Jade fish are a characteristic find in
Han tombs. In the third month of the Chinese year the
rainbow carp (zacco platypus) and another species, the
"huang chuan" (elopichthys bambusa, Richardson), go up the
Yangtze River to spawn.[3] To reach their spawning grounds

[1] Lafcadio Hearn. In Ghostly Japan, p. 125.
[2] See Ku Kung Shu Hua Chi, Fishing:
Vol. 1, No. 1. "Fishing amid snow," by an anonymous painter of
Five Dynasties.
Vol. 1, No. 9. "Fishing from a punt in autumn woods," by Ma Yüan.
Yüan.
Vol. 9, No. 9. "Fishing among reeds," by Yeh Kuang-T'sung. Ming.
Vol. 11, No. 6. "Fishing in loneliness on the Tung-t'ing Lake," by
Wu Chên. Yüan.
Vol. 13, No. 17. "Fishing," by Ho I-Ch'ing.
Vol. 22, No. 3. "Catching fish," by a Sung artist.
Vol. 23, No. 20. "Fishing fleet," by Tung Jung. Ch'ing.
Vol. 25, No. 16. "Fishing in a boat on autumn lake," by Tsou I-Kuei.
Ch'ing.
Vol. 26, No. 11. "Fishing in concealment in a flower-covered ravine,"
by Lu Chih. Ming.
Vol. 29, No. 12. "The joy of fishing," by Chang Ling. Ming.
[3] Falsely referred to as salmon.—Sowerby, A. de. China Journal,
Dec. 1932, p. 321.

they have to leap the Wu Mên cataracts and swim the rapids of Lung Mên. The Chinese have it that those which succeed become dragons. As a result the carp has come to represent vigour, endurance and accomplishment, and is applied to those who have succeeded in their literary examinations. It is strange that the Chinese confine their painting of fish to the freshwater species, and almost entirely to the carp and its relations. The goldfish (*Carassus auratus*) is a member of this family. It is still found in a wild state. Sowerby mentions having seen red specimens taken by fishermen in the lakes between Tientsin and Paoting-fu, Chihli. Li Shih Chên in his *Materia Medica*[1] observes that they were not domesticated or reared artificially till the Sung.[2] They seem to have first reached England during the reign of James I. Chinese paintings often represent the strange artificial breeds that the ingenuity of the Chinese have devised, such as the "dragon eyes," which have been kept in vessels from which all light is withdrawn except from the top, so that the eyes protrude and turn upwards, and the "lion headed" which, because it has no dorsal fin, lacks equilibrium and swims upside down. It was said of Yuan I of the Five Dynasties, who was skilled in this genre of painting, that his were not the kitchen fish (*i.e.* dead fish) of ordinary artists.[3] The painting of fish was a fashionable academic subject under the Sung. Prince Chun,[4] the fourth son of the Emperor Ying Tsung of the Sung who abdicated in 1066, was a celebrated painter of shrimps (as is Chi Pai Shi to-day). Fan An-Jên,[5] (Lai Tzu), a member of the academy between 1253–58, was fond of painting fish, also

[1] Published, 1570–1600.
[2] *Notes and Queries on China and Japan*, vol. ii, No. 8, p. 123.
[3] Giles, H. A. *Chinese Pictorial Art*, p. 83.
[4] *Ibid.*, p. 94.
[5] Sirén, O. *A History of Early Chinese Painting*, vol. ii, p. 108.

Lai-An of the Yüan. Pictures of fish and vegetables in monochrome were in vogue in the Ming.

The Chinese "lion" is a fantastic but far from intimidating animal, not unlike a Pekingese dog, which must have been bred in imitation; there is a closely allied Tibetan variety which is called the "lion dog." Male specimens are represented playing with a ball of brocade and females at play with a cub. The lion was not indigenous to China but was certainly known by Han times, when it was brought to the country as tribute. It must have always been a rare spectacle, for at a far later date we find in the reign of Chêng Hua records of some lions sent as a present from Turkestan refused with these comments, "Lions are strange animals unknown to China and either genuine or spurious; if genuine we do not know how to rear them and if spurious we are being made sport of."[1] Yet it is difficult to believe that they were not well known in the imperial menageries before that date. Moule has collected a number of references to their arrival as tribute.[2] During Han times the lion motive was introduced into Chinese art, both by the Scythians from the north and by the Buddhists from India. The Scythian lion, which can be detected on the friezes of some Han jars, is a perfectly natural representation, but the Buddhist lion was already conventionalized before the Chinese adopted and developed it. Both in India and China stone lions were placed outside Buddhist temples as guardians and owing to this rôle they have been called the Dogs of Fo (Buddha). Pairs of porcelain figures of the animals are particularly common in white Fukien porcelain, and with a turquoise blue glaze; and *famille verte* animals were made to adorn the altars of

[1] *China Review,* vol. x, p. 70.
[2] Moule, A. C. *Royal Asiatic Society Journal,* April, 1925, pp. 247–261: "Some Foreign Birds and Beasts in Chinese Books."

Buddhist temples and for decoration; they are often confused with kylins (Chinese unicorn). In China the lion is also found outside the official yamens and in the courtyards of magistrates, for it became a symbol of justice and an upholder of the dignity of the law. The lion, like the tiger, was used to devour or scare away devils.[1] In Canton it is said "the dancing lion drives away plague," and when a severe scourge sweeps the city a man (or men) shaking a lion mask dances down the main thoroughfares accompanied by the beating of gongs and firing of crackers. The exorcisms of the Japanese artist Hokusai, two hundred and nineteen in number, done in 1849, seven years before his death, are from the same theme.[2]

The monkey appears in different rôles in Chinese and Japanese paintings. In Chinese paintings, particularly in those of the Zen school, the gibbon is represented as a symbol of gentleness and benevolence. The sad cry of the gibbons along the Yangtze gorges is constantly referred to in Chinese poetry. "Listen out there in the country whitened by the moon, hear the monkeys—weeping as they crouch on the abandoned tombs."[3] The bee and the monkey are sometimes used in painting to point the rebus *fêng hou*, "to be raised to the peerage." I-Yuan Chi painted a famous picture of a hundred gibbons,[4] a copy of which still survives in the Peking Palace.[5] The cult of Hanumoi (the monkey god), who was supposed to have helped to bring

[1] A lion was once painted one evening by Ku Chiu Chih on the bedroom door of a sick friend; next morning the sickness had left him but the jaws of the lion were seen to be red with blood. (Giles, H. A. *Chinese Pictorial Art,* p. 26.)

[2] This was the charming old man who signed himself "The old man mad about drawing."

[3] Ball, K. *Decorative Motives of Oriental Art,* p. 124 (quotation from Li Tai-po, T'ang poet, translated by Joerissen).

[4] Giles, H. A. *Chinese Pictorial Art,* p. 45.

[5] Sirén, O. *A History of Early Chinese Painting,* vol. ii, p. 112.

the Buddhist scriptures from China, made some headway in China. His birthday on the 23rd of the 2nd month used to be observed; he was said to have control over hob-goblins and witches. The monkey that appears in the Japanese painting is an entirely different creature; to the Japanese he is an emblem of intelligence.

The festival of the moon in China is held on the 15th day of the 8th moon about the same time as our Easter, and the cakes that are eaten to celebrate it are stamped with the figure of a hare. In an Indian Buddhist legend the hare is supposed to have offered its life to Buddha and to have received as a reward for its devotion a reincarnation as the old man of the moon. It has been suggested that this is the original of the Chinese motif, but in China the hare is probably a Taoist not a Buddhist symbol. Jade hares dating from the Chou period are excavated from tombs, and the worship of the hare probably goes back to a very much earlier period.[1] In Chinese folklore a mythical figure Chang O, daughter of one of the officers of Shun, is sup-posed to have stolen the elixir of immortality and fled to the moon, where she is represented either in the form, or company, of a white hare, which sits in the moon under the cassia tree with mortar and pestle grinding the drugs of immortality. The expression "the jade hare" is constantly used in Chinese literature to indicate the moon. He is also thought to be the special friend of the married girl, and should the mother of an unmarried girl cut a picture of a hare to fit the shoe of her daughter, and place it under the lining so that she will wear it without knowing it, she will certainly be married during the New Year. There were many painters of the hare in China. We are told that T'sui K'o of the Sung specialized in them, carefully distinguishing between the "hare of the mountain forest, which has scant

[1] Hentze, C. *Chinese Tomb Figures*, p. 64.

XXXVI. HILL FLOWERS AND A BLACK HARE
(? Part of a Painting)
Artist unknown. Sung dynasty (960–1279).
The National Collection, Peiping.　　　　　　　　($5' 4'' \times 2' 2\frac{1}{2}''$)

fur and which has not a white belly, and the hare of the plain, where the vegetation is shorter, and which has plenty of fur and a white belly." [1]

Pictures of hawks and eagles are not uncommon in Chinese paintings. The word ying (鷹), used for falcon or eagle, is a homonym for ying (英), heroic. Pictures of white eagles by Hui Tsung have been referred to in another chapter. The hawk was as popular as the dog and the horse among the Mongol tribes. Its swift flight, and its penetrating vision commanded general admiration. The "falcon banners" of Chinese armies are mentioned in the *Shu Ching*. There is probably no mention of hawking in Chinese literature prior to the Han. The oldest representations of hawking are probably the Han bas-reliefs of Hsiao T'ang Shan.[2] It must have originated somewhere on the steppes of Mongolia and Siberia and was not introduced into Europe until after the Crusades (A.D. 560). Laufer believes Turkestan to have been its mother country. The method used in China and Japan was similar to that of Persia and Arabia. Falconry with sparrowhawks is still indulged in by the dilettantié of Peking. Marco Polo [3] gives a vivid description of "hawking" expeditions of Kublai Khan, and the Jesuit fathers record that the Manchu emperors revived the habits of their predecessors. The sport was introduced into Japan towards the end of the fifteenth or beginning of the sixteenth century; in the Ashikaga period the Soga school specialized in the painting of falcons.

"Man is judged by his clothes, a horse by his saddle," runs a Chinese proverb. In China the horse is constantly referred to as an emblem of speed, perseverance and nobility. A quick-witted youth was referred to as a

[1] Giles, H. A. *Chinese Pictorial Art*, p. 118.
[2] Laufer, B. *Chinese Pottery Figures of the Han Dynasty*, p. 233.
[3] *Yule*, vol. i, pp. 389–390.

"thousand *li* colt." "Horse riding" was used as a term for the competition in the literary examination; and "horses' sheds," slang for the halls where the examination took place. The horse was also an emblem of rank, power and wealth, for in China and Japan it was reserved for the chase and warfare, and limited to the aristocracy. In the *Shu Ching* [1] a description of his carriage horses is used to extol the greatness and wealth of the Marquis of Lu. The Tartars and the Mongols relied on the horse to carry them vast distances. Marco says of the latter, "In cases of great urgency they will ride ten days on end without lighting a fire or taking a meal. On such an occasion they will sustain themselves with the blood of their horses, opening a vein and letting the blood jet into their mouths, drinking till they have had enough, then staunching it." [2] The Manchus supposed themselves to have been descended from horses and perpetuated the legend by the cut of the cuff (in the form of a hoof) and the plaited queue (the horse's tail). The horse is the favourite of all nomad peoples. It was the natural tribute of the border tribes of the north-west frontier, who from time to time invaded and conquered China. The mobility of their cavalry was a constant menace. In Han times the emperor sent a delegation to Ferghana to obtain superior horses to meet the raids of the Hsiung Nu. [3] There are scarcely any stone engravings of the Han which do not contain horses. The T'ang dynasty was mad about horses. The six reliefs representing the six battle chargers of T'ai Tsung, erected at his mausoleum ten miles north-west of Li Chuan near his capital Ch'ang an (Sian fu) are specimens of the finest T'ang modelling; [4] pottery tomb

[1] *Praise Odes of Lu*, Book ii, Pt. iv, Ode i, p. 611 (Legge).

[2] Yule. *Marco Polo*, vol. i, ch. liv, p. 254.

[3] Yetts, W. P. *The Horse a Factor in Early Chinese History*.

[4] Waley, A. *Burlington Magazine*, Sept. 1923, pp. 117 and 118: "Tai T'sung's Six Chargers."

figures of horses from the same dynasty are justly famous. Polo was probably introduced in the T'ang. The first record of a match is in A.D. 709 in the reign of Ching Tsung. Ming Huang, who was devoted to it, played on horses decorated with tassels, bells and mirrors, with balls of vermilion wood, and members of his harem were also players. One of the relatives of T'ai Tsu of the Posterior Liang (907–912) was killed on the polo ground, where-upon all the participants in that particular chukka were executed.[1] Giles, in *Adversaria Sinica* (p. 95), quotes from a poem by Ch'ao Wu-Chiu, who laments on Ming Huang's addiction to the sport. He went so far as to play in torchlight:

"The thousand doors of the palace are open
  When in broad daylight
  Sang Lang comes back very drunk from polo, . . .
  Ah! Chiu-Ling is old and Han Hsiu is dead;
  To-morrow there will be none to come forward
    with remonstrance."

In 881 Hui Tsung put to death a minister who remonstrated on his love for polo, cock-fighting and football. Another T'ang prince, Giles tells us, taught his ladies to play polo on donkey back, providing them with inlaid saddles and jewelled bridles. It is not then surprising that a large number of Chinese painters should have concentrated upon the horse. Ts'ao Pa, Han Kan, Li Lung-Mien, Chao Mêng-Fu were all horse painters. Li Lung-Mien spent so much time in the stables that he was chidden by a priest, who told him he would be reborn a horse.[2] But Tao Lin, a poet of the first century, who was rebuked for the same reason, replied, "The company of horses is not incongruous

[1] Laufer, B. *Polo*, April 1932, p. 44.
[2] Golobew, V. *Gazette des Beaux Arts,* 4me période, tome xi: "Li Lung-Mien," pp. 275–296.

with the sacred calling; there is a divinity in their fleetness."
The name of the phœnix-headed horse of Khotan, the
Brocade-legged horses of T'ung Tan and of other mysterious
inmates of the imperial stables that Li Lung-Mien painted
has survived.[1] Han Kan began his life as a pot-boy near
Chang-an at an inn where Wang Wei and his brother were
accustomed to stop and drink wine; while the boy held
their horses he drew pictures of them in the dust. Wang
Wei was so struck by his talent that he paid for his training.
Chao Mêng-Fu, a lineal descendant of the Sung dynasty
and a hereditary official, retired from public life after the
fall of the Sung dynasty till 1286, when he returned to
court and was appointed to the Board of War. He was very
popular with the first Yüan emperor, who addressed him
by his pen-name, Tzu-ang. His beautiful pictures of horses
must have endeared him even more to the Mongols.[2] He
had a talented family; Kuan Tao-Sheng (Fu-Jên), his wife,
painted in monochrome, bamboo, orchids and plum and
landscape. We are told that for "an inch of silk of her work
or a slip of paper" [3] people would offer large sums. His
son Chao Yung-Tzu (Ching Ma), born 1289, was well
known; and his grandson Wang Mêng one of China's
greatest landscape painters. But Chao Mêng-Fu was both a
painter and a successful courtier. It is related that on seeing a
painting of bird and bamboos by Hui Tsung he remarked,
"What a joy for trivial things to be limned by a hand that
is divine." The Chinese never forgave him for serving an
alien dynasty.

While the horse was an emblem for the high and mighty,
the ox (and particularly the water buffalo) typified the

[1] Mayer, A. *Chinese Painting as reflected in the Thought and Art of
Li Lung-Mien,* p. 128.
[2] Giles, H. A. *Chinese Pictorial Art,* p. 159.
[3] *Ibid.,* p. 170.

overladen peasant. "The ox ploughs the field but the horse eats the grain. The concubine bears a son, but the great mother (the first wife) enjoys his services." [1] The picture of a herd-boy playing his flute astride a buffalo's back is one of the commonest representations of rural life. The domestic buffaloes do all the hard work of the small farms in the south of China. It was considered a great crime to slaughter the ox or the buffalo for food; candles of buffalo tallow were forbidden and the Buddhists wrote tracts against beef-eaters, and drew vivid pictures of their suffering in hell. [2] The *San Tzu Ching* made a plea especially for the ox and the dog. "One can plough the fields and the other can guard the house. It is to obscure your natural goodness of disposition to kill them or expose them for sale." "Do not kill draught oxen or throw away written paper" is another saying. The sacrifice of a real buffalo or a paper or mud model was part of the ancient spring ceremonies. Representations of the God of Fertility and Vegetation in the form of a bull are widespread. [3] The *Shih niu chih sung* [4] uses a bull to express the fundamentals of Zen, and the ten steps by which the bull (human nature) is caught and subdued, are illustrated and explained. The Taoist sage, Lao Tzŭ, rode a black bull; and Ning Chi, [5] a poor but ambitious scholar, [6] rode a buffalo, beating time on its horns to the tune of a song he composed on his misfortunes. Huang Kung, Lord of Chi (685–645 B.C.), who heard it, was so pleased with it that he made him his prime minister. Hu

[1] *North China Review,* vol. iii, p. 369.

[2] Dolittle. *Social Life of Chinese,* vol. ii, p. 18–21.

[3] Frazer's *Golden Bough,* 2nd edition, vol. ii, p. 277 *et sequitur.*

[4] Written by Tsê-Kung Chuan and illustrated by Ching-Chu-Ch'an Shih of the Sung. Ball, K. *Decorative Motives of Oriental Art,* p. 85.

[5] *Kokka,* No. 283: vol. xxv illustrates a picture of him by Yen Tzu Ping of Southern Sung.

[6] He was reputed to have lived in the seventh century.

Yen and Ch'ao Fu, advisers to the Emperor Yü, rode bullocks when the great worthy suggested that he should abdicate; the former ran to the nearest pool to wash his ears lest even listening to such an idea should defile him and his friends, and led away his animal from the infected waters.[1] There were many cattle painters. Tai I of the T'ang specialized in painting buffalos in rapid motion.[2] It was said of Tai Sung, "the muzzles of his oxen he made moist and shiny, a special feature which I cannot explain."

The stag is an emblem of happiness or official emolument. Pictures of a "hundred deer" Pai Lu (百鹿), "the white deer" Pai Lu (白鹿), or "the cypress and the stag" Pai Lu (柏鹿), represent Pai Lu (百樂) a hundred blessings. A Taoist philosopher, Liu Hsiang of the first century, is quoted[3] to the effect that the stag turns blue after a thousand years of life, and Ko Hung, another Taoist author,[4] that it is able to live for a thousand years and turn white after five hundred. On account of the stag's reputed longevity, and because it lives among the hills and mists, it has become the special companion of the immortals. Its sad cries heard on mountain sides betoken its loneliness, when the genii have forsaken it for their own paradise.[5]

The sheep is used as an emblem of filial piety. "Even lambs have the grace to suckle kneeling." A picture of three sheep or goats entitled "San yang k'ai t'ai" (三羊開泰) is often used to convey wishes for the New Year. It has been suggested that it is a phonetic trope, *San yang* being the diagrammatic names of the three last months of the old year, while *k'ai t'ai* stands for the opening of the first month of the new, *i.e.* it conveys a meaning

[1] Ball, K. *Decorative Motives of Oriental Art,* p. 89.
[2] *Kokka,* No. 263, p. 217.
[3] De Groot. *Religious System of China,* vol. i, p. 56.
[4] Of the fourth century B.C.
[5] Ball, K. *Decorative Motives of Oriental Art,* p. 109.

XXXVII. TIGER
Artist unknown. Ch'ing dynasty (1644–1912).
The British Museum.
(5′ 0″ × 2′ 10″)

the last three months of the old year are but a prelude to the new. But *K'ai tai* (開泰) is also a homonym for *K'ai tai* (開胎), "opening the womb." The Taoist priest, Huang Ch'u-P'ing, was sent to tend sheep, but deserted them for a Taoist monastery. When he was discovered forty years later by his brothers and asked to return to his charge he took them to a pile of stones on the hill-side, which he turned into sheep. He is often the subject of Chinese and Japanese paintings.

The tiger was an emblem of courage. It occupies a most important place in the fable and folklore of China. In the mountainous country of Fukien, where it is common, the peasants worship it as a god. The tiger's claws and the tiger's whiskers were charms against fear; and tiger meat conveyed strength, cunning and ferocity to those who ate it. Generals are supposed to have partaken of its blood mixed with a powder ground from its teeth. "The dragon tread and tiger glance" of which they boasted was a charmingly ferocious phrase. Highly conventionalized jade tigers are continually excavated from Chou tombs, and bronze tiger heads from Han graves. There are tiger tallies inlaid with turquoise and supposed to date from the Ming. Chinese folklore is full of were-tigers that assume human form [1]; they are the ghosts of men that tigers have devoured which can never find relief until they kill some one to take their place. Yet the tiger can be a destroyer of evil spirits; pictures of tigers are painted on the walls of magistrates' yamens to ward off demons. The god of wealth is sometimes mounted on a tiger, and a picture of a tiger standing on its hind legs grasping a cash entitled "His Excellency the cash-grasping tiger" is the trade sign of gambling dens.[2] "A wooden tiger" is a term for an

[1] De Groot. *Religious Systems of China*, vol. v, ch. 5, pp. 544–548.
[2] Dolittle. *Social Life of the Chinese*, vol. i, p. 289.

unsuccessful plan to frighten an enemy, a "paper tiger" for uninforced regulations, and a "tiger eating a fly" for disproportion. It was said of Pao Ting of the Sung dynasty, who was famous for his tigers, that "when working he cleared his rooms, closed the doors and windows, obtaining light from a hole in the roof, drank freely of strong wine, removed his garments, crept on the ground, crouched, lay, glared about, imagining himself to be the very beast he was about to limn. Having thus stirred his imagination he would seize his brush and paint furiously until his picture was completed."[1] The tiger is generally drawn in company with the bamboo; emblematic, it has been suggested, of the hospitality of the weak to the strong, but more probably a symbol for a combination of endurance and courage. A quasi-scientific system of geomancy called *fêng shui* ("wind and water") has sprung up in which the dragon and the tiger represent two counter influences in nature which must be propitiated. The tiger symbolizing the west (fire, heat and wind), and the dragon the east (rain and pools, rivers, mists, thunder). Unless these influences are properly balanced,[2] it is impossible to build a grave, a temple or a dwelling-house under auspicious circumstances. The doctors of geomancy, by interpreting the position of water, hills, trees and buildings in the vicinity, professed to be able to find sites which would be free from any hostile influences.

As Elliot Smith has said, to write a history of the dragon motive would involve[3] a survey of all the important civilizations of the world; for the dragon appears in the

[1] Strehlneek. *Chinese Pictorial Art,* p. 303.

[2] In 1867 a serious drought near Peking called forth a suggestion from a censor that a white tiger should be sacrificed by the Emperor to the dragons so that the rain should be liberated: S. W. William's *Middle Kingdom,* vol. ii. p. 204.

[3] Elliot Smith. *Evolution of the Dragon.*

legends of Egypt, Assyria, Israel, Greece, Rome and South America and India as well as in China and Japan. Probably its origin lies in some form of snake worship, which was a common religion all over the world at a very early stage in the world's history; traces still exist in Naga worship, in the Himalayas, Burma and Siam to-day. Professor Eitel has remarked that in Sanskrit Buddhist texts the Chinese invariably render the term *naga* (snake) as *Lung* (dragon). The Chinese believe that dragons live in the sky, the river, the wells and the sea, and that they control the rain clouds. Elliot Smith points out that a liking for water is common to dragons from all over the world. The importance of rain in the eyes of an agricultural people like the Chinese cannot be over-estimated, and perhaps the dragon came to be worshipped originally as a Rain God. Even to-day the Chinese in times of drought make a paper dragon, carry it about in procession, invoke it, and, if no rain is granted, execrate and destroy it. Other ways have been found to cajole, provoke or if necessary restrain recalcitrant dragons.[1] In all mythologies the dragon is represented as a guardian of forbidden treasure. Precious stones, particularly pearls, are to his taste. The *Pen T'sao* says, "a dragon has whiskers at the sides of his mouth and a bright

[1] The Pên Ts'ao (*Materia Medica*) says: "The dragon's nature is rough and fierce, and yet he likes beautiful gems, and the K'ung ts'ung and is fond of (roasted) swallows. He is afraid of iron, of the wang plant, of centipedes, of the leaves of the *lien* tree, of five-coloured silk thread. Therefore those who have eaten swallows avoid to cross the water, and those who pray for rain use swallows; those who suppress calamity (inundations) use iron, those who stir up dragons (to cause them to make rain) use the *wung* plant, and those who offer to Kuh Yuen use leaves of the Melia Azederack and coloured silk thread, wrapping dumplings in them which they throw into the river. Also when physicians use dragon bones, they must know particulars about the dragons' nature as to their likings and hatreds. (Dr. M. W. De Visser. *The Dragon in China and Japan*, Kon. Akademie van Wetenschappen, vol. xiii, No. 2, pp. 67 and 68.)

pearl under his chin." The Chinese dragon is invariably represented chasing a pearl, which probably represents a cosmic symbol.[1] The author of the *T'ien ching ki* suggests that the eyes of the dragon are hurt by the pungent nature of iron and that they flee to protect their eyes. "In A.D. 762 the dyke of a river was broken and each time when the repairs were finished it broke again. At last somebody told them that in a similar case in the home of the Emperor Wu of the Liang dynasty thousands of pounds of iron were buried under the dyke, and the work completed. On hearing these words the superintendent of the work ordered men to do the same, and lo ! the thundering noise under the ground was no longer heard at the spot where the iron was laid, but gradually went away and the dyke was soon repaired." [2] Flood and drought are both the direct consequences of recalcitrant dragons, who must be bribed by offerings, or bullied by iron or the *wung* plant into renewing their normal duties. But whereas the dragon in Europe became a symbol of the devil, in China it became the emblem of beneficial government, and eventually a symbol of the emperor himself. His throne was the "dragon seat," his anger "the reversal of the dragon's scales." Huang Ti, the mythical yellow emperor, rode a dragon; and the great Yü is depicted with a pair harnessed to his carriage at a very early date. Late emperors adopted the symbol, and had it embroidered on their clothes and painted on their utensils. It is not surprising that there should be many painters of dragons.

It was said of Chin Tsung, the great dragon painter of the Southern Sung, that "When he was drunk he shouted aloud, threw off his cap, dropped it in the ink and then smeared and rubbed, making a rough picture which he afterwards

[1] See De Groot. *The Religious System of China.*
[2] See De Visser, M. W. *The Dragon in China and Japan,* p. 70.

completed with the brush. Sometimes the whole body of the dragon was shown, and sometimes only a leg or head. The clearly defined shapes were beyond description, almost inaccessible yet truly divine and mysterious." [1] T'ang Yin wrote that "the dragons should rise towards the sky through dense mist and layers of clouds, or plunge into the bottomless depths of the turbulent waters where no human eye can reach them. Ancient as well as modern painters have found it difficult to pursue their forms and shapes. The dragon's form may be divided into three sections and nine similarities: the first is from the head to the neck, the second from the neck to the belly, the third from the belly to the tail; these are the three sections. The nine similarities are: the head like that of a bull, the muzzle like a donkey's, the eyes like a shrimp's, the horns like those of a deer, the ears like an elephant's, the scales like those of fishes, the beard like a man's, the body like a serpent's, the feet like the Fêng-bird's. Such are the similarities. . . .If you want to make them with the sweeping brush and flowing ink bring out the life of the muscles and bones, but in order to express perfectly the essence and spirit of the dragon you must give him awe-inspiring bloody eyes, impetuously moving red beard, mist-hoarding scales, bristling mane, hair on the knees, claws, and teeth. Make him spit and hide in the rain and the dew, make him skip and gambol as he soars through space—then, when the eyes are put in, he will fly away like the dragons of Chang Sêng-Yu and master Yeh." [2]

The natural companion of the dragon were the *fêng huang* (incorrectly called the Chinese phœnix). The *fêng huang* (male, *fêng*, female, *huang*) are fabulous birds which belong

[1] Sirén, O. *History of Early Chinese Painting,* vol. ii, p. 107, quoted from the *Shu Hua P'u,* vol. li.
[2] *Ibid.,* p. 106.

to the same race as the Persian simurgh, the Indian garuda and the European phœnix. The Jesuits christened them phœnix, to which in fact they bear some resemblance for they are in one capacity also a cosmic symbol. The red bird or heavenly chicken (which in China is associated with the southern quarter of the four signs of the Zodiac) is the symbol of fire, heat and summer; it is supposed to crow up the sun each morning from the tree of life on the top of the world, and is generally represented as the three-legged crow or cock, or in a form resembling the golden pheasant; but it is also represented as the *fêng huang*. All four species are almost interchangeable symbols. Yet the Chinese phœnix has come to represent, in another rôle, the *yin* or female element, and the cock more than any other bird, the *yang* (masculine) element.

Efforts to identify the *fêng huang* with the ocellated pheasant (*Reinardus ocellatus*) [1] are not satisfactory. It remains a composite creature, with the wattle of the cock, the plumage curling from the neck in the manner of a mandarin teal (*aix galericulata*), legs with spurs like a cock, toes arranged like a parrot's and a mixture of the argus pheasant and the peacock in its tail plumes. According to the *San Ts'ai T'u Hui*, Part 13, Chüan, 6: "The *fêng* is a divine bird, commonly called the king of birds. Of the three hundred and sixty birds and insects the *fêng* is the chief. Before it is like the swan and behind like the *lin*. (Chinese unicorn). Its neck is like a snake and its tail like a fish, its forehead like a stork's, and its temperament like a mandarin duck's. It has dragon markings, a back like a tortoise, a throat like a swallow, a bill like a fowl and five colours completely distinguishable. It comes from the gentlemen's country in the East. When it appears there will be peace everywhere in the land. On its head is the character

[1] Marquis Hachisuka. *Royal Asiatic Societies' Journal*, Oct. 1934.

XXXVIII. PHŒNIX
By Lin Liang (*b.* 1500).

Shokokuji Temple, Kyoto.

$(5'\,4\tfrac{7}{8}'' \times 3'\,2'')$

for ceremony, on its back the character for righteousness, on its stomach the character for loyalty. Its voice is like a flute. It does not peck at living insects or trample on living grass. It does not go in flocks. It does not perch where there is no *wu t'ung* tree, nor eat anything but bamboo or drink anything but clear spring water." [1] The *Kin King,* a work devoted to ornithology and purporting to date back to the Tsin (A.D. 263–317), describes it thus : "Its head is supposed to have impressed on it the character for virtue, the poll that for uprightness, the back that for humanity, the heart is supposed to contain that for sincerity and the wings to enfold in their clasp that of integrity, its foot imprints righteousness, its low notes are like a bell and its higher notes are like a drum. It is said that it contains all the five colours (black, red, azure, white, yellow). Wherever it flies crowds of birds follow. Wherever it appears the monarch is equitable, and the kingdom has moral principles." [2] Its occasional and highly questionable appearances were hailed with delight by Chinese chroniclers as an auspicious augury, for it was only seen in the gardens of equitable princes in time of peace and plenty. The *Annals of the Bamboo Books* tells us that the *fêng* and *huang* visited the emperor's Eastern Gardens in the 7th month of the 5th year of Huang Ti (2647 B.C.) and that some built their nests in the galleries of the palace and others sang in the courtyard, the females gambolling to the note of the males. The commentary adds that the *fêng* appeared in the 7th year of the reign of Yao (2286 B.C.) and again in the 1st year of the reign of Shun (2235 B.C.). Kùo P'o states that during the reign of the Han dynasty the *fêng* appeared constantly. During the good old days of antiquity it was a frequent visitor, "in the times of

[1] The translation is my own.

[2] Giles, H. A. *Adversaria Sinica*, pp. 9–13. See also Gould, C., *Mythical Monsters*, p. 369.

Shun and Yü the unicorn and phœnix wandered about."
In the *Shi Ching* [1] the Duke of Shao, congratulating King
Ching on the happiness of his people and his admirable
officers says, metaphorically, that in his country—

" The male and female (*fêng huang*) phœnix give out their
notes

> On that lofty ridge;
> The Azandras (*wu t'ung*) grow
> On their eastern slopes;
> They grow luxuriantly;
> And harmoniously the notes resound."

The critics of later times were quick to point out that it
has never been seen since the Han period; courtiers were
eager to identify the appearance of any strange bird with
this species. In the *Shan hai ching* its home is indicated in the
caves where cinnabar is mined, in the Tu Hueh Mountains, a range in the south, and also south and west in the
great desert west of K'un-Lun. The *Erh ya* says that it
lives in the mountains of northern Chou (Szechuan), where
mountains are so steep that even a monkey cannot climb
them. Another tradition states it came from Korea where
General Sieh Jan-Kwei saw one in A.D. 668.[2]

The *Shang li jen wei* records five different varieties. But
in Chinese mythology the only important variety of the
fêng is the *luan* which is described as a green fêng (identified
by Hachisuka as the argus pheasant (*argusianus argus*)).[3]
"The *Shuo wen* says the *luan* is the essence of divinity. Its
red feathers are variegated with five colours. Its appearance
is like a fowl. It possesses all the five notes. When the
panegyrics are sung then it appears. One name for the *luan*
is the green *fêng*. The female of the *luan* is called the *Ho*,

[1] Book ii, Ode viii, Pt. iii, p. 494. Decade of Shang Min (Legge).
[2] Gould. *Mythical Monsters*, p. 371.
[3] Beebe. *Monograph of Pheasants*, vol. iv, p. 118.

the male the *luan*. It is an ancient saying that the blood of the *luan* was used as glue to piece together bows and crossbows and the strings of musical instruments. Some people say the *luan* is inferior to the *fêng*. When it first appeared it was as the *fêng*, but the five colours deteriorated. In former times when the State carriage moved, then the birds collected and gathered on the top of the carriage. The males called in front, the females answered from behind. Later ages were unable to make it appear, so they made a *Ho luan* to resemble it." [1] The *Shang li jen wei* says that when the world is peaceful then the notes of the *luan* can be heard tolling like a bell. The *Shu king* says that it is fond of music and comes to the sound of the flute; when it sings *Wu t'ung* trees flourish. During the Chou it was customary to hang bells from the tops of vehicles which were supposed to emit a sound like that of a *luan*. Both these birds have been a symbol of the empress, just as the dragon became that of the emperor, and these motives were extensively used in headdresses, ear-rings and the silk brocades of the royal princesses. They are among the three "supernatural creatures" and like the crane they are used as steeds of the immortals. In this rôle they are associated with Hsi Wang Mu, the Queen of the Taoist Fairyland, who is seldom painted without at least one *fêng huang*. But perhaps the poet, T'ao Yuan-Ming (A.D. 365–427), was right when he wrote: "The divine *fêng* dances among clouds, the spiritual *luan* trills its pure notes. Although these varieties are not of this world, yet they are beloved by (Hsi) Wang Mu." [2]

A humbler relation of the phœnix is the pheasant. China is the home of nearly all the pheasants [3] and they frequently appear in Chinese paintings. The bird is also particularly

[1] Chuan. *San Ts'ai T'u Hui*, Pt. 13.
[2] Giles' translation.
[3] Sowerby, A. de. *China Journal,* May 1933, pp. 310-311.

associated with women. Granet [1] speaks of it as a fecundity
symbol. He says it was embroidered on the ritual gowns of
princesses and queens, and speaks of the crying of the
pheasants imitated by girls in their spring dances. The
phrase "he lightly esteems the domestic fowl but loves the
wild pheasant" is used of a man who forsakes his wife and
spends his days with ladies of easy virtue. Pheasant feathers
were used in dances [2] and to decorate the ritual chariots of
the queen. The immense tail feathers of the Reeves pheasant
(*Syrmaticus reevesii*), which has a reputation for pugnacity,
and which is indigenous to the wooded country north of
Ichang, were once used to decorate official hats, and are still
part of the headdress of military characters on the Chinese
stage. The flesh of the golden pheasant (*Chrysolophus
pictus*), which abounds in the western Hupeh and eastern
Szechuan, where it is captured and kept as a pet, is eaten
to make people clever. It is very commonly met with in
Chinese painting. Temminick's Tragopan (*Tragopan Tem-
minicki*), which comes from northern Hupeh and Szechuan,
has a wattle which is supposed to resemble the character for
longevity. Pictures of the quail, invariably combined with
the millet, are common.[3] They were a speciality of Li An
Chung and Li Hsuan and other artists of Hui Tsung's
academy, perhaps because the emperor favoured them himself. The quail is another bird of the *yang* principle and
particularly associated with fire. Another bird which may
be confused with the phœnix is the peacock. The peacock

[1] Granet. *Danses et légendes de la Chine ancienne*, Tome ii, p. 570.

[2] *Shi Ching*, Pt. i, Bk. iii, Ode xiii, V. iii, p. 62.

[3] This motive was adopted by the Japanese potter Kakiemon in red,
blue and yellow enamels to decorate his wares in the late seventeenth
and early eighteenth centuries. These in turn were copied in Europe—at
Meissen in Germany, and Chantilly, St. Cloud and Mennecy in France.
The partridge pattern of Bow, Chelsea and Worcester was the result in
England.

in India was the emblem of Kārtikeya, the God of War, and a favourite emblem among Rajput warriors.[1] This may or may not be the direct origin of the Peacock Feather, a Manchu order originally conferred solely for active service in the field. There were various degrees of this order—the flower feather, the green feather, and the one-, two- and three-eyed feather. It was first conferred upon Prince Li, second son of Nurhachu, and was still a very real honour in the time of K'ang Hsi, but by the beginning of the nineteenth century, and especially since the T'ai p'ing rebellion, it lost all significance.[2] The *San Ts'ai T'u Hui* says, "the peacock's character is jealous and spiteful. It is very vain of its tail and although domesticated or kept in captivity for a long time, when it meets women and boys wearing embroidered silks it must choose to peck them. Whenever it wishes to alight on the hills it first chooses a place to arrange its tail." In Chinese painting it is generally depicted with the peony. Peacocks from Burma seem to have been an article of tribute at least as early as the T'ang.

Next to the *fêng huang* the crane is the commonest of all the birds in Chinese painting. Several species of crane visit China, but it is only one species, the Manchurian crane (*Grus Japanensis Muller*), which occupies an honoured position in legend and symbolism. It is distinguished from the other cranes by its white plumage, dark face and neck, a bare crimson patch on its bill and the long black falcated plumes of the tertiary wing feathers that droop over the tail.[3] Sowerby says its breeding grounds are Eastern Siberia and Northern Manchuria, but it ranges from Chihli to the lower Yangtze where it winters. It is supposed to be remarkable for its power of longevity, and it is the most frequent

[1] Ball, K. *Decorative Motives of Oriental Art*, p. 220.
[2] Li Ung Bing. *Outlines of Chinese History*, p. 284.
[3] Sowerby, A. de. *China Journal*, May 1935, p. 284.

companion of the *hsien* in their mountain retreats, and the
steed of the Immortals in their voyages across the sky from
their island paradises. With the tortoise and the spotted
deer it is found in constant attendance on Shou Lao, the
God of Longevity. In painting it is often combined with
the fir and the sun to suggest everlasting years. "The crane
has grey legs and white wings. It often calls at midnight,
and its cry is high and clear and can be heard for eight or
nine *li*. Its character is very wary. In the eighth month the
white dew falls, whereupon it gives a clear and high call
to give warning to move (migration?), for wherever it
is, it invariably has a foreboding of possible evils. After two
years it moults its baby feathers, after three it sits and
broods, after seven it flies right up to the Milky Way. After
another seven years it learns to dance and after another
seven years to respond to cadence, and after a further seven
years it calls day and night and its cries correspond to the
twelve musical notes. After sixty years it does not eat living
things; its big feathers fall out and are replaced by down
white as snow. Mud and water do not dirty them. After
one hundred and sixty years the male and female gaze at
each other, the pupils of their eyes fixed unblinkingly. In
this way the females become pregnant. After six hundred
years they drink but do not eat." [1]

The domestic cock *chi* (鷄) (a homophone for *chi* (吉)
fortunate) was a symbol of the *yang* principle, for it crows
at dawn to welcome the sun. The Chinese believe that the
heat of the sun is particularly concentrated in the bird or it
would not become so excited at sunrise.[2] The *San Ts'ai
T'u Hui* says: "Of old it was said there was a cock that
lived in the sun. The cock is the emblem of the Western
quarter. When there is at night a light in the East then the

[1] San Ts'ai T'u Hui.
[2] *Notes and Queries of China and Japan,* vol. ii, No. ii, p. 22.

cock appears. The *Book of Changes* says that the cock is the symbol of the sun trigram . . . it is always good at detecting evil influences." As in English symbolism it is an emblem of courage and aspiration. The Chinese believe that its presence keeps away evil spirits. Hence pottery figures of cocks and hens were buried in tombs; a live white cock often accompanies the coffin to the grave, and white sugar cocks and hens are often eaten at a marriage ceremony. We say "a whistling maid and a crowing hen are fit for neither God nor men." The Chinese believed that a crowing hen was a fatal augury of petticoat government and heralded the downfall of the dynasty. Ta Chi, who overthrew the Yin dynasty, was called the "hen who heralded the dawn of the day." Williams tells us that pictures of a red cock were pasted on the walls of houses in a belief that this bird was a protection against fire; and De Groot that cocks were killed in Fukien in the spring and their blood sprinkled on the doorposts to scare away devils. The Chinese eat eggs from shells dyed with a red pigment on New Year's day, and at the celebration of the birth of a son, for good luck, and to ward off pestilential vapours. Our custom of eating Easter eggs is of pagan origin and was originally part of the ritual connected with the return of spring. The Chinese at the Ch'ing Ming Festival [1] eat eggs in memory of the resurrection of the sun, just as the Easter egg is eaten to celebrate Christ's resurrection.[2] The cock is renowned for other qualities. It has a cap on its head as a sign of literary ambition, it has spurs on its feet which speak of its military spirit, it is benevolent because it calls the hens together, it is always vigilant because it never forgets the hour.[3]

[1] 105 days after the winter solstice; it usually falls about the 5th after April.
[2] *Notes and Queries,* China and Japan, vol. ii, No. ii, p. 22.
[3] Stewart Lockhart. *Manual of Chinese Quotations,* p. 227.

Pictures of geese are not uncommon.[1] To the Chinese the wild geese were remarkable for their fidelity to the *yang* principle. They thought that they followed the sun south in their migrations as a woman should follow her husband. As early as the Chou dynasty they were enumerated among the betrothal presents to the bride as a symbol of conjugal fidelity.[2] The Chinese also admired their powers of organization. They noticed their annual migration at regular intervals under leaders; their system of sentinels; the compact formation of a flock in flight, which is said to have been adopted by the Japanese in warfare. "One name for it is the Scarlet bird. In the frosts it flies south. When the ice melts it returns north. Its nature is to hold to the heat and so in China at the beginning of the winter it comes from the north. The Chou Kuan says the birds may be used as one of the six presents, and so officials catch them. Geese seek islands and marshy country at night. They pick out one of their number to serve as a sentinel. When in flight they carry reeds in their beaks,[3] and so on the wing they avoid darts and such is their method of avoiding harm; hence they are presented as a gift because they manage the procedure of going and coming to the best advantage." [4] Chinese painters often represent them by

[1] *Geese.* See Ku Kung Shu Hua Chi.
Vol. 1, No. 2. By Ts'ui Po. Sung.
Vol. 2, No. 10. By a Yüan artist.
Vol. 4, No. 10. By Chu Fei. Ming. (A flock amid reedy islands.)
Vol. 14, No. 1. By Ts'ui Po. Sung.
Vol. 15, No. 1. By Hui Tsung. Sung.
Vol. 16, No. 13. Geese in reeds. By Hsiang Shêng-Mo. Ming.
Vol. 19, No. 9. Pair of geese on snowy shore. By Lu Chih. Ming.
Vol. 20, No. 2. By Ts'ui Po. Sung.
Vol. 29, No. 9. Shooting at wild geese. By a Sung artist.
[2] Williams, C. A. S. *Outlines of Chinese Symbolism*, p. 180.
[3] Presumably in order to keep their mouths shut.
[4] San Ts'ai Tu Hui.

XXXIX. GEESE
By Lin Liang (c. 1500).

The British Museum. (6′ × 3′ 5″)

the side of some icebound lake with crows sitting in the snow-laden branches overhead, dreaming of the spring; a suitable gift to some old couple who have passed through many years together. The famous calligraphist Wang Hsi Chih was so fond of geese that those who wanted specimens of his calligraphy would bring him presents of these birds. He is supposed to have traded a flock of four from a Taoist priest for a copy of the *Canon of Reason and Virtue*.[1] Su Wu, after he had been captured by the barbarians outside the wall sent a message to Wu Ti of the Han dynasty tied to the leg of a wild goose, declaring his intention to put an end to himself. This goose was shot in the imperial pleasure grounds and the message found its way to the emperor who took steps to obtain his release.[2] Pien Shou Min (who signed himself Wei Chien Chü-Shih "the scholar living among the marshes") who lived at the end of the eighteenth and beginning of the nineteenth century, was famous for his pictures of geese in black and white. Other goose painters were Tsung-Han (tzǔ, Hsien Fu), a prince of the imperial house of Sung, Ts'ui P'o the academician, Li Ling of the Ming dynasty, Hui Ching, Mu Ch'i and Lo Ch'uang.

The Mandarin duck outstrips the goose as a symbol of conjugal faithfulness and affection. It is supposed to be monogamous and of a gentle, peaceful, affectionate disposition. The Japanese say that Kuanyin, the Goddess of Mercy, on her visits to this world sometimes takes the shape of an Oshidori,[3] and the Chinese trackers along the banks of the Yangtze, where the ducks are found in their wild state, wear amulets carved in the shape of the duck, in the belief that on one occasion when a tow-line broke and

[1] Strehlneek, *Chinese Pictorial Art*, p. 102.
[2] Williams. *Outline of Chinese Symbolism*, p. 180.
[3] Ball, K. *Decorative Motives of Oriental Art*, p. 233.

a man fell from a ledge into the Yangtze he was kept afloat by the help of two of the birds.[1] De Groot[2] remarks on the reputed attachment of the drake and the duck, which are supposed to sleep with necks interlocked; the one will not survive the death of the other. Hence it has come about that a certain kind of cangue in which the arms of two criminals are confined at the same time has been nicknamed a *yüan yang*. The *Materia Medica* says that the flesh of the Mandarin must be taken secretly to cure marital unhappiness.

"Crows are black all the world over," runs a Chinese proverb; but the magpie, which is called the devil's bird in Scotland and equally disliked in Ireland,[3] and which in Germany is supposed to be the steed of witches, is in China a bird of good omen. It is often referred to as the bird of joy. Pictures of the five happinesses (longevity, children, health, wealth, peace) may be represented by five magpies. Its chatter is used for purposes of divination. This bird was particularly sacred to the Manchus.[4] Legend says that the Emperor Shun Chih was saved by a magpie perching on his head, so that his enemies mistook him for a stump. Tradition has it that in the evening of the 7th day of the 7th moon the magpies make a bridge to unite the cowherd (Aquila) with the spinning damsel (Lyra), who are separated for the rest of the year by the Milky Way.

"Old age," say the Chinese, "and faded flowers no remedies can revive." They love to compare the delicate and fleeting blossom with the life of man, and the painting and fragrance of the opening bud with the first years of

[1] Nance, F. N. *China Journal,* Jan. 1934: "Chinese Symbolism," p. 17.
[2] Vol. iv, p. 228.
[3] "Ireland will never be rid of the English while the magpie remains."
[4] Gutzlaff. *History of China,* vol. ii, p. 2.

maidenhood. The Chinese frequently refer to their country as the "Flowery Land"; they are very fond of flowers and make use of them whenever ceremonies or festivities permit. The flowers of the four seasons are one of the commonest subjects in painting or on porcelain or embroidery. Usually the peony is selected to represent spring, the lotus summer, the chrysanthemum autumn and the plum winter. Other species have by tradition become associated with certain characteristics, festivals, or felicitous greetings, and appear again and again in Chinese painting. The large pink or crimson blossoms of the tree peony (*paeonia arborea*) is a favourite emblem of rank and wealth. In Canton it is called the "Fu Kuei Hua" (Flower of Wealth and Honour). In both Chinese and Japanese paintings it is often combined with the lion and the peacock. This flower is discussed at great length in all Chinese works on botany and is probably indigenous to Szechuan, but it has been cultivated for so long that it is unknown in a wild state. In Han times Loyang was famous for its peonies. Its vivid flowers are supposed to be imbued with the *yang* principle. The figure of Nan T'ien *alias* Yün Shou-P'ing (1632–90), who painted in the so-called "boneless" style after Hsu Chung of the northern Sung, is particularly associated with paintings of the peony. It was also the favourite of Ch'en Nan-P'en, a Ch'ing artist who went to Japan in 1731 and painted at Nagasaki when Japan was shut to foreign intercourse, and opened the eyes of the Japanese to flower and bird paintings of the Ming and Ch'ing.

The lotus blossom (*nelumbium speciosum*), whose dazzling whiteness is not affected by the mud and the stagnant waters from which it grows, became a symbol of purity. It is one of the eight precious symbols of Buddhism. Johnston suggests that it has come to play a part in the Buddhist imagination almost analogous to that to the cross in Chris-

O

tianity. "Just as the lotus, born in the water, bred in the water overcomes water and is not defiled by water, even so I (Buddha) born in the world, bred in the world have overcome the world." [1] Both Buddhas and bodhisattvas were invariably depicted standing enthroned on the open calyx of a lotus blossom, and the souls of the dead were wafted by Kuanyin to the lotus blossoms on the sacred lake in Amitābha's paradise; it is the flower that has lent its name to one of the most important Buddhist sutras. The pod and stem of the plant are peddled about the streets of Canton in summer and ground into flour, for it is supposed to rid the body of any noxious poisons.

The chrysanthemum blooms in mid-autumn, and is associated with the dying year. "The chrysanthemum in autumn and the peach in spring" is a Chinese metaphor for everything in its due season. It is frequently compared to the retired scholar, and it has always been the favourite of the official who devoted his last years to his garden, his book, and his wine, in some country retreat. The poet T'ao Chien (A.D. 365–427) refused an official post and devoted himself to the cultivation of chrysanthemums, to music, poetry and wine. Lin Ming, of the eleventh century, wrote a work on this species distinguishing thirty-five varieties, one of which he christened "Drunk with wine made for the paradise of the immortals." Sun K'an, of the Ming, was "exceedingly fond of the flower and cultivated it in his garden. Morning and evening he was looking at his chrysanthemums, the result being that when he came to paint he painted their souls." [2] The flower was also associated with the yang principle, and an old name was jih ching (日 精), "the soul energy of the sun." Chrysanthemum wine was quaffed by the immortals and by the Taoists generally because

[1] Reginald Johnston. *Buddhist China*, p. 104.
[2] Giles, H. A. *Chinese Pictorial Art*, p. 183.

it engendered longevity. "There was at Nan Yang in the hills of the Lo District (Honan) a sweet brook, which got its taste from sweet chrysanthemums growing at its source on both banks; indeed the flowers having dropped into it for a long series of generations had changed its taste. The people in the valley by the spot where the brook entered it had no wells, but they all drank the sweet brook water so that they all reached a great age varying between 145 years and 80 or 90; premature death was unknown to them. They obtained these blessings from the powers of those chrysanthemums mixed in wine." [1] "In my opinion," wrote Chou Tun-I, "the chrysanthemum is the flower of rank and wealth, the water-lily the lady *sans pareille*. Alas! few have loved the chrysanthemum since Tao Yüan-Ming and none now love the water-lily like myself; whereas the peony is the favourite of all mankind." [2]

"Coloured paintings of the peony, the hibiscus and the poppy are the favourites of academicians. Sketches of the plum, orchid, narcissus and the lotus in ink appealed to the literary painter. The Chinese invariably depict the orchid (*cymbidium ensifolium*), which sports an insignificant green flower with a delicate smell. 'Tall grass may hide a fragrant orchid, a thatched cottage may cover the heir to a throne.' Its perfume and its modesty made it beloved of the scholar class. Chêng Ssu-Hsiao, a famous painter of orchids, when ordered to paint under arrest, replied 'You may have my head, but not my orchids.' " [3]

The peach and plum attract more attention than any of the other flowering trees. There is a legend that is constantly referred to by Chinese poets that in the Han dynasty a fisherman, in pursuit of his occupation, lost his way and

[1] Ko Hung from the *Pao P'o tsze chi*. (De Groot, vol. iv, p. 323.)
[2] Giles, H. A. *Gems of Chinese Literature*.
[3] Giles, H. A. *Chinese Pictorial Art*, p. 146.

O*

travelled up the banks of a river lined with peach trees until he came to a happy land, where the descendants of the Ch'in dynasty (third century B.C.) lived cut off from the rest of the world. He returned without thinking much of his discovery, but when at a later date he tried to retrace his steps he could not find the way. His friends told him that he had paid a fleeting visit to paradise.[1]

"The peach possesses more vitality than any other of the four trees, it suppresses and subdues evil influences and combats hundreds of demons."[2] Its fruit and its bark are among the substances, according to the Taoists, which form the basis of the elixir of life. In the realms of Hsi Wang Mu, the Taoist queen of the Western Paradise, grew a peach tree whose fruits bequeathed eternal life. "The branches of the east and south side of the peach tree are particularly detested by spirits." In Canton amulets of peach stones are hung round the neck by children to prevent their being molested by evil spirits; cradles and idols are made of peach wood. Chung K'uei, the demon dispeller, is invariably shown wearing a wreath of peach blossoms. On the 1st day of the 1st moon when demons are abroad, sprigs of peach are hung over the door. The insane are sometimes beaten with peach switches to drive out the evil spirit.[3] "If the village

[1] Chinese poets and men of letters continually refer to this peach-spangled heaven—
  1. Lao Tzǔ in the Tao Tê Ching; fifth century.
  2. T'ao Yüan Ming, A.D. 365–427, "Narrative of Peach Flower Spring."
  3. "Ravine of Flowering Peach Trees," Chang Hsu; eighth century.
  4. Li T'ai Po, "A Decalogue in the Mountains"; A.D. 705–762.
  5. "Peony Flower Felicitation," Hsieh Fang-Ti; A.D. 1226–1289.
See Sowerby, A. de. *China Journal*, May 1934, pp. 220–22.
[2] Plopper, C. H. *Chinese Religions seen through the Proverb*, pp. 137–8.
[3] Dennys, N. B., *Folklore of China*, p. 57.

possess virtue what need is there for the wooden-tongued bell? If thoughts be free from impurity what use is the peach charm?" [1] The peach blooms in spring when marriages are arranged, and it has become the equivalent of a young bride.

> "The peach tree is young and elegant
> Brilliant are its flowers
> The young lady is going to her future home
> And will order well the chamber and house." [2]

Peach-flower wine is used to celebrate wedding feasts and the man à bonnes fortunes is said to possess "peach flower luck." In the vernacular, the peach is used to describe the private parts of a woman, and the phrase "to go into the peach garden" expresses sexual union. De Groot has even suggested that the Chinese love of red and their habit of flanking the lintels of their houses at New Year with strips of red paper bearing antithetical phrases, and of decorating their children with red silk clothes, springs from a representation of the colour of the "peach blossom." [3]

The painting of plum in monochrome is first associated with the name of the Taoist priest Chung Jên of the Sung (eleventh century), whose pen-name was Hua Kuang. In the Mei P'u (Book of the Plum) attributed to him we have an ethical and philosophical treatise in which the author compares the blossom to the yang principle and the stalk to the yin, and discovers a metaphysical relation of its petals, stamens and calyx. "The branches combine the power and the refinement respectively of arms and letters, and the flowers stand in relation of retainers to a lord; the twigs, some long and others short, signify parental relation and the petals and

---

[1] *China Repository*, vol. xiv, p. 231.
[2] *Shi Ching*: Ode of Chou and the South, Pt. i, Bk. i, Ode vii, 13.
[3] *China Review*, vol. ix, p. 20–28.

stamens that of wife and husband." [1] It goes on to lay down especial rules for painting this lofty subject and enumerates six stumbling blocks for the unwary. The treatise concludes with remarks by Yang Pu-Chih: "Painting of plum blossoms in monochrome started with Hua-Kuang. The virtuous old man was extremely fond of plum-trees. He planted a great number of such trees at his temple retreat, and when they were in bloom, he removed his couch under the trees and lay there chanting poems the whole day. When the moon was bright, he could not sleep, but looked at the play of the happy and lovable shadows on the window, imitating their shapes with the brush. When morning dawned, his pictures were filled with the thoughts of moonlight; exquisitely beautiful. They became appreciated everywhere. When Shan-ku (Huang T'ing-Chien) saw the pictures, he said: 'They give me the impression of walking in a cool and clear morning among some peaceful farmsteads; only the odour is missing.' Many scholars and officials asked him in vain for such pictures, but on the other hand, those who did not ask received them easily. Whenever Hua-Kuang painted, he burned incense, entered into the happiness of perfect *Ch'an* (meditation), and then completed the whole thing with one sweep of the brush. Some one said to him jokingly: 'Wang Tzu-Yu of old liked bamboos; why do you have such a weakness for plumtrees?' To which Hua-Kuang answered gravely: 'Their beauty can never be esteemed equal,' an answer which pleased those who heard it very much." [2] The painting of the plum blossom is supposed to have reached its zenith in the work of Tang Pa-Chih, and there have been many painters of plum blossom ever since. Liu Fu of the Ming (whose picture "Pearls (*i.e.* plum blossom) dancing before

[1] *Kokka*, No. 195, p. 405.
[2] Sirén, O. *A History of Early Chinese Painting*, vol. ii, pp. 110, 111.

the wind " was famous) called himself the "Plum blossom master."

The pine and the cypress are more often represented than any other trees except the bamboo. They have become emblems of endurance; for while the winter gales strip other trees of their foliage, it leaves them evergreen. Hence the phrase for friendship in time of need, "the pine and the cypress in the cold of the year." Chuang Tzǔ says "Pines and cypresses alone are endowed with life, in the midst of winter as well as summer they are evergreen." It is related that Su Tung-P'o wrote [1] of the pine that "the blessings it bestowed on mankind are very numerous. Its flowers, its juice, and the fungus which grows at its roots, if consumed, all prolong life." De Groot tells us of the legend of a certain Ch'ao Ku who was abandoned by his relatives as a leper in a cave on a hillside, "he lived on the juice of pine trees until his body became light and his breath a hundred times as strong as it had ever been before, and he reached his 170th year without his teeth dropping out or his hair turning grey." "In the time of Ch'ing, an emperor of the Han dynasty (32–6 B.C.), some huntsmen saw in the Tsung-nan mountains a naked human being, with black hairs on its body. They were going to pursue it, but across glens and vales it fled, as if carried by wings, and it could not be reached. So they secretly watched where the abode of that being was; they besieged it there, and caught it, and then discovered that it was a woman. On their interrogating her, she related as follows: 'I was a harem dame of the Ch'in dynasty. Hearing that the Kwan-tung rebels were coming, and that the king, on marching his troops against them, was forced into submission, as also that they had set fire to the palace-building, fear made me flee into the hills. I was hungry, but found nothing to eat;

[1] In the spring of 1099.

and when on the point of dying, an old man told me to eat pine-leaves and pine-seeds. I found them bitter and acrid, but I got accustomed to that taste, and they caused me to feel no hunger or thirst, neither any cold in winter, nor any heat in summer.' Admitting that this woman was a harem lady of a prince of the Ch'in dynasty, I calculate that in Ch'ing's reign she must have been over three hundred years old. They took her home, and gave her cereal food to eat; but she vomited when she smelled corn, and it took her several days to overcome her aversion for it. She lived then on such food for more than two years, in which time she cast the hairs that covered her body, became old, and died."[1]

The bamboo is one of the most rapidly growing plants in existence and it spreads in clumps just as the Chinese clan extends, hence it has become emblematic of filial piety. The Chinese say "Good bamboo shoots spring up outside the fence" (i.e. Good daughters marry and leave the home), and "Young bamboos are easily bent" (i.e. one must educate when young). Pages could be filled with the uses of the bamboo.[2] The shoots of some varieties are stewed and eaten as a vegetable, the roots used as divining blocks for the temple altar, the stems for baskets, scaffolding, lanterns, birdcages, flutes, stools, and for tablets, for painting and writing, before the introduction of paper. Bamboo branches were carried at funerals to drive away devils. Dennys [3] suggests that the crackers, with which the Chinese celebrate every festival, were inspired by the crackling of dry bamboo on the fire, and served the same purpose, i.e. to scare away hostile spirits. As the bamboo is green all the

[1] From *Pao P'o Tzü*, ch. ii. De Groot. *Religious System of China*, vol. iv, p. 298.

[2] Ball, D. *Things Chinese*, p. 48.

[3] *Folklore of China*, p. 46.

XL. BAMBOO
Attributed to Wu Chēn (b. 1280, d. 1354).
The British Museum (Eumorfopoulos Collection). (8¾″ × 8½″)

year round it is often combined with the fir as a symbol of endurance and constancy. "The hollow bamboo has drooping leaves," is a description of a Chinese gentleman; it suggests that he is as unprejudiced as the hollow stem and as modest as the drooping leaves. By its symbolism and its elegance the bamboo has lent itself most happily to Chinese painting. The bamboo motive appears as early as the Han.[1] Hsiao Yueh devoted himself to the bamboo but only painted one variety. He was very chary of parting with his paintings and it took a year to obtain a few stalks from him.[2] Large sums were offered for the bamboo sketches of Kuan Tao-Sheng [3] (the wife of Chao Mêng-fu). Wen T'ung, Wang Wei and Su Tung-P'o were all famous painters of this genre.[4] Li Kan, a president of the Board of Civil Office and member of the Privy Council under Jên Tsung (1312–1320), wrote the Chu P'u or the Bamboo Essay. He tells us: "The painting of ink-bamboos started in the T'ang

[1] Laufer, B. *Chinese Pottery of the Han Dynasty*, p. 284.
[2] Giles, H. A. *Chinese Pictorial Art*, p. 74.
[3] *Ibid.*, p. 170.
[4] Paintings of bamboos from the first twenty odd numbers of the *Ku Kung Shu Hua Chi*—
   Vol. 1, No. 8. By Ku An P'êng. Yüan.
   Vol. 2, No. 8. "Bamboos and stones" by Wu Chên. Yüan.
   Vol. 3, No. 7. By Ko Chiu-Ssu. Yüan.
   Vol. 5, No. 6. "Bamboos and stones" by Ku An and Ni Tsan in collaboration.
   Vol. 6, No. 8. By Hsia Ch'ang. Ming.
   Vol. 6, No. 16. "Bamboos and orchid" by Yüan Chi and Wang Yüan-Ch'i. Ch'ing.
   Vol. 7, No. 6. By Wu Chên. Yüan.
   Vol. 10, No. 10. "Orchids and bamboos" by Hsiang Yüan-Pien. Ming.
   Vol. 11, No. 13. "Orchid and bamboos" by Wên Chêng-Ming. Ming.
   Vol. 12, No. 5. By Chao Mêng-Fu.
   Vol. 12, No. 6. By Kuan Tao-Sheng.
   Vol. 13, No. 9. "Red bamboos" by Wên Chêng-Ming. Ming.

period, but the origin of it has not been investigated. According to tradition Li Shih (Li P'o) of the Five Dynasties traced the shadows on the window and the others imitated him. Huang T'ing-Chien thought that Wu Tao-Tzŭ started to paint bamboos (but these were in colour). Until Sung there was a gradual development; then at last Wen T'ung appeared."[1] One of the most famous bamboo painters was the Sung poet Su Tung P'o.

It would be possible to extend this list of motives to include many others but it is suitable to conclude with the bamboo. For it is graceful, flexible and adaptable; it can flourish under almost any conditions except that of extreme cold. It bends under the sun as a nation may bend under adversity or foreign rule, but it does not break. The Bamboo symbolizes far better than any other plant the spirit of the people whose artists still love to trace the delicate pattern of its leaves.

Vol. 14, No. 8. "High stems in a gentle wind" by Hsia Ch'ang. Ming.

Vol. 16, No. 7. By Hsia Ch'ang. Ming.

Vol. 16, No. 8. "Red bamboos" by Wên Chêng-Ming. Ming.

Vol. 18, No. 14. "The five purities" by Yün Shou-P'ing. Ch'ing. (Here combined with pine and plum, rocks and water.)

Vol. 20. No. 11. By Lu Tuan-Chün. Ming.

Vol. 21, No. 11. By Wên Yuan-Shan. Ming. (Combined with rocks, bamboo, chrysanthemum and fungus in a picture entitled "Congratulations on Pine Tree Age.")

[1] Sirén, O. *A History of Early Chinese Painting*, vol. ii, p. 146.

LIST OF AUTHORITIES

Ars Islamica. Michigan, 1934.
AYSCOUGH, F. The connection between Chinese Calligraphy,
poetry and painting. (Wiener Beitrage zur Kunst and
Kultur Asiens, Band VI, 1931.)

BALL, KATHERINE. Decorative Motives of Oriental Art.
London, 1927.
Bijutsu Kenkyu.
BING, LI UNG. Outlines of Chinese History. Shanghai, 1914.
BINYON, LAURENCE. Painting in the Far East. London, 1934.
—— The Flight of the Dragon. London, 1911.
—— Chinese Paintings in English Collections. Paris, 1927.
—— Catalogue of the Eumorfopoulos Collection of Paintings.
London.
Burlington Magazine of Fine Arts, The. London.
BUSHELL, STEPHEN. Chinese Art. London, 1906.

CHANG, T'IEN-TSÊ. Sino Portuguese Trade from 1514–1644.
Leiden, 1934.
CHAVANNES, EDOUARD. Sculpture sur pierre en chine. Paris,
1893.
China Journal, Shanghai.
China Review, The. Hong Kong.
Chinese Art. Burlington Magazine Monograph. London,
1925.
Chinese Repository The. Hong Kong, 1844.
CLAPPERTON, R. H. Papermaking by hand. Oxford, 1934.
Connoisseur The. London.
COULING, SAMUEL. The Encyclopædia Sinica. Oxford, 1917.

DE GROOT, J. J. M. The Religious System of China. Leiden,
1901, 1902.
DENNYS, N. B. The Folklore of China. London, 1876.
DOOLITTLE, Rev. J. The Social Life of the Chinese. New
York, 1867.

203

ECKARDT, A. History of Korean Art. London, 1929.

FABER, E. Chronological Handbook of the History of China. Shanghai, 1902.
FENOLLOSA, E. F. Epochs of Chinese and Japanese Art. London, 1912.
FERGUSON, J. C. Chinese Painting. Chicago, 1927.
FISCHER, O. Die Chinesische Malerei, der Han-dynastie. Berlin, 1931.
—— Chinesische Landschaftmalerei. Munich, 1921.

Gazette des Beaux Arts. Paris.
GETTY, A. The Gods of Northern Buddhism. Oxford, 1914.
GILES, H. A. Chinese Pictorial Art. London, 1918.
—— A Chinese Biographical Dictionary. London and Shanghai, 1898.
—— Adversaria Sinica. Shanghai, 1905.
GOULD, CHARLES. Mythical monsters. London, 1886.
GRANET, MARCEL. Danses et Légendes de la Chinese Ancienne. Paris, 1926.
GRANTHAM, A. E. Hills of Blue. London, 1927.
GROUSSET, RENÉ. The Civilizations of the East—China. [trans.] London, 1934.

HIRTH, FREDERICK. Native Sources for the History of Chinese Pictorial Art "Chinese Painters." [trans.] New York, 1917.
—— Scraps from a collector's note-book. Leiden, 1905.
HUC, M. L'Empire Chinois. Annotated by J. M. Planchet. Peking, 1926.

JOHNSTON, Sir REGINALD. Confucianism and Modern China. London, 1934.
—— Buddhist China. London, 1913.

Kokka The. An illustrated monthly journal of the fine and applied arts of Japan and other Eastern countries. Tokyo.
Ku kung shu hua chi. Peking.
KUROSAWA, R. Imperial Chinese Art. Shanghai, 1917.

LAUFER, BERTHOLD. Chinese Pottery of the Han dynasty. Leiden, 1909.

—— T'ang, Sung and Yüan Paintings belonging to various collectors. Paris and Brussels, 1924.

LEGGE, JAMES. The Chinese Classics. Hong Kong, 1871.

LOCKHART, STEWART. A manual of Chinese Quotations. Hong Kong, 1893.

MAYERS, W. F. The Chinese Readers Manual. Shanghai, 1874.

MOULE, A. C. T'ai Shan, [1908].

—— Christians in China before the year 1550. London, 1930.

Museum of Fine Arts (Boston) Bulletin.

Notes and Queries on China and Japan. Hong Kong.

Ostasiatische Zeitschrift. Berlin.

PETRUCCI, R. Encyclopédie de la Peinture Chinoise. Paris, 1918.

PLOPPER, C. H. Chinese Religion seen through the Proverb. Shanghai, 1926.

READ, B. E. Translations from the Chinese Materia Medica. Peiping, 1931, etc.

REICHELT, K. L. Truth and Tradition in Chinese Buddhism. [trans.] Shanghai, 1927.

REICHWEIN, A. China and Europe. London, 1925.

Royal Asiatic Society, The Journal of the. London.

SAKANISHI, SHIO. An Essay on Landscape Painting by Kuo Hsi. London, 1935.

San T'sai tu hui.

Sei-ichi Taki. Three Essays on Oriental Paintings. London, 1910.

Shimbi Taikan. (Selected Relics of Japanese and Chinese Art.) Kyoto, 1899.

SIRÉN, OSVALD. History of Early Chinese Painting, Vols. I and II. London, 1933.

STREHLNEEK, E. A. Chinese Pictorial Art. Shanghai, 1914.

TOMITA, K. Portfolio of Chinese Paintings. Museum of Fine Arts. Boston, 1933.
T'oung Pao. Leiden.

WADDELL, L. A. Lamaism. London. 1895.
WALEY, ARTHUR. Catalogue of Paintings recovered from Tun-Huang by Sir Aurel Stein. London, 1931.
—— An introduction to the Study of Chinese Painting. London, 1923.
—— The Way and its Power. London, 1934.
—— An Index to Chinese Artists. London, 1922.
WIEGER, L. Moral Tenets and Customs in China. Ho-Kien-fu, 1913.
WILLIAMS, C. H. S. Outlines of Chinese Symbolism. Peiping, 1931.
WILLIAMS, S. WELLS. The Middle Kingdom. New York, 1883.
WYLIE, A. Notes on Chinese Literature. Shanghai, 1902.

YULE, Colonel HENRY. The Book of Marco Polo. London, 1875.

ZEN, S. H. CHEN. Symposium on Chinese Culture. Shanghai, 1931.

INDEX

∴ *The names of only the more important Chinese artists are included in the index.*

207

INDEX

THE END

PRINTED IN GREAT BRITAIN BY WILLIAM CLOWES & SONS, LTD., LONDON AND BECCLES.